*The Coming FORERUNNER ʌ
America's end-time calling
Reconciliation and Fullness.*

Cover design by Donald De Jesus

ISBN 9781460958490

Printed in the United States of America.

Dedication

To my parents Franklin & Sandra Mathis who passed away in 2006, and 2001 respectively. I proudly dedicate this book to both my parents, to whom I owe all that I am, and all that I do. Daddy, thank you for being the most humble, faithful man I ever met. Thank you for the example of your commitment to God, family and ministry in that order. Mommy! Thank you for showing me a love that only a mother can give. Your last words you spoke to me right before you passed. "I love you Brondon," still rings in my ears as words from heaven to my heart.

Table of Contents

PREFACE

PRE-PRAYER-ING FOR THE COMING SHAKING OF THE NATIONS

> *Zeph. 3:8 Therefore wait ye upon me, says the LORD, until the day that I rise up to the prey: for my determination is to gather the nations, that I may assemble the kingdoms, to pour upon them mine indignation, even all my fierce anger:* **for all the earth shall be devoured with the fire of my jealousy.**

As we approached the year 2011, in November of 2010 the Spirit of God began inviting me into his heart for what he wanted to do in the earth in the coming year. I immediately begin capitulating with God, saying, "Who am I Lord that you would want to speak to me about what you want to do in the earth? I'm not the head of a major ministry. I'm not on television etc, etc. In actuality, I was telling the Lord, I'm not a major leader in the body of Christ today, why would you want to tell me what you want to do in the earth in the coming year. Tell someone else that is a major leader, who can speak to the masses. He said to me, I use the base things of the world to confound the wise. I don't tell my secrets to the wise and prudent, I reveal my secrets to babes (Luke 10:20). Most of those that can speak to the masses are too busy saying what the masses want to hear. Once I submitted to the fact that he wanted to tell me, I felt him invite me to enter into an end of the year consecration, fasting for the last forty days of the year, not eating meats or sweets.

This was especially painful for me since it was right before Thanksgiving, and Christmas, the two largest meals of the year in most homes in the United States. However, once I yielded to this invitation of the spirit of God the grace to fast and seek his face came upon me. At the beginning of this consecration God spoke into my spirit the above verse from Zephaniah 3:8-10, *for my determination is to gather the nations, that I may assemble the kingdoms, to pour upon them mine indignation, even all my fierce anger:* **10 From beyond the rivers of**

1

Ethiopia my suppliants, even the daughter of my dispersed, shall bring mine offering.

This verse might as well had been God speaking in Chinese to me, because I couldn't remember the last time I had read the book of Zephaniah. At the end of the consecration, which was the beginning of 2011, he gave me another verse from Ezekiel 30:20.

> *And it came to pass in the eleventh year, in the first month, in the seventh day of the month, that the word of the LORD came unto me, saying, 21 Son of man, I have broken the arm of Pharaoh king of Egypt; and, lo, it shall not be bound up to be healed, to put a roller to bind it, to make it strong to hold the sword. 22 Therefore thus saith the Lord GOD; Behold, I am against Pharaoh king of Egypt, and will break his arms, the strong, and that which was broken; and I will cause the sword to fall out of his hand.*

From these verses God began speaking to me about the divine purpose of the continent of Africa, and specifically North, East and Central Africa becoming cities of Refuge for worshippers of the Lord - the remnant of Israel, to be offered up as an offering to the Lord. He said to me, "I'm positioning my people on the continent of Africa to have my heart of unity and oneness with my chosen people, that they might stand shoulder to shoulder with the apple of my eye, becoming a continent of glory and refuge as a forerunner continent to take in my people in the time of trouble and distress during times of great tribulation in the earth.

One of the main strategies God is employing in His church on the continent of Africa in preparation for this day of the Lord is the coming forth of the original, final and eternal expression of his church as a House of Prayer for all nations. During the day of the shaking and judgment of the nations, before the coming of the Lord, those that come to his holy mountain, to his house of prayer will become a place of refuge for persecuted Jews during the time of the release of the fire of God's jealousy (Isaiah 2:2-5 Isaiah 56:6-8). This coming day of the Lord is going to have negative and positive dimensions in the nations and will coincide with the final restoration movement and expression of Prayer being restored in the church. We will share more about in a later chapter.

What's coming in the nations of the earth in the years to come requires the type of preparation of the First Testament (OT) priests that were to prepare to come into the presence of the Lord before they would go before the mercy seat to sacrifice for the sins of the children of Israel. God is coming in a glory like we've never seen or experienced before. He wants to do more than visit Africa with revivals and mass gatherings of prayer and power, he wants to dwell with Africa with His presence and His people. Which will totally revive the ecological, geological landscape of the continent of Africa. But Africa must PRE-PRAYER for His presence.

I believe 2011 initiated our year to begin praying prayers and specific scriptures that will pre-prayer Africa and the nations for his presence and His people. It was our year to begin praying and asking him to get us ready, doing whatever he has to do, and shaking whatever needs to be shaken now for his presence to dwell among us and we not be consumed later. In the Appendix at the end of this book are some scriptures we can begin praying for Africa, for Israel and the Church, for God to fulfill His promises of protection, provision and prosperity at the end of the age. We must stop asking just for the experiences of revivals of the past but look ahead to what God has prepared for his people, that no eye has seen, nor ear heard.

The Coming Baptism of Fire in The Earth

Zep 3:8 Therefore wait ye upon me, saith the LORD, until the day that I rise up to the prey: for my determination is to gather the nations, that I may assemble the kingdoms, to pour upon them mine indignation, even all my fierce anger: for all the earth shall be devoured with the fire of my jealousy.

Luk 12:49 I am come to send fire on the earth; and what will I, if it be already kindled? 50 But I have a baptism to be baptized with; and how am I straitened till it be accomplished! 51 Suppose ye that I am come to give peace on earth? I tell you, Nay; but rather division:

When God shows up in all of his glory there is no precedent of what Africa will experience of His presence and His power. But there's also no precedent for what will be experienced of his judgment and his indignation when the fire of His jealousy is released against sin in Africa and the nations. When God shows up to dwell amongst his people, what happened in the early church with Ananias and Sapphire will be magnified and multiplied many times over. The greatness and the awesomeness of this day together with the terribleness and dread of this day is a scenario that we must equally prepare and position ourselves for in the coming days.

Act 2:17 And it shall come to pass in the last days, saith God, I will pour out of my Spirit upon all flesh: and your sons and your daughters shall prophesy, and your young men shall see visions, and your old men shall dream dreams: 18 And on my servants and on my handmaidens I will pour out in those days of my Spirit; and they shall prophesy:

There are several unbalanced tendencies that most of the body of Christ ends up in when we read about and begin desiring the glory of God, revival in our day as it was in former days. One of them is, we often quote Acts 2:17 without finishing the quote with Acts 2:22

Most preachers when preaching from this verse, stop right there and preach on revival coming in the last days when the Holy Spirit is poured out on all flesh. However, the scripture verses that Peter is quoting from in Joel 2 go on to say;

19 And I will shew wonders in heaven above, and signs in the earth beneath; blood, and fire, and vapor of smoke: 20 The sun shall be turned into darkness, and the moon into blood, before that great and notable day of the Lord come: 21 And it shall

4

come to pass, that whosoever shall call on the name of the Lord shall be saved.

The revival described here is describing a return to the Lord of God's chosen people, the Jews, and of all the children of God that have been scattered from the nations of the earth. As the Lord releases his Spirit of mercy and judgment in the earth through the increase of the prophetic gifts there's going to be unprecedented power released, as well as unprecedented darkness, sin and Judgment in the earth.

It is at this time and in this context that God is going to pour His spirit out on His chosen people, Israel, that they may see Yeshua as their Messiah. Before this happens there will be a shaking of the nation of Israel of the Jews in their promised-land. This shaking of time Judgment is called in scripture, the time of Jacobs trouble (Jeremiah 30:6). The sign of the coming of this shaking listed in Acts 2:20 will be the sun turned to darkness – *A solar eclipse*, and the Moon turned to blood – *A Lunar eclipse*. These two occurrences are both scheduled to happen in 2014-15 during four successive Jewish Holidays of Feast of Passover and Feast of Tabernacles. Consequently, His chosen people in the land, both Jews and Christians will be scattered from the land once again and driven to the nations of the world. Where will the majority of them go? I believe many of them will end up on the continent of Africa. This persecution and tribulation are what will cause His people to look to Him, again, eventually saying, "Blessed is He that comes in the name of the Lord.

> *O Jerusalem, Jerusalem, thou that kills the prophets, and stones them which are sent unto thee, how often would I have gathered thy children together, even as a hen gathers her chickens under her wings, and ye would not! 38 Behold, your house is left unto you desolate. 39 For I say unto you, Ye shall not see me henceforth, till ye shall say, "Blessed is he that comes in the name of the Lord."*

This is what Joel 2:28, Acts 2:17 is speaking of – *shaking of the nation's towards the return of the Jewish Messiah back to His people and back to the land.* But most Christians don't associate God's presence coming with power and darkness, tribulation and signs in the heavens and the earth. They just associate this release of God's spirit and presence with the power seen on the day of Pentecost. And while there was a partial fulfillment of this prophecy. Most Christians don't associate His presence coming with life and death, just life. But the coming baptism of fire is a baptism of the fiery presence of God to purge and purify the earth, and to bring everlasting righteousness to the earth. Luke 12:49 says it like this;

Luk 12:49 I am come to send fire on the earth; and what will I, if it be already kindled? 50 But I have a baptism to be baptized with; and how am I straitened till it be accomplished!

John the Baptist says it like this;

Luk 3:16 John answered, saying unto them all, I indeed baptize you with water; but one mightier than I cometh, the latchet of whose shoes I am not worthy to unloose: he shall baptize you with the Holy Ghost and with fire: 17 Whose fan is in his hand, and he will throughly purge his floor, and will gather the wheat into his garner; but the chaff he will burn with fire unquenchable.

The winnowing fork in the hand of the Lord is the instrument of sifting and separating the wheat and tares by the hand of the Lord. This is what the baptism of Fire releases. This is what the Baptism of Fire is unto, the fiery presence and judgment of God to clear his threshing floor and gather his wheat into his barn, but the chaff he will burn with unquenchable fire. This separating of the wheat and tares explained by Jesus in His parable in Matthew 13.

Mat 13:24 Another parable put he forth unto them, saying, "The kingdom of heaven is likened unto a man which sowed good seed in his field:

25 But while men slept, his enemy came and sowed tares among the wheat, and went his way.

26 But when the blade was sprung up, and brought forth fruit, then appeared the also.

27 So the servant's tares of the householder came and said unto him, Sir, didst not thou sow good seed in thy field? from whence then hath it tares?

28 He said unto them, an enemy hath done this. So, the servants said unto him, then do you want us to go and gather them up? But he said,

*"No, lest in gathering the weeds you root up the wheat along with them. 30 **Let both grow together until the harvest, and at harvest time I will tell the reapers, Gather the weeds first and bind them in bundles to be burned, but gather the wheat into my barn."***

Jesus gives the explanation of this parable to His disciples as they left the crowds and returned to their lodging for the night.

Mat 13:36 Then Jesus sent the multitude away and went into the house: and his disciples came unto him, saying, Declare unto us the parable of the tares of the field. 37 He answered and said unto them, He that soweth the good seed is the Son of man;

38 The field is the world; the good seed are the children of the kingdom; but the tares are the children of the wicked one; 39 The enemy that sowed them is the devil; the harvest is the end of the world; and the reapers are the angels.

40 Just as the weeds are gathered and burned with fire, so will it be at the end of the age. 41 The Son of Man will send his angels, and they will gather out of his kingdom all causes of sin and all law breakers, 42 and throw them into the fiery furnace. In that place there will be weeping and gnashing of teeth.

Jesus was explaining, not only the process of how the wheat and tares grow together until the end of the age, but how the wheat and tares would be separated by the fiery presence of the baptism of fire, purging His threshing floor and bringing His wheat into the barn.

This baptism with fire is another baptism, which is a part of the Holy Ghost baptism, but is a distinct and separate baptism with distinct differences in its application and its characteristics just like in the Godhead, the father, Son and Holy Ghost are one with distinct and separate characteristics and manifestations. The Baptism with fire is a baptism of manifestation and fulfillment of the word of God that has been sown with the baptism with water unto repentance, and the baptism with the Holy Ghost.

The Water Baptism – Baptizing the Earth with the Word of God

John's water baptism represents the baptism with the word of God, or the submerging in the water of the word of God. Water in scripture represents the word of God.

Eph 5:26 That he might sanctify and cleanse it with the washing of water by the word...

When we are baptized in water, it's because the word of God has convicted our hearts and brought us to a saving knowledge of Jesus Christ. This is how man repents and turns to Jesus – by the word of God that we are washed with – by the forerunners that God puts in our lives to feed us the word of God. Once we get that word in us we can turn or repent, coming back to Jesus. This is the goal of true repentance – Jesus – not just the forgiveness of sins.

Act 3:__19 Repent ye therefore, and turn back__, that your sins may be blotted out, when the times of refreshing shall come from the presence of the Lord; 20 __And he shall send Christ, appointed for you, Jesus__:

When Jesus comes, He shall baptize with the Holy Ghost and with Fire...*but he who is mightier than I is coming, the strap of whose sandals I am not worthy to untie. He will baptize you with the **Holy Spirit** and with **Fire** (Luk 3:16).*

8

Again, I must reiterate that these are three distinct baptisms – the Word, the Spirit, and the Fire Baptism, that are representative of the one Spirit. It's like the godhead – One God in three manifestations, or personifications. So, it is with the spirits designations, functions and applications. There are three separate administrations of the Spirits baptism, beginning with the water of the word of God, which is spirit of life. *John 6:63 says, it is the Spirit who gives life; the flesh is no help at all. **The words that I have spoken to you are spirit and life.*** Going on to the Holy Ghost baptism, which is the baptism that releases the spirits revelation and mysteries of the words of Christ, and then to the fire baptism, which releases the manifestation and presence of the words of Christ, or word of God.

*Joh 1:1 In the beginning was the Word, and the Word was with God, and the Word was God. Joh 1:14 **And the Word was made flesh, and dwelt among us,** (and we beheld his glory, the glory as of the only begotten of the Father,) full of grace and truth.*

The fire baptism is the baptism that manifests and spreads the word throughout the earth. The baptism of fire that manifests and spreads the word throughout the body of the believer, and the earth is what purifies and purges the earth, or man's selfish heart, sinful attitudes, and motives, enabling both to receive the heart of God. This is what is coming in this millennium.

Through the restoration of the baptism of fire and the manifestation of the heart of God in man throughout His body, were going to see the coming of the Lord and His kingdom come to the earth, as it is in heaven. This baptism is going to bring together in the earth, God and man, causing a supernatural uniting of all races, tribes and ethnicities that will accomplish all of the will of God for the earth. This is the revival that is coming in this century that will make this century unlike any century in human history. God has an inheritance of revival for our generation that will supersede all the previous generations combined.

9

The Baptism with Fire Revelation Restored

If I were to ask what the baptism of the Holy Ghost was most people in the church would be able to tell me, even if they had differing views on its manifestations of evidences. Most people could tell me that it involved the speaking in tongues (unknown tongue). But if I were to ask

"Who can tell what the baptism in fire is? Most people would not be able to say. This is because we have not seen the restoration of the fire baptism returned to the body. We have thought that the Holy Ghost baptism and the fire baptism were one in the same.

Another Baptism

*Luke 3:15,16 and as the people were in expectation, and all men mused in their hearts of John, whether he were Christ, or not; or not; John answered, saying unto them all, I indeed baptize you **with** water; but one mightier than I comes, the latchet of whose shoes I am not worthy to unloose: he shall baptize you **with** the HOLY GHOST and **with** FIRE. (KJV)*

He Shall Baptize You With....

While the baptism with the Holy Ghost has been widely recognized and regarded as part and parcel of the Pentecostal outpour, the baptism with fire has been overlooked and lightly regarded as just a part of the baptism with the Holy Ghost. While it is a part of the spirits work in the believer, it is also a baptism distinct and separate from the baptism with the Holy Ghost. *"He shall baptize you **with** the Holy Ghost and **with** fire." (KJV) The* Baptism with the Holy Ghost is one function of the spirits working in the believer or in the earth, and the baptism with fire is another function of the spirits working. The key word in this verse is *"with."* It is stated three times in this 16th verse (KJV) *"He shall baptize you with....and with...and with"* denoting three baptisms.

10

We know from the past century's restoration of the truth of the baptism with the Holy Ghost, that the Holy Ghost deals with leading the believer into all truth, which is Jesus. (John 16:13) *Howbeit when He, the spirit of truth, is come he will guide you into all truth.*

What then is it that the baptism with fire deals with? What is the function of the baptism with fire? What are the major attributes of the baptism with fire? What have we not seen more of the baptism fire, with its evidences and manifestations in the life of the believe in the modern church. Why have we not made a smoother transition from the baptism with the Holy Ghost to the baptism with fire before now? These are some of the questions this book will begin to reveal for the century's believers to come to know and receive. This is the next revival that is coming in the earth through the church.

The Purpose of the Baptism with Fire

Acts 1:4 and beings assembled together with them, commanded them that they should not depart from Jerusalem, but wait for the promise of the father, which saith he, ye have heard of me. 5. For John truly baptized with water; but ye shall be baptized with the Holy Ghost not many days hence.

When you've gone through a period of waiting of the Lord for the promise of the father which he said, then you shall be baptized with water, the spirit and the fire for the promise to come through you to you. God is releasing the fulfillment of the promise of the father into the earth through the church, the promise of the baptism with fire. This promise will first manifest itself through you with power, signs, wonders and fruitfulness and multiplication of the nature and purposes of God. As a result of this season of birthing and the subsequent release of the promise of the fire baptism will see and increase and multiplication of the nature of God (love) in the earth, the people of God, and the works of God. The spirit of prayer will increase in the earth, and the spirit of covenant and reconciliation will increase in the earth, the works of God will increase in the earth. There will be a proliferation of houses of prayer being raised up all over the earth. There will be the release of the true expression and purpose of the house of God; my house shall be called the house of prayer.

Acts 1:7 and he said unto them, it is not for you to know the times and seasons, which the father has put in his own power. 8. But ye shall receive power, after that the Holy Ghost is come upon you: and ye shall be witnesses unto me both in Jerusalem and in all Judea, and in Samaria, and unto the uttermost part of the earth.

The promise of the father which he said unto you is manifested by the power of the spirit that he releases through you to be a witness of his death burial and resurrection in the earth, when you wait on him to receive the water, spirit, and fire. Why didn't Jesus finish John's statement in Act 1:5 that ye shall be baptized with the Holy Ghost and fire? He stopped short of saying ye shall be baptized with fire as is recorded in Matt 3:11, and Luke 3:16. Why is that? I believe it was because the main function in the earth at that time was going to be the release of the baptism with the Holy Ghost for them to be witnesses in the entire world, but the fire baptism would be released at the end of the age...at another separate and distinct time, to fulfill verse 6. The question they asked him, *Lord will thou at this time restore again the kingdom to Israel?* The Holy Ghost baptism is for the power to be a witness to the uttermost parts of the earth of what's coming in the fire baptism when Jesus' coming consummated.

The fire baptism is for the power to restore the kingdom to Israel in the end at Jesus' second coming. It is a part of the fiery judgment and tribulation of the world at the coming of the Day of the Lord at the end of the age. The fire baptism is for the bringing back of the kingdom of God to the earth in Jerusalem, for the king Jesus being enthroned as king of kings and Lord of lord, and for the Jews to return to Jesus as their messiah.

The Baptism with Fire is a baptism that release the presence of God's Judgment on the earth to divide and separate evil from righteousness, the holy from the unholy. Jesus further explains this characteristic of this baptism with Fire in Luke 12:51

Luke 12:51 Do you think that I have come to give peace on the earth? No, I tell you, but rather division. 52 For from now on in one house there will be five divided, three against two and two against three.

53 They will be divided, father against son and son against father, mother against daughter and daughter against mother, mother-in-law against her daughter-in-law and daughter-in-law against mother-in-law.

Before the offering up of the offering of the Lord's people there will come a shaking in the earth of the nations of the world, specifically to this African continent. We saw the beginnings of this in North Africa over the last few months of the year when this book was being written in January 2011, but we will see a whole lot more of the fire of the Lord's jealousy before he makes Africa a place of refuge for His chosen people.

God gave me 7 things His body needed to do in order for her to be prepared for the release of the fiery shaking of the nations in His presence. He gave me an interesting play on words to best describe what the church must move towards in 2011 to be ready for the coming of the Lord.

He said, "IN 2011 MY BRIDE MUST ***PRE-PRAYER*** FOR MY PRESENCE." 2011 is the year of shaking, disorder, confusion, and judgment. I said to myself, how can that be God's presence? He then took me to Hebrews 12 which says, in the presence of the consuming fire of God He will shake everything that can be shaken so that the things that can't be shaken can remain. In Zephaniah I began seeing what the shaking of the nations in the earth looked like, and from Ezekiel 30:20 I began seeing specifically the breaking of the King of Egypt, (North Africa) as the presence of the Lord began to increase in the earth on unto the coming of the Lord to set up his kingdom in the earth. I began to have revealed to me what it really looks like when God's presence truly comes to a people, to a church, to the earth, and what it's unto. He began by saying. "My body, the church in 2011 must be re-conditioned to prepare for my presence. We must be re-conditioned to be positioned to truly host my presence. Zephaniah 1:7-9 gives us an aspect of what it looks like when the presence of the Lord comes, and the day of the Lord is at hand. Then Zephaniah 3:8, 9 tells us what to do.

> *Zeph. 1:7-9 says, hold thy peace at the presence of the Lord GOD: for the day of the LORD is at hand: for the*

> *LORD hath prepared a sacrifice, he hath bid his guests. And it shall come to pass in the day of the LORD'S sacrifice that I will punish the princes, and the king's children, and all such as are clothed with strange apparel. In the same day also will I punish all those that leap on the threshold, which fill their masters' houses with violence and deceit.*

INTRODUCTION

THE 7 THINGS AFRICA MUST TO DO TO PRE-PRAYER FOR
THE MINISTRY OF HIS PRESENCE

Three-fourths of the scriptures that speak of the presence of God speaks of the terribleness of his presence, the awesomeness of his presence, the judgment of his presence, the shaking of the things of the earth in his presence. To be ready for his presence we must adequately prepare in prayer. When the presence of God comes it's not something that we should take lightly or flippantly. Nine times out of ten, nor is it something we're ready for. It's something that we must prepare for, or like the word I've made up for this season, "WE MUST PRE-PRAYER FOR." There are many scriptures that speak of his presence coming in judgment, shaking, or trembling that man was not prepared to stand in his presence. Then there are as many scriptures that speak of things we are to do, or what we are to be, in order to be prepared to stand in his presence. One of the main releases from God that is being released in the earth for His church in preparation for this day is going to be the coming forth of the original, final and eternal expression of his Church as a House of Prayer for all nations.

During this day of shaking and judgment of the nations, those that come to his holy mountain, to his house of prayer will be covered, protected and provided for in his house of prayer. (Isaiah 2:2-5 Isaiah 56:6-8). This coming day of the Lord is going to coincide with the final restoration movement and expression of Prayer being restored in the church. We will share more about this in a later chapter. When the spirit of God is released into the earth from God to pre-prayer for His presence it is God's mercy giving us forewarning that his presence is coming and to get ready because it won't be pretty. It requires the type of preparation of the Old Testament priests that were to prepare to come into the presence of the Lord when they would go before the mercy seat to sacrifice for the sins of the children of Israel. God is looking for a company of priests in the House of prayer that will not only pre-prayer to come into His presence in 2011 and beyond, but that will make sacrifice for His people, lest he consume them in the fiery judgment of His presence. God wants to do more than visit us with revivals he wants to dwell with us with His presence. But we must PRE-PRAYER for his presence. We must pray prayers that will prepare us in advance for the shaking, the judgment, and the trembling of his presence, as well as the joy of his presence or the peace of his presence that will come out of the Judgment. If we are not PRE-PRAYER-ED we will be offended when he comes with his presence and it doesn't look like what we thought it would look like.

Looking to God for experiences of revivals of generations past represents seeking God after the old ordinances of the Moses Generation. Moses in the mount experienced a lesser glory than we have today. When Moses went into the mount of God he saw God's backside, as he was given the Pentateuch representing the past works of God. Moses, in receiving the Pentateuch, was shown the past, from creation to the Exodus. This was the backside glory of God. We need to begin asking for the experience of St. John, where Jesus reveals his front side, his face, to reveal his future plan for the judgment of the nations. It's this revelation of Jesus' face to his church that will enable us to partner with him for the coming of the Lord to dwell with man.

This revelation of Jesus as Christ, the bridegroom, king and Judge was left in the earth by the Holy Spirit for the church, revealed to Peter in Matt 16:14 in a moment, but further revealed and explained in detail and in all of his glory to the Apostle John on the isle of Patmos. The rock that the church is founded upon is speaking of *The Book of the Revelation of Jesus Christ*. It's this book that Jesus revealed to the Church of the glorified Christ and His plan to transition the earth through the unique dynamics at the end of the age, to the establishing of His coming kingdom in the earth.

The 7 Things to Do to Pre-Prayer for His Presence

What should we do when we are confronted with the fiery presence of the Lord, associated with the baptism with fire? How should we respond to His presence when we know that judgment is coming swiftly in the earth with this final baptism?

These 7 things are what God spoke to me in 2011, from these verses in Zephaniah, concerning pre-prayer-ing for the presence of His fire to the earth, beginning with Africa, the Middle East and the uttermost part of the earth.

Zep 3:8 Therefore wait ye upon me, saith the LORD, until the day that I rise up to the prey: for my determination is to gather the nations, that I may assemble the kingdoms, to pour upon them mine indignation, even all my fierce anger: ***for all the earth shall be devoured with the fire of my jealousy***

The 7 things from Zephaniah 3:8, 9 are:

1. **Wait upon the Lord** – Zeph. 3:8 (*Worship*)

2. **Pre-prayer for the gathering of the nations** – Zeph. 3:8b (*Pray for and partner w/ other nations*)

3. **Pre-prayer for the judgment of the nations** – Zeph. 3:8b *(Pray the peace and safety of the people of God during a time of severe Judgment in the nations)*

4. **Pre-prayer for the release of the spirit of God** to unite the nations shoulder to shoulder; to worship the Lord with a pure language - Zeph.3:9 (*Pray For revival and Outpour of His spirit on all Flesh*)

5. **Pre-prayer to call upon the name of the Lord** – Zeph. 3:9 (*Pray for day & Night Worship & Intercession - 24/7Houses of Prayer to be raised up in the earth.*)

6. **Pre-prayer for the nations to serve him in unity** with one accord shoulder to shoulder with all ethnicities – Zeph. 3:9 (*Pray for the release of the*

ministry of reconciliation within all the nations in
the earth)

7. **Pre-prayer for Africa to offer an offering** of
worshippers to come from beyond the rivers of
Ethiopia (Africa) – Zeph. 3:10 (*Pray for the
establishing of whole cities of refuge in Africa to
pray for peace and protection for Israel & other
oppressed nations during these times of
Judgment*).

When God shows up in all his glory there is no precedent of what we
will experience of His presence and His power. But there's also no
precedent for what we will experience of his judgment and his
indignation when the fire of His jealousy is released against sin in the
earth. When God shows up to dwell amongst his people, what
happened in the early church with Ananias and Sapphire will be
magnified and multiplied many times over. The greatness and the
awesomeness of this day together with the terribleness and dread of
this day is a scenario that we must equally prepare and position
ourselves for in 2011. There are two unbalanced tendencies that most
of the body of Christ ends up in when we read about and begin desiring
the glory of God or revival in our day as it was in former days. Number
one, we often quote Acts 2:17 without finishing the quote with Acts
2:22.

Acts 2:17 says, *And it shall come to pass in the last days,
saith God, I will pour out of my Spirit upon all flesh: and
your sons and your daughters shall prophesy, and your
young men shall see visions, and your old men shall
dream dreams: 18 And on my servants and on my
handmaidens I will pour out in those days of my Spirit;
and they shall prophesy:*

Most preachers when preaching from this verse, stop right there and
preach on revival coming in the last days when the Holy Spirit is poured
out on all flesh. However, the scripture verses that Peter is quoting
from in Joel 2 go on to say;

18

19 And I will show wonders in heaven above, and signs in the earth beneath; blood, and fire, and vapor of smoke: 20 The sun shall be turned into darkness, and the moon into blood, before that great and notable day of the Lord come: 21 And it shall come to pass, that whosoever shall call on the name of the Lord shall be saved.

The revival described here is describing a return to the Lord of God's chosen people, the Jews, by the power of the Spirit (dreams and visions) and of all the children of God that have been scattered across the nations of the earth. As the Lord releases his Spirit of mercy and judgment in the earth through the increase of the prophetic gifts there's going to be unprecedented power released, as well as unprecedented darkness, sin and Judgment in the earth. It is at this time and in this context that God is going to pour His Spirit out on His chosen people, Israel, that they may see Yeshua as their Messiah. When this happens simultaneously and at the same time there will be a shaking of the nation of Israel of the Jews in their promised-land. This shaking or time of Judgment is called in scripture, the time of Jacobs trouble (Jeremiah 30-6). His chosen people in the land, both Jews and Christians will, once again, be scattered from the land and driven to the nations of the world. This persecution and the tribulation are what will cause His people to look to Him again and say, *"Blessed is He that cometh in the name of the Lord.*

O Jerusalem, Jerusalem, the one who kills the prophets and stones those who are sent to her! How often I wanted to gather your children together, as a hen

gathers her chicks under her wings, but you were not willing! ___See! Your house is left desolate; "For I say to you, you shall see Me no more till you say, "Blessed is He who comes in the name of the Lord!"___

This is what Joel 2:28, Acts 2:17 speaking of - *the shaking of the nation towards the return of the Jewish Messiah back to His people and back to the land.* But most Christians don't associate God's presence coming with power and darkness, tribulation and signs in the heavens and the earth. Most Christians don't associate His presence coming with life and death, just life. They just associate this release of God's spirit and presence with the power, like what was seen on the day of Pentecost. But we must remember the judgment of Ananias and Sapphire, when they fell dead in the presence of God in the midst of the outpour of the spirit of God in the book of Acts Church, because they lied to the Holy Ghost.

In Store for More than Past Revivals

The number two imbalanced tendency of most believers in a God of revival is that we often cry out for revival based on what we have seen of His past moves simply referring to the greatness of his power and the awesomeness of the spirit's move in the midst of those in days gone by. (*A spiritual/mystic experience*) But we seldom pray for Him to do whatever He has to do in us now (*Shake us*); to be prepared for Him to live and dwell amongst us in the earth, not just visit us with an experience. Why is this the case? because this calls for having to experience and explain his terribleness and his judgment for sin in us. It also entails having to come up with palatable answers to the world as to why things are happening that are uncomfortable for us to attribute to a God of love; like earthquakes, Tsunami's, Hurricanes and other natural disasters. These characteristics of God's presence cause whole scale death and devastation. Most church folk don't know how to explain when God shows up and it doesn't look like a pretty picture of the God of mercy and Love. However, I heard the spirit say in 2011 it's time for the church to PRE-PRAYER for His presence and be ready to give an answer to the nations concerning the coming shaking to the earth.

Everything that can be shaken will be shaken in His Presence

Hebrews 12:18-28 records these words concerning one of the purposes of his presence coming in our midst right before his kingdom comes at the end of the age.

Heb 12:18 *For ye are not come unto a mount that might be touched, and that burned with fire, and unto blackness, and darkness, and tempest,*

Heb 12:19 *and the sound of a trumpet, and the voice of words; which voice they that heard entreated that no word more should be spoken unto them;*

Heb 12:20 *for they could not endure that which was enjoined, If even a beast touch the mountain, it shall be stoned;*

Heb 12:21 *and so fearful was the appearance, (or presence) that Moses said, I exceedingly fear and quake:*

Heb 12:22 *but ye are come unto mount Zion, and unto the city of the living God, the heavenly Jerusalem, and to innumerable hosts of angels,*

Heb 12:23 *to the general assembly and church of the firstborn who are enrolled in heaven, and to God the Judge of all, and to the spirits of just men made perfect,*

Heb 12:24 *and to Jesus the mediator of a new covenant, and to the blood of sprinkling that speaks better than that of Abel.*

Heb 12:25 *See that ye refuse not him that speaks. For if they escaped not when they refused him that warned them on earth, much more shall not we escape who turn away from him that warns from heaven:*

Heb 12:26 *whose voice then shook the earth: but now he hath promised, saying, Yet once more will I make to tremble not the earth only, but also the heaven.*

> ***Heb 12:27*** *And this word, Yet once more, signifieth the removing of those things that are shaken, as of things*
>
> *that have been made, that those things which are not shaken may remain.*
>
> ***Heb 12:28*** *Wherefore, receiving a kingdom that cannot be shaken, let us have grace, whereby we may offer service well-pleasing to God with reverence and awe:* ***Heb 12:29*** *for our God is a consuming fire.*

The Coming Forth Of 3rd World Missionaries

When this time of the shaking of the nations comes upon the nations of the world as God manifests his presence in a way we are not used to, those that have learned how to live supernaturally by divine prophetic direction and provision from God will be the ones that will begin to lead in the earth. Many of the third world and persecuted nations in Africa, India, Asia, that have learned to live by every word that proceeds out of the mouth of God in the face of persecution, starvation and devastation will come to the forefront.

Very soon what has been the American Dream is going to turn into a nightmare, as what Americans and the world economy have been standing on is shaken to collapse. There's an economic, political and financial shaking that's coming to America and the nations of the world that's going to change the landscape of the world power structure. When this economic shaking hits the world economy, only those that have learned to live by another system will be able to thrive during these times. Many nations in Africa that have tapped into this realm of the miraculous divine provision of God, are going to be raised up to lead the body of Christ and the world during these times.

God is getting ready to raise up African missionaries and send them to America and the nations of the world as forerunners to teach the nations how to live in the realm of the miraculous supernatural of God when all they have is God. America and the West have not seen the supernatural in the way that they're going to need to experience it during these times of shaking, because of the conveniences and luxuries that have been characteristic of the American dream, and the prosperity of the western world. God, and living by the Word of God has been the 2nd and 3rd options in the church of west because of the modern conveniences in those regions. However, those in the 3rd world nations of Africa and other 3rd world countries have learned how to trust God for everything, because God has been all these countries had to lean on. Therefore, these nations see more supernatural occurrences of signs, wonders and miracles. When this shaking comes it will be the time of the raising up of those that have trusted in the Lord for everything.

We must get ready NOW for what God wants to manifest of his presence in the days to come. He doesn't just want to visit us with a move of the spirit; he wants to stay with us with a habitation of his presence. This requires God doing whatever he has to do to remove sin, and evil from our hearts, and from the earth, and turn hearts back to him. Living in this state of preparedness requires living totally dependent on God, and with a continual awareness that God is in our midst, that God lives amongst us, by which we serve God acceptably with reverence and godly fear. This requires us realizing as Hebrews 12:28, 29 says, *Our God is a consuming fire.* We come boldly before the throne of Grace that we might obtain mercy and find grace to help in our time of need. We must focus our prayers on what's coming, not just on what's been. We must get PRAYED UP; praying in advance of what's coming to the earth.

A Shaking unto Unity & Love

From this coming shaking from Zephaniah 3, I believe God wants to do 3 things in particular. 1) He wants to gather the nations in position to be totally dependent on him, to fulfil their eternal purposes connected to His kingdom coming, 2) He wants to unite the nations shoulder to shoulder to become more dependent on one another, and to prepare them for world-wide corporate worship. 3) He wants to raise up places of refuge on the African continent for His Church and His chosen people Israel, during the time of the shaking coming in the land of Israel. Just as he did in Egypt during the time of Joseph's journey into

Egypt as a slave to preserve his brothers and the nations of the world, he's doing it again at the end of the age. He's going to raise up Africans that have already been through the oppression of slavery and colonialism in foreign lands and in their own land and raise them up to a place of prominence and authority in these countries for the purpose of preserving his people, the Church and Israel.

> *Psa. 113:5 Who is like unto the LORD our God, who dwelleth on high... 7 He raises up the poor out of the dust and lifts the needy out of the dunghill; 8 That he may set him with princes, even with the princes of his people. 9 He makes the barren woman to keep house, and to be a joyful mother of children. Praise ye the LORD.*

CHAPTER 1

THE BEGINNING OF THE END – THE COLLAPSE OF THE EGYPTIAN PRESIDENT MUBARAK'S 30 YEAR REGIME

After the 40-day consecration at the end of 2010, as we came into the New Year, the Lord gave me Ezekiel 30:20 concerning a coming change in the landscape of the nation of Egypt in the coming year.

> *20 And it came to pass in the eleventh year, in the first month, in the seventh day of the month, that the word of the LORD came unto me, saying, 21. Son of man, I have broken the arm of Pharaoh king of Egypt; and, lo, it shall not be bound up to be healed, to put a roller to*

> *bind it, to make it strong to hold the sword. 22 THEREFORE THUS SAITH THE LORD GOD; BEHOLD, I AM AGAINST PHARAOH KING OF EGYPT, AND WILL BREAK HIS ARMS, THE STRONG, AND THAT WHICH WAS BROKEN; AND I WILL CAUSE THE SWORD TO FALL OUT OF HIS HAND.*

In the first month of 2011, not long after the seventh day of the first month, the nation of Egypt on the continent of North Africa begin revolting against their government and their dictator, President Hosni Mubarak. Could it be that the change in leadership and the government of this nation is a sign post for the preparation of the nations for a shaking of God in the region? I'm not sure, but here is what happened not long after this time frame enumerated in Ezekiel 30:20. Here is a copy of a newspaper article from the New York Times, 2 weeks after the 7day of the first month of the eleventh year, which detailed the beginning of the end for Egypt's modern-day Pharaoh, President Hosni Mubarak.

25

By KAREEM FAHIM and MONA EL-NAGGAR
Published: January 25, 2011

CAIRO — Tens of thousands of people demanding an end to the nearly 30-year rule of President <u>Hosni Mubarak</u> filled the streets of several Egyptian cities on Tuesday, in an unusually large and sometimes violent burst of civil unrest that appeared to threaten the stability of one of the United States' closest Arab allies.

Protesters Call for End of Mubarak's Rule

The protests, at least partly inspired by the toppling of the authoritarian government in Tunisia, began small but grew all day, with protesters occupying one of Cairo's central squares. Security forces, which normally prevent major public displays of dissent, initially struggled to suppress the demonstrations, allowing them to swell. But early Wednesday morning, firing rubber bullets, tear gas and concussion grenades, the police finally drove groups of demonstrators from the square, as the sit-in was transformed into a spreading battle involving thousands of people and little restraint. Plain clothes officers beat several demonstrators, and protesters flipped over a police car and set it on fire.

Protests also flared in Alexandria, Suez, Mansura and Beni Suef. There were reports of three deaths and many injuries around the country. Several observers said the protests represented the largest display of popular dissatisfaction in recent memory, perhaps since 1977, when people across <u>Egypt</u> violently protested the elimination of subsidies for food and other basic goods. It was not clear whether the size and *intensity of the demonstrations — which seemed to shock even the protesters — would or could be sustained.*

The government quickly placed blame for the protests on Egypt's largest opposition movement, the Muslim Brotherhood, which is tolerated but officially banned. In a statement, the Interior Ministry said the protests were the work of "instigators" led by the Muslim Brotherhood, while the movement declared that it had little to do with them.

The reality that emerged from interviews with protesters — many of whom said they were independents — was more complicated and reflected one of the government's deepest fears: that opposition to Mr. Mubarak's rule spreads across ideological lines and includes average people angered by corruption and economic hardship as well as secular and Islamist opponents. That broad support could make it harder for the government to co-opt or crush those demanding change.

"The big, grand ideological narratives were not seen today," said Amr Hamzawy, research director of the Carnegie Middle East Center. "This was not about 'Islam is the solution' or anything else."

Instead, the protests seemed to reflect a spreading unease with Mr. Mubarak on issues from extension of an emergency law that allows arrests without charge, to his presiding over a stagnant bureaucracy that citizens say is incapable of handling even basic responsibilities. Their size seemed to represent a breakthrough for opposition groups harassed by the government as they struggle to break Mr. Mubarak's monopoly on political life.

Modern Day Background on the Egyptian Crisis

Egypt is a heavyweight in Middle East diplomacy, in part because of its peace treaty with Israel, and as a key ally of the United States. The country, often the fulcrum on which currents in the region turn, also has one of the largest and most sophisticated security forces in the Middle East. Mr. Mubarak has been in office since the assassination of Anwar el-Sadat on Oct. 16, 1981, whom he served as vice president. Until the recent unrest, he had firmly resisted calls to name a successor. He had also successfully negotiated complicated issues of regional security, solidified a relationship with Washington, maintained cool but correct ties with Israel and sharply suppressed Islamic fundamentalism and terrorism — along with dissent in general.

The government has maintained what it calls an Emergency Law, passed first in 1981 to combat terrorism after the assassination of Mr. Sadat. The law allows police to arrest people without charge, detain prisoners indefinitely, limit freedom of expression and assembly, and maintain a special security court.

In 2010, the government promised that it would only use the law to combat terrorism and drug trafficking, but terrorism was defined so broadly as to render that promise largely meaningless, according to human rights activists and political prisoners. While Mr. Mubarak's regime had become increasingly unpopular, the public long seemed mired in apathy. For years, the main opposition to his rule appeared to be the Muslim Brotherhood, which was officially banned but still commanded significant support.

In 2010, speculation rose as to whether Mr. Mubarak, who underwent gall bladder surgery that year and appeared increasingly frail, would run in the 2011 elections or seek to install his son Gamal as a successor. Mr. ElBaradei, the former director of the International Atomic Energy Agency, publicly challenged Mr. Mubarak's autocratic rule, but the Mubarak political machine steamrolled its way to its regular lopsided victory in a parliamentary vote.

Ancient Egyptian History

Though Egypt today is made up of primarily Arabs, this does not preclude its African ancestry. Nor does it take from the fact that Egypt is Africa, by its geographical setting, located on the continent of Africa. Its history of foreign domination and colonization can be traced back through all the three sons of Noah, from Ham, during the times of the great Pharaoh's, and building of the great pyramids, onto Shem, and finally to Japheth. History tells us that from an ancient African civilization which developed writing and agriculture, Egypt underwent several periods of foreign domination: starting with Alexander the Great in 330 BCE, cycling through the Ptolemaic Greeks, Romans, Byzantines, Arabs, Mamelukes, Ottoman Turks, and French, and ending up under British authority until independence was achieved in 1936.

The regularity and richness of the annual Nile River flood, coupled with semi-isolation provided by deserts to the east and west, allowed for the development of one of the world's great civilizations. A unified kingdom arose circa 3200 B.C., and a series of dynasties ruled in Egypt for the next three millennia. The last native dynasty fell to the Persians in 341 B.C., who in turn were replaced by the Greeks, Romans, and Byzantines. It was the Arabs who introduced Islam and the Arabic language in the 7th century and who ruled for the next six centuries. A local military caste, the Mamelukes took control about 1250 and continued to govern after the conquest of Egypt by the Ottoman Turks in 1517. Following the completion of the Suez Canal in 1869, Egypt became an important world transportation hub, but also fell heavily into debt. Ostensibly to protect its investments, Britain seized control of Egypt's government in 1882, but nominal allegiance to the Ottoman Empire continued until 1914. Partially independent from the UK in 1922, Egypt acquired full sovereignty with the overthrow of the British-backed monarchy in 1952. The completion of the Aswan High Dam in 1971 and the resultant Lake Nasser have altered the time-honoured place of the Nile River in the agriculture and ecology of Egypt. A rapidly growing population (the largest in the Arab world), limited arable land, and dependence on the Nile all continue to overtax resources and stress society. The government has struggled to meet the demands of Egypt's growing population. The results of this struggle culminated in riots that started in January 2011.

The Coming Alliance of the African Continent and Israel

In this present-day uprising in the northern continent of Africa, I believe one of two scenarios is being set in motion. One scenario could see many Muslim, anti-Semitic groups attempt to arise to positions of power in North Africa making life difficult for Israel in the middle-east.

If this happens there will be fewer and fewer alliances and friendships in and around Israel. The other scenario is what I believe God wants to position the countries of this region for. God is revealing his heart concerning areas in North, East and Central Africa that are going to be safe havens and cities of refuge for his chosen people Israel during the unique dynamics at the end of the age. God wants to raise up forerunner ministries from this continent to begin to stand with Israel in prayer, for Egypt and all of North Africa to continue to stay pro-Israel.

Israel and Africa were aligned with one another when the sons of Jacob were given refuge during the time when Joseph went down to Egypt as a slave strategically positioned to deliver them during the world famine. When Joseph was sold into slavery he became an Egyptian, he married an Egyptian wife, and he had Egyptian children. I believe those from the sons of Ham (Africa) were forever aligned with those from the sons of Shem (Israel) when Joseph's two sons, Ephraim and Manasseh, born in Egypt to Joseph's Egyptian wife, were grafted into the 12 Sons of Jacob in Genesis 48:5.

> *Gen 46:20 And unto Joseph in the land of Egypt were born Manasseh and Ephraim, which Asenath the daughter of Potipherah priest of On bare unto him.*

> *Gen 48:5 And now thy two sons, Ephraim and Manasseh, which were born unto thee in the land of Egypt before I came unto thee into Egypt, are mine; as Reuben and Simeon, they shall be mine.*

I believe God will once again use Africa and those of African descent to stand with Israel, and consequently have Israel end up being a blessing to the continent of Africa again at the end of the age. The judgment or shaking of the nations has begun, for the purpose of returning the nations back to God and back to one another to fulfill their end-time purpose in the earth. It is quite possible that this shaking has begun in North Africa because God wants to raise up a people with a pure language that will call upon him with one consent, shoulder to shoulder, from this forerunner continent and forerunner people, to be cities of refuge for his chosen people Israel.

The phrase from Zephaniah 3:10 *"From beyond the rivers of Ethiopia,"* speaks of somewhere in the continent of Africa. *"My worshipers, the daughter of My scattered ones, shall bring My offering,"* speaks of Jews that have been scattered from their promised inheritance coming back to the Lord and their inheritance from cities of refuge in Africa as an offering. I believe God is going to use this continent and the people from this continent to pray for Israel, to stand with Israel and to be a covering for Israel, as the release of God's fiery Jealousy is kindled to return His people back to him and one another, calling upon name of the Lord.

CHAPTER 2

THE ORIGIN OF THE NATIONS AND RECONCILATION

Acts 17:26 And he hath made of one blood all nations of men for to dwell on all the face of the earth, and hath determined the times before appointed, and the bounds of their habitation.

How do the nations with ethnic diversities, and cultural distinctions and particular and different strengths, weaknesses and purposes come into unity within one body? We must understand the position we are called to fulfill within the body of Christ. Furthermore, we must understand that our individual and national destinies - where we're going, and what we're called to do as a people in the earth, is connected in some degree to our heritage in the earth - where we've come from in the earth. God always deals in geographic regions when dealing with people. People and their prophetic destinies and promise in scripture are always tied to a geographic region or plot of land. As many different people groups coming together in one body there are 3 main things we must come to understand if we're going to come together and realize our individual, corporate and national destinies in Christ. When we do, we will realize our significance as a people, recognizing our need for one another and coming together into fullness. The 3 things we must understand are:

1. Where we've come from as a people, both in heaven and the earth, not just heaven.

2. We must know where our story and plight is in scripture.

3. In understanding the origin of all people groups, we must understand that in the formation of the nations all people groups were originally created to be in unity in the earth.

The Origin of the Nations

To understand this origin of unity within the nations Acts 17:26 gives us a launching pad to explain how the nations were all made from one blood. We further see after the formation of the nations, how we were all separated at the tower of Babel. In that separation we've all gone on to have a separate place of habitation in the earth where we've developed our own individualities, our own culture and our own distinct physical features based on our geographical proximity to the sun. In that separation we've all had an appointed time of leadership in the earth where we developed and excelled over and above the other, instead of together and with the other in mind. In this appointed time we've all attempted to find God separated from each other. However, in our reconciliation we will all truly find God and the fullness of who we are by coming together in one body again to love God, and one another, even as we love ourselves and how God made us.

Acts 17:26 And he hath made of one blood all nations of men for to dwell on all the face of the earth, and hath determined the times before appointed, and the bounds of their habitation; Acts 17:27 That they should seek the Lord, if haply they might feel after him, and find him, though he be not far from every one of us: Act 17:28 For in him we live, and move, and have our being; as certain also of your own poets have said, For we are also his offspring.

These verses in Acts 17:26-28 say a lot. Firstly, it says He hath made of one blood ALL nations. Secondly it says, ALL nations were made to dwell on ALL the face of the earth. Next it says He hath determined an appointed time of leadership in the earth for the nations. (I believe to develop their individual leadership traits).

Next it says, there would be boundaries given for these nations to live within (I believe to form their individual identities and features). Next it says, these nations would seek after God within these boundaries, but they would not find him fully until THEY CAME TOGETHER to live, move and have their being in HIM. And lastly it says, we are ALL from Him, (his offspring) born and made with certain individualities as an expression of His diversity. This scripture depicts for us the ultimate purpose and destiny of the scattering and uniting of the nations in the beginning formation of the races, and at the end of the age. It depicts the purposes of our boundaries that were given and the goal of our scattering over the expanse of the earth, with the eventual results of our coming together at the end of the age- that we would find the fullness of God in and through one another.

What Blood do all Nations come from?

Acts 17:26 says, All nations come from one blood. Who is the one blood that all nations have come from? The one blood that all nations come from is found in the table of the nations in Genesis Ch. 10.

1 Now these are the generations of the sons of Noah, Shem, Ham, and Japheth: and unto them were sons born after the flood. Gen 10:5 By these were the isles of the Gentiles divided in their lands; everyone after his tongue, after their families, IN THEIR NATIONS.

It is from one blood, the blood of Noah, that all nations were made. Noah's three sons were the foundation for the new world after the flood. In Genesis 9 the bible says, that Noah and his three sons were blessed and told to be fruitful and multiply and replenish the earth. The three sons of Noah were Ham, Shem and Japheth. FROM THESE THREE SONS ALL NATIONS HAVE ORIGINATED.

Dominion is based on Communion and Relational Connectedness

The three sons of Noah were mandated to be fruitful and multiply and replenish the earth and have dominion. This was God's original command to Adam in the beginning. But because Adam did not stay connected with God in heaven because of sin, he was unable to accomplish this mandate. He was fruitful, and he multiplied, those two commands required his connection to the earth. However, Adam having dominion and subduing the earth required righteousness – right standing with God and man. The dominion in the earth of man is directly connected to man's ability to be together in unity with God who created the earth and man whom he gave individual purpose in the earth. Without a relational connection with the God of heaven and earth, and with individual persons that God put in the earth to corporately bring about the purpose for the earth, mankind is unable to have dominion and subdue the earth. Thusly, these two failures led to the destruction of all men in the earth. However, Noah was spared the judgment of the flood because he was righteous in an unrighteous world.

Gen 7:1 And the LORD said unto Noah, Come thou and all thy house into the ark; for thee have I seen righteous before me in this generation.

If the three sons of Noah were going to be able to accomplish the mandate of God to have dominion they were going to have to stay together in unity and intimacy with God and one another. God created the 3 sons in the earth to be in unity so as to rule and reign in the earth as the God-head ruled in heaven. As God is a triune God, Father, Son and Holy Ghost ruling the heavens as One God, so mankind was created to rule and reign in the earth as a triune people from the three sons of Noah, Ham, Shem, and Japheth. We will prove this from scripture later in this chapter.

The dominion of Noah's three sons was going to be based on their communion, or relational connectedness (unity with God & Man). They were to go forth with the vision of God for the earth, not their own individual visions. They were to go forth to prepare the earth for God to enter it with His righteous seed to produce righteous fruit in the earth. As God in heaven is Father, Son and Holy Ghost - One God, they were to be in the earth, Shem, Ham and Japheth - One man. But because of their unrighteous nature, they were unable to stay in unity with God or one another to accomplish his vision and purpose for the earth. Therefore, they were unable to subdue the earth in preparation to have dominion in the earth. Again, our dominion in the earth is contingent upon our continued relational connectedness with God and with one another. However, there can be no communion, no oneness, no relational connectedness, or unity without an understanding of purpose amongst the subjects involved.

Understanding of Purpose Dispels Strife

Understanding of individual purpose dispels strife. Understanding of national purpose dispels competition and wars. Nations were not created to be like one another. People, families, and countries were not created to be like one another. Nations were created to be themselves and do what God created them to do, together with the other doing what God created the other to do, coming together to fulfill the total plan of the earth through mankind in right relationship with God and one another. Instead of ruling and reigning together in unity they went forth separately at different intervals of times in the earth in the 6000 years of man's lease on the earth to attempt to have dominion, ruling and reigning apart from the other. At the same time, they attempted to hold the other down, when they should have been working together to subdue the earth for the purpose of preparing the earth for God's presence to return.

The Times Before Appointed

In the year 2000 the earth became approximately 6000 years old. Man was created on the 6th day to subdue and have dominion in the earth to prepare the earth for heaven to inhabit it. When Adam sinned he surrendered his authority in the earth to Satan, and Satan went about preparing the earth for his habitation. For thousands of years Satan has been attempting to exercise his authority with this lease he received from man, trying to establish his kingdom in the earth. The purpose of the Church is to receive back this authority Jesus took from Satan at Calvary, to take back the lease and bind Satan and His kingdom and loose the kingdom of God in the earth.

Mat 16:18 And I say also unto thee, that thou art Peter, and upon this rock I will build my church; and the gates of hell shall not prevail against it. 19 And I will give unto thee the keys of the kingdom of heaven: and whatsoever thou shalt bind on earth shall be bound in heaven: and whatsoever thou shalt loose on earth shall be loosed in heaven.

Jesus regained the right and authority to the title deed of the earth on the cross and gave its keys back to man in the church. In other words, for man to receive authority back in the earth to subdue it for God's coming habitation he's going to have to be in Christ. All three sons from which all nations come from would have to be reconciled in one - Christ Jesus - in order for man to take back the earth to offer it up to God for His throne to be established in it.

In the days and years to come, as we go further into the 21st century we're going to see this lease of authority on the earth fully restored back to man, as together with his Church, Jesus takes the scroll during the unique dynamics of the end-times to judge the earth and establish his righteous kingdom in the earth. Only a mature united church can be positioned with Christ to repossess the earth for the Lord and fill it with his glory. This will begin the day of Christ and His Church's reign in the earth.

A Day with the Lord is as a Thousand Years

The 6000 years of the earth from Adam's Creation can be equated with the six days of creation in Genesis 1 and 2.

Gen 1:31 And God saw everything that he had made, and behold, it was very good. And the evening and the morning were the sixth day.

2 Peter 3:8 says, But, beloved, be not ignorant of this one thing, that a day is with the Lord as a thousand years, and a thousand years as one day.

The 6th day is the day of mans' creation maturity. The 6 thousand years is the time of the earth's creation maturity, where mankind's time of developing a heart and mind after God will come to its perfection and he will be prepared to host the presence of the God in the earth. This is what Romans 8 speaks of when it says, the earth, all of creation is groaning waiting for the manifestation of the Sons of God. The Earth knows that it's not in its rightful possessors' hands, and it's groaning (shaking) to be possessed by the sons of God. It is during this time, when man repossesses the earth at the coming of Christ, that God will establish His millennial reign in the earth with Jesus ruling and reigning through his united Church in the earth. This will begin the day of rest in the earth, the 7th day. The 7th day is the day of God, and of restoration. Gen 2:1 Thus the heavens and the earth were finished, and all the host of them. 2 And on the seventh day God ended his work which he had made; and he rested on the seventh day from all his work which he had made.

I believe that in the year 2000A.D, we entered the beginnings of the 7th day. From the time of Adam to the time of Abraham is approximately 2000 years. From Abraham to Jesus Christ is approximately 2000 years, and from Jesus Christ to the 21st century is approximately 2000 years, totaling approximately 6000 years of mankind in the earth. All three of the Sons of Noah have had approximately a 2000-year span of time when nations from one of the three sons ruled and reigned in the earth over the nations from the other two sons, a time appointed by God to find and seek after God.

Act 17:26 and hath made of one blood all nations of men for to dwell on all the face of the earth, AND HATH DETERMINED THE TIMES BEFORE APPOINTED, AND THE BOUNDS OF THEIR HABITATION: 27. THAT THEY SHOULD SEEK THE LORD, IF HAPLY THEY MIGHT FEEL AFTER HIM, AND FIND HIM, THOUGH HE BE NOT FAR FROM EVERY ONE OF US: 28 for in him we live, and move, and have our being; as certain also of your own poets have said, For we are also his offspring.

I believe that since the year 2000, the beginning of the 21st century, humanity has been in a state of preparation and positioning, being prepared and positioned to enter the great and terrible day of the Lord, which will culminate in the transition of the earth to the day of rest, known as the millennial reign. In the church we are not only preparing to enter the 7th day as we've gone from the 6 day to the 7th on God's calendar, but we are entering the 3rd day of Resurrection from Pentecost, as we go from the two thousand years from Pentecost into the 3rd thousandth year of the church's existence in the earth from Jesus' ascension. Hosea 6:1-3 says after two days will he revive us: in the third day he will raise us up, and we shall live in his sight.

This will represent the time where man is completely restored to the unity it lost at the tower of Babel. God scattered the nations through the scattering of their tongues, as Nimrod, the son of Cush, the son of Ham, attempted to build a tower to heaven to make a name for himself. However, God, on the day of Pentecost released His spirit on the Church to birth His Church and begin the time of the restoration of all things, where all nations would return to unity with God and man, and the earth would be prepared for God to inhabit her once again. As a result of the birthing of the Church on the day of Pentecost, as God poured out his spirit upon all flesh the sons of Noah, Ham, Shem and Japheth will begin to flow back into the House of Prayer as the body of Christ begins to arise and shine to be the light of the nation's leading the nations back to her original purpose in God's body as a House of Prayer for All Nations. How will this flow take place? What will be the process that leads the nations from Noah back into unity in Gods' house of Prayer? How will we come to the place of fullness - reconciliation, healing and unity for the release of unprecedented power in God's house of prayer? Let's continue on to see how God has been shaping history to accomplish his purposes for His house of prayer in the earth.

The 3 separate two Thousand Year Reigns of Each Son of Noah in the Earth in History

Within the six days, or six thousand years of man's perfection and maturing in the earth, mankind has been being prepared to rule and reign in the earth in unity. Each nationality from Noah's three sons have exercised a two-thousand-year period in which they would attempt to be in authority in the earth, while holding the other two under their domination. During this time, they would come to the realization that apart from one another mankind is incapable and unable to accomplish the calling of God for having dominion in the earth. We were made, both as individuals in the beginning and at the formation of the nations, to need God and one another to live and have our being. The latter verse from Acts 17:26 that speaks of God making from one blood all nations, ends in Acts 17:28; saying, for in him we live, and move, and have our being; as certain also of your own poets have said, for we are also his offspring.

In these verses describing the formation and arranging of the nations it ends with an interesting acknowledgement. It states, "For in Him WE live, and move and have our being," not I, or they. For the nations to live and accomplish their individual callings and responsibilities they must come together in HIM (Christ) to live, move and have their being. The word "being" in the original Greek text of the bible, means to exist, it means "WE ARE." Each Son of Noah has attempted to rule and reign irrespective of the other, and each one has failed in that period and time frame.

It is it very important for this study for it to be established and continually reiterated that the three sons of Noah - Ham, Shem and Japheth have each had a two-thousand-year reign in which they held down their other two brothers while attempting to have dominion in the earth. The order and position of their individual rule in the earth began with Ham, from which the nations listed below established the first great civilizations in the earth – Egypt, Babylon, Ethiopia, etc. After Ham's attempt to reign, rule and have dominion in the earth failed, the baton was passed to Shem when Melchizedek blessed and released the promise of the land of Canaan to Abraham in Genesis 14:18

Gen 14:18 And Melchizedek king of Salem brought forth bread and wine: and he was the priest of the most high God. 19 And he blessed him, and said, Blessed be Abram of the most high God, possessor of heaven and earth:

Shem, through Abraham, Isaac, and Jacob, and the Kings of Israel attempted to reign, rule and have dominion the 2nd two-thousand years. And though during the second two-thousand years the seed of God was birth through Jesus Christ being born as the seed of Abraham, seed David, this attempt also failed, as Jesus the seed that would crush the head of the serpent, came to his own and his own received him not. (John 1:12) So from Shem the baton was passed onto Japheth, in the book of Acts, as Peter was summoned by the Roman Centurion Cornelius, to speak unto him the words of life in Acts 10, and as Paul, the Apostle of Jesus Christ declared His intention and call to the be a light to the Gentiles. It was here that the European nations of the

Japhetic line would begin the preaching and spreading of the gospel in the 3rd two-thousand-year period. Peter unlocks the door to the Gentiles to receive the message and mantle for the spreading of the gospel in Acts 10:1

Acts 10:1 There was a certain man in Caesarea called Cornelius, a centurion of the band called the Italian band, 2 A devout man, and one that feared God with all his house, which gave much alms to the people, and prayed to God always. 3 He saw in a vision evidently about the ninth hour of the day an angel of God coming in to him, and saying unto him, Cornelius. 4 And when he looked on him, he was afraid, and said, what is it, Lord? And he said unto him, Thy prayers and thine alms are come up for a memorial before God. 5 And now send men to Joppa, and call for one Simon, whose surname is Peter: 6 He lodges with one Simon a tanner, whose house is by the sea side: he shall tell thee what thou oughts' to do.

Paul's Call to the Gentiles in Acts 13:46-48

Then Paul and Barnabas waxed bold, and said, It was necessary that the word of God should first have been spoken to you: but seeing ye put it from you, and judge yourselves unworthy of everlasting life, lo, we turn to the Gentiles. 47 For so hath the Lord commanded us, saying, I have set thee to be a light of the Gentiles, that thou shouldest be for salvation unto the ends of the earth. 48 And when the Gentiles heard this, they were glad, and glorified the word of the Lord: and as many as were ordained to eternal life believed.

Once this release and baton handoff was made the Japhethic - European nations went forth to rule and reign and attempt to take dominion in the earth. And even though the Roman Empire and many other European dynasties went forth to conquer and overrun the nations from Ham and Shem in the 3rd two-thousand years, they also carried the mantle and message of the gospel in this 3rd two-thousand-year period, keeping the light of the message of salvation through Jesus Christ shining to be given to the ends of the earth. Each son from Noah has taking turns attempting to overthrow, overtake and oppress the other two sons, to have dominion in the earth.

The Order of Their Dominion Began as Follows:

1. **Ham -1st 2000-year reign** — Nations from Babylon, Ethiopia, Egypt, Canaan (By-in-large Africans) are the first great civilizations in the earth. Beginning with Nimrod building the tower of Babel the descendants from Ham begins the reign of the first two-thousand years of the nations from the sons of Noah in the earth. (Genesis 2:11-13; 10:1-8).

2. **Shem — 2nd 2000-year reign** - the Middle-eastern nations of the Mesopotamia area of Shem's descendants from Abraham (Jews, Arabs and some Asians) reigned the second two-thousand years, with the possessing of the promised land (of Canaan) and the reign of the Kings of Israel. (Genesis 14:18-20; Melchizidek baton hand-off from Hametic/Canaanites to Abraham of the Semitic descent for the possessing of the promise land.)

3. **Japheth — 3rd 2000-year reign** — Western, European and some of Asiatic descent have reigned for the third two-thousand years from Christ to the 21st century, beginning with the coming of the great Roman Empire and the Destruction of Jerusalem in 70AD. (Acts 13:46-49, Christ, and Paul baton hand-off to gentile believers from Semitic descent to the Gentiles of Japhetic, European descent).

All of the nations of the world come from one of these three sons of Noah. (Acts 17:26-30). Below is a list of the Table of Nations with the origin of each nation.

Ancestry	Nation	Notes
Japhethic Line:		
Japheth (Europe)	Greeks	Became known as Gentiles
Gomer	Russians	
Britons	Britains	
Magog	Scythians	
Madai	Medes	
Javan	Greeks	
Tubal	Iberians	
Meshech	Muscovites	
Tiras	Thracians	
Ashjenaz	Germans	
Togarmah	Armenians, Turks	
Elisha	Hellenists	All of Greece
Tarshish	Spanish	
Kittim	Cyprus	
Hametic Line:		
Cush	Ethiopia	
Mezraim	Egyptian	
Put (Phut or Punt)	Libya	
Canaan	Canaanites - *one Ham's sons w/o a homeland*	
Seba	Sudan (Sabeans)	Only one of
Heth	Hittites	
Ham	American Indian Mongoloids	
Semetic Line:		
Shem	Jews	Genesis 10:21
Elam	Elamites	
Asshur	Assyrians	
Lud	Lydians	
Arphaxad	Chaldeans	
Aram	Arameans	Aramaic
Sin	China	

44

CHAPTER 3

FORERUNNERS COMING OUT OF AFRICA FOR THE LAST DAYS

> Isaiah 40:3,5 The voice of one crying in the wilderness:
> "Prepare the way of the LORD; make straight in the
> desert a highway for our God... 5 The glory of the LORD
> shall be revealed, and all flesh shall see it together [at
> Jesus' Second Coming... Isaiah 62:10-11 Prepare the
> way for the people; build up the highway! Take out the
> stones, lift up a banner for the peoples! 11 Say, "Surely
> your salvation is coming..."

I believe that during the slave trade as Africans were taken from their homeland by Europeans and Americans, they were actually being sent by God to these nations throughout the world. *Psalm 105:17, 18 says concerning Joseph, God sent a man before them, Joseph, who was sold as a slave.* Just as God sent Joseph as a man sold into slavery as a forerunner to preserve his father's household, I believe our African forefathers were sold into slavery, but sent by God to the nations as forerunners. They were sent to these nations all over the world that they may be forerunners in bringing forth God's expression that the nations should come together shoulder to shoulder to worship Him in His house of prayer. Zephaniah 3:8, 9 says it like this;

> 8 Therefore wait ye for me, saith the Lord, until the
> day that I rise up to the prey; *for my determination is
> to gather the nations, that I may assemble the
> kingdoms...* 9 For then will I turn to the peoples of a
> pure language, that they may all call upon the name of
> Lord, to serve him shoulder to shoulder. 10 From
> beyond the rivers of Ethiopia my suppliants, even the
> daughter of my dispersed, shall bring mine offering.

Joseph – A Forerunner to Africa

These Forerunners out of Africa will be instrumental not only in reconciling the nations of the world, but in praying for the preservation and the reconciliation of the nation of Israel to God and to the nations during the most tumultuous times the world has ever seen. What does it mean to be a Forerunner? Forerunners prepare the way of the Lord by preparing people to prepare the nations for Jesus' return. A forerunner speaks of a person that is to go before to lead the way, or one that goes first. A forerunner is one that leads others into his current place and position. The Webster's definition of a forerunner reads as follows:

1. A messenger sent before to give notice of the approach of others; a harbinger somebody or something that announces something: somebody or something that foreshadows or anticipates a future event. 2. An ancestor or predecessor. 3. A prognostic; a sign foreshowing something to follow. A *runner ahead*, that is, *scout* (figuratively *precursor*): - forerunner - to *run forward*, that is, *outstrip*, *precede*, outrun, run before. Forerunners are always a step ahead leading the way into what the rest will eventually come into.

At the beginning of the formation of God's chosen people, when it was time for Israel to become a great and mighty nation, the Lord called a 17-year-old boy named Joseph. Psalm 105:18 tells us that the Lord sent Joseph to another people and into slavery in a land called Egypt. At that time Egypt was the greatest civilization in the earth. Joseph was sent as a slave, but he eventually would arise to second in command to the Pharaoh, King of Egypt. Joseph would help prepare that nation for the greatest famine the world had ever seen. He would also preserve his father's house by bringing them out of their land to the nation that he had helped prepare for this famine. He then would oversee the birthing forth of the nation of Israel as a great people. Seventy people came into the land and they grew and multiplied numerically, as well as in favor and prosperity in the land of Egypt until they were fastly growing greater in number than the Egyptians. Joseph was sent ahead

46

into that foreign country as a forerunner, to help preserve his people from the coming world famine, and bring forth the destiny of his people, as well as the nations of the world.

Egypt Is Africa

This geographical tract of land that God chose to use in Egypt to preserve the people that would become his chosen people Israel, we know today to be on the continent of Africa. When most Christians of African descent, and European descent alike, read about Egypt or hear a message preached from the bible about Egypt, and how Israel was in slavery in Egypt for 400 years, they rarely, if ever, relate Egypt with Africa. Since

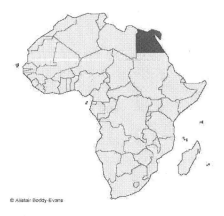

© Alistair Boddy-Evans

God began healing my heart by revealing this truth to me about the origins of race-based slavery beginning in Egypt, I have asked many people, both believers and unbelievers, both theologians, ministers and Christians who have been saved for decades, this same question; *"Have you ever thought about the fact, that Egypt is on the continent of Africa, and according to scripture, Israel was enslaved in Africa for 400 years? "I* have not met one person who was aware of this fact, and did not pause and say, *"No, I never considered that."* Some have gone so far as to vehemently deny the fact, even with geographical evidence like the map above. However, Egypt, the nation that Joseph was sent into by God as a slave, and the nation that Israel was born in, preserved in, as well as enslaved in, is on the continent of Africa.

Whatsoever a Man sows that also shall He Reap

Therefore, this northern part of the continent of Africa, right outside of the Children of Israel's promised land, not only became the womb to preserve and birth forth God's chosen people, Israel, but two generations later, it was the cradle of race-based slavery. I don't believe It's a coincidence that Africans in Slavery were enslaved the same 400 years that Israel was enslaved on the African Continent in Egypt. I know I'm going to offend many African-American people, and especially some of our leaders in the political and social arena's, as well as the African-American Church, with this statement you're about to read. But I'm going to write it anyway. I believe that these two events were directly related. The Bible declares in Galatians 6:7 *Be not deceived; God is not mocked: for whatsoever a man sows, that shall he also reap.* Africans in the Americas and Europe between the years of the 1400s – 1800s went through the same type of race-based economic exploitation in slavery, for the same amount of time as the Jews did in Africa – 400 years - building Pharaoh's pyramids, and enhancing and building His economy, approximately four thousand years ago. I know many argue that our slavery was more severe than any slavery since the beginning of time. However, the verses I read that day, which kept jumping off the page into my heart, felt eerily similar to what I heard and read about African oppression during the era of slavery and Jim Crow: ....*And they made their lives bitter with hard bondage, in mortar, and in brick, and in all manner of service in the field: all their service, wherein they made them serve, was with rigor.* (Exodus 1:14)

This nation of Egypt, which is on the African Continent, was identified in the bible in Psalm 105:23 as the land of Ham, saying; *Israel also came into Egypt; and Jacob sojourned in the land of Ham.* Ham is the youngest son of Noah. Ham had four sons – *Cush, Mizraim, (Egypt) Phut, and Canaan.* We will learn in more detail later in this book that those from African-Descent come from one of the four sons of Ham, Noah's youngest son. However, for this chapter, suffice it to say that it is not a stretch to say that those from Egypt were quite probably dark-skinned Africans. Not necessarily because of the color of their skin though. Even if they were not dark skinned, because of the geographical region they were from they should still be called Africans because of the land mass they were from. This brings us to another major point in the formulation and perpetuation of racism in modern civilization in this generation – the skin color paradigm of viewing people groups.

The Patriarchal-Land Paradigm of Viewing People Groups Verses the Skin Color Paradigm of Viewing People Groups

The color of our skin is not how we should identify people groups, when we speak of races, or nations. Africans and those of African-descent are not so because of skin color, but because of the continent they are from. This is what I call **The Patriarchal-Land Paradigm of mankind** – *viewing people groups through the lens of their earthly heritage and/or land they're from, as opposed to by the color of their skin.*

Most people in the western world, and particularly in the United States, have a skin color paradigm in relation to racial (ethnic) groups, and not a regional, land, or Patriarchal paradigm (which is the people group paradigm of scripture). In relation to racial groups, we see and call people from the different regions and ethnic groups of the earth by their skin color, as black, white, yellow, or red, as opposed to calling people groups by the land they originate from. For example, when we think of Africa we think of Black or dark colored people from Central Africa, and we call all of these nations or people, Africa. However, when we think of North Africa we don't think of a people with dark skin, we think of a particular people group called Arabs, and we call the people of these lands by their nation, i.e. Egypt –Egyptians, Libya-Libyans, almost as if they are not a part of the African continent. Most people lump these countries from North Africa into the region called *The Middle-East*, as opposed to their continent – Africa. Rather than seeing them all as Africans because of the land, continent they live on or come from called Africa, we call North Africans primarily by their nation, subconsciously, I think, because the majority in Egypt or Libya, etc, do not have black skin.

The Perpetuation of White Supremacy in the Church

This way of viewing humans, by labeling people black, white, yellow, etc, by the color of their skin, did not come from God or scripture. Our skin color paradigm of viewing people groups, as opposed to the land, or Patriarchal paradigm in scripture of viewing people groups, causes us to see scripture and the people of the scriptures based on whatever we look like, whatever skin color we are, or whatever skin color or ethnicity the people presently living in those various biblical lands are right now. This is known as creating God or people of the biblical lands after our own image, rather than after the image of God, or after the image of their Patriarchal Fathers, as its' stated in Genesis 1:26, 27 about the creation of mankind.

> *Gen 1:26 And God said, let us make man in our image, after our likeness: and let them have dominion over the fish of the sea, and over the fowl of the air, and over the cattle, and over all the earth, and over every creeping thing that creepeth upon the earth. 27 So God created man in his own image, in the image of God created he him; male and female created he them.*

Creating God in our own image is one-way white supremacy was given justification in the Christian Church in the earth in the middle-ages, during the translation of the bible by King James. For example, if we are in Europe or America and we see a portrait of Jesus, he will be White with blond hair and blue eyes. If we are in Africa and you see a picture of Jesus, in most cases, He will also be blond hair and blue eyes, even in Africa, where the majority of the people are dark skinned.

We will see clearer in later chapters that all nations come from one of the three sons of Noah, Ham, Shem and Japheth. And each of Noah's sons had a two-thousand-year period where one of the three sons attempted to exert their dominion over the other two, instead of together exerting their dominion over the earth, as God commissioned them to in Genesis 1:26; 9:1. The first two thousand years Ham's descendants, from whence Africans descend from, ruled over the other two sons from Noah. This was when Egyptians, descendants from Ham

(Ps.68:31), was the dominant, most advanced civilization in the earth. Concerning Egypt, the bible calls this nation the land of Ham.   The second two thousand years Shem's descendants ruled over the other two sons, through Abraham and the kings of Israel, with David conquering all the nations of the earth during His reign.   Notice, however, that the bible called the promised-land in the first two-thousand years, the land of Canaan – *After Ham's fourth son who was in possession of the land.*   However, the promised-land in the second thousand years is called after the Patriarch, Israel, otherwise known as Jacob, from Noah's son Shem, with the land being renamed the "Land of Israel." The third two-thousand years Japheth, Noah's oldest son ruled over the land, and over the other two sons, through the Roman-European possessors of the land. During their rule they renamed the Land of Israel, Palestine, after the Japhetic people that lived there after Israel was removed from the land in 70 A.D. The bible never identifies the skin color of the people of these lands, nor does it recognize any lands in scripture by a predominant skin color of those people in a particular region. It only recognized these lands by the name of their Patriarchal fathers – Canaan, Israel, Palestine. This is known as the **Patriarchal – Land paradigm** of recognizing people groups.

We don't know definitively what skin color most biblical characters were in these lands, unless we dig deep beneath the surface of scripture. This was one of the reasons God told the Children of Israel to make for you no graven images of God (Exodus 20:4). God knew that man would try to make God in their own image, instead of man being in the image of God. I believe it is the wisdom and ingenuity of God and His Word that we don't know definitively what skin color the biblical characters were, unless we go into a deep word study of the biblical meanings of certain names of the biblical characters. And even then we're still hypothesizing. But most Christian believers today believe that the people of the biblical lands two-thousand years ago are the same color as the people that live in the biblical lands today. Most European Christians believe that most of the people of scripture where White, or light complexioned.   Most African or African-American Christians believe the same way - that most biblical personalities were white, or light complexioned – as a result of the skin color of the European Kings and rulers that translated the bible into English in the middle-ages, or as a result of the European Missionaries that evangelized these in the last two-thousand years of European-Japhetic rule in the earth, from the beginning of civilization. This way or lens of viewing people groups or racial groups, through a color paradigm, or after our own or present image, adds to the racial divide and the prejudiced way of relating to those of differing races, which further exacerbates the racial divisions within the body of Christ; Further disparaging Jesus' purpose of the Church, that we would all come into the unity of the faith, and be a place for all ethnicities.

Can Arab-Egyptians also be Africans

Because of this skin color paradigm, when dealing with Egypt many Christians, white and black alike, have a hard time seeing the biblical land of Egypt as Africa, because today Egypt is primarily made up of Arab speaking, olive colored people, and when we think of Africa, we think of black, dark complexioned people. However, when seeing people through the Patriarchal-land paradigm, skin color designations are not emphasized or highlighted.

Being an Arab does not exclude one from being an African, if they live on the land mass called Africa. Again, Africa is not necessarily a designation of the color of the skin but of the people that presently live on the continent called Africa. Even today in the Sub Sahara section of Africa there are different people groups with different skin colors that live on this section of the continent of Africa. A people group of a particular patriarchal origin presently in that part of the region of Africa can vary in skin color mainly because of European Colonization back in the middle ages. Today there are olive colored Arabs, European Arabs, dark skinned, black Arabs, etc, that live in Egypt, on the continent of Africa. Just like there are, European Jews, Ethiopian, black Jews and olive colored Jews living in Israel. There are dark skinned, black African-Americans, brown African-Americans, light skinned (white) African-Americans that live in America. There are dark skinned, black Africans; light skinned Africans, as well as white Afrikaans in South Africa, and within many of the other nations on the continent of Africa, because of the era of Colonization. However, in the original formation of the nations those from Egypt came from what the bible calls the land of

Ham, which is located on the continent of Africa. Psalm 68:31 bears this out, referring to Cush and Egypt (brothers and sons of Ham) together, saying; *Envoys will come from Egypt; Cush (Those traditionally labeled as those from a darker hue) will submit herself to God* (NIV). Therefore, Egypt was and still is an African nation.

Africa – A Forerunner People to the birthing of Israel

During the formation of the nation of Israel these people on the African continent in the nation of Egypt were forerunners in every sense of the word. They were the pioneers of civilization in the earth. They produced some of the present wonders of the world, the pyramids, over 3000 years ago. They went before the nations to prepare and preserve Gods chosen nation Israel, which would bring forth the Messiah into the world at Jesus' first coming into the earth. This great nation of Egypt preserved and blessed what would become known as the nation of Israel during the time of the great world famine, in order to bring forth God's chosen people as a great nation. This was during a time when all the earth was in travail and the powers of darkness were released in the earth, arrayed against and assigned to stop the coming forth of God's chosen people. Those from the land of Ham went before Israel as a covering and a place of refuge.

Forerunners at the End of the Age

I believe at the end of the age God is going to once again use this continent of Africa as a forerunner continent to his chosen people Israel, to preserve, prepare and offer up a people of worship from God's first-born son to the Lord. (Zephaniah 3:8,9). I believe he will establish forerunner nations on the continent of Africa as cities of refuge for Jews in flight during a coming time of persecution and tribulation, once again coming to God's chosen people before their Messiah is revealed to them. Just as the persecution of the Holocaust was instrumental in the restoration of the nation of Israel, and Jews returning to their homeland, the bible speaks of another persecution and scattering of God's chosen people in their homeland called *Jacobs Trouble* (Jeremiah 30:7), which the Holocaust will pale in comparison to. I believe that this persecution and scattering in the land of God's chosen people will be instrumental in the coming revealing and manifesting of the Jewish Messiah in the land of Israel. I believe that during this time, known as *Jacobs Trouble*, God is going to raise up pockets of this African continent and its people with a message of comfort and peace (reconciliation to God and man) to His chosen people.

Forerunners are sent to make ready the way of the Lord by helping people to prepare the nations for Jesus' return. In Isaiah 40:3, forerunners prepare a highway "for God" whereas in Isaiah 62:10 they prepare the highway "for the people." It is one highway seen from two points of view. Forerunners represent God and His interests in Isaiah 40, whereas in Isaiah 62, the intercessors represent the people. The highway God walks on is the voluntary agreement of His people as they partner with Him. Forerunners are messengers who proclaim "now" what the Holy Spirit is "soon" to emphasize in a universal way across the nations. They are "one short step" ahead of what the Holy Spirit is about to openly release, so they can prepare the people to respond rightly to Jesus by making known God's plans. They help other people make sense of what will happen before it actually happens. Forerunners bring new paradigms of God and His end-time activity and plans through his house of prayer.

Seven Theological Premises of the Forerunner Message in His House of Prayer

There are seven theological premises of the Forerunner message that I believe God is going to release in the earth at the end of the age. This forerunner message is going to have an expression from those from the continent of Africa, as well as from all the nations of the world. Forerunners are "messengers" who are prepared in the place of intercessory prayer in their wilderness seasons of suffering and affliction, to function with a specific message in different spheres of life and geographical regions. Africans and the Diaspora world-wide have been in centuries of preparation in their wilderness seasons of suffering and affliction through slavery, racism and discrimination, to function with a specific message of forgiveness, comfort, peace and reconciliation to God and man at the end of the age in the different spheres of life in the nations. For example, forerunners are preachers, evangelists, artists (singers, musicians, actors, etc.), writers (internet), media, marketplace or intercessors as well as those who disciple people one-on-one in the church, university or home (moms and dads are some of the most important forerunners). They are called and sent to the nations to disciple those nations and leaders for the preparation of the coming of the King of kings to the earth. Their message will come forth clearest and precise during the generation right before the Lord returns to prepare the way for the coming of the Lord. There are seven theological premises of their message.

Premise #1: There will be *"unique dynamics"* in the generation the Lord returns. It will witness the *greatest demonstration of power* both God's and Satan's (Rev. 13). The three "supernatural generations" in Scripture are the generation of Moses (Ex. 7-10), the generation of the apostles, and the generation Jesus returns in which the miracles done by Moses and the apostles will be combined and multiplied on a global level. It is the generation *most described* by God in His Word. It is the generation that is *most populated*. Some estimate that there will be more people alive in this one generation in one life span (70 years) than in all history combined. After the Great Harvest, there will be more of God's people on earth than in heaven. The greatest number of people at the time of the greatest manifestation of power will require a unique preparation, focus and understanding. The unique dynamics of the generation in which history transitions to the Millennial Kingdom is the "new thing".

> *18 Do not remember the former things, nor consider the things of old. 19 Behold, I will do a new thing, now it shall spring forth; shall you not know it? (Isa. 43:18-19)*

Premise #2: The Spirit is emphasizing the *revelation of the Father* in bringing God's family to maturity. God will raise up those who release the Father's heart in the home, church, marketplace and government (Ps 68:5-6). The Spirit is also highlighting care for the fatherless (orphans, etc.), and the unborn.

> *5 I will send you Elijah the prophet before the coming of the great and dreadful day of the LORD. 6 And he will turn the hearts of the fathers to the children, and the*

> *hearts of the children to their fathers, lest I come and strike the earth with a curse. (Mal. 4:5-6)*

Premise #3: The Holy Spirit will emphasize *3 facets of the beauty of Jesus* as clearly seen in Scriptures that describe God's End-Time plans (Rev. 19; Mt. 24-25; Isa. 60-62). There will be no contradiction in Jesus' heart and ministry as He manifests His glory as a Bridegroom, King, and Judge. He does not suspend one attribute to exercise another.

1. Jesus as a *passionate Bridegroom*: has great tenderness and deep desire for His people
2. Jesus as a *powerful King*: releases power in confronting darkness and winning the lost
3. Jesus as a *righteous Judge*: upholds the standards of conduct (holiness)

Premise #4: Forerunners will participate in the *3 unprecedented activities of the Holy Spirit*:

1. *To restore the First Commandment to first place* worldwide as the Church is prepared as a worthy Bride (Mt. 22:37; Rev. 19:7).
2. *To gather the Harvest* through an unprecedented release of God's power (Rev. 7:9, 14).
3. *To release Jesus' End-Time judgments* described in Revelation (Rev. 6; 8-9; 16).

Jesus' end-time judgments will remove everything that hinders love in preparing the Church as a Bride. The principle of God's love in judgment is: God uses the least severe means to reach the greatest number of people at the deepest level of love without violating our free will.

Forerunners will aid in gathering the Harvest by bringing eternity to bear on the hearts of multitudes of lost humanity and by manifesting God's power.

Forerunners will release God's vengeance on those who hate Jesus and persecute His people. God's End-Time judgments will shake 7 spheres of human life as recorded in Haggai 2:6, 7. *1) The heavens:* the sky, atmosphere, weather patterns; *2) The earth:* earthquakes, volcanoes, etc.; *3) The sea:* tidal waves, tsunamis, etc.; *4. The dry land:* vegetation and plant life; *5) All nations:* national and social infrastructures will be shaken; *6) Religious institutions:* multitudes come to Jesus as the Desire of All Nations; *7. Economic disruption:* commercial turmoil as God transfers wealth.

> *6 I will shake heaven and earth, the sea and dry land; 7 and I will shake all nations, and they shall come to the Desire of All Nations, and I will fill this temple with glory...8 The silver is Mine, and the gold is Mine,' says the Lord of hosts. (Hag 2:6-8)*

Premise #5: God is *preparing forerunner ministries ahead of time* in the wilderness that they may prepare others for the Day of the Lord activities. It takes a clear sense of mandate and identity as a forerunner to stay faithful long-term to grow in understanding (Dan. 11:33-35). God is raising up "friends of the Bridegroom" type forerunner ministries like John the Baptist who will fast and pray as they "stand and hear" Jesus' voice as the Bridegroom God.

> *The friend of the Bridegroom, who stands and hears him, rejoices greatly because of the Bridegroom's voice. Therefore, this joy of mine (John the Baptist) is fulfilled. (Jn. 3:29)*

Premise #6: Forerunners must *live a fasted lifestyle* in the grace of God as seen in Mt. 6:1-18. This is God's way to position ourselves to tenderize our hearts to receive more revelation in faster time frames with a deeper impact on our hearts.

Premise #7: Forerunners are *best trained in context to the End-Time prayer movement*. God is raising up forerunner ministries in local congregations that are rooted in prayer that flows in the spirit of the Tabernacle of David.

The Coming Forerunners out of Africa

In order for these forerunner purposes of God to be fulfilled in every people group, whatever or whoever has been holding God's people in prescribed boundaries must be broken, before that people group can be released to realize God's eternal purposes for their lives or region. For over 500 years God has been bringing Forerunners out of Africa and dispersing them throughout the nations of the world to take this message and ministry to the masses. We will see in this book how God used slavery and oppression to prepare and form a people for this forerunner calling at the end of the age. During the times of slavery in the middle-ages though many Africans were sold and bartered like chattel for work in the European-American cotton, grain, and rice fields, God was actually positioning Africans in the nations of the world, bringing forerunners out of the wilderness of the dark continent of Africa to eventually be sent throughout the nations with a message and ministry of reconciliation at the end of the age.

Though they were bound and kept in chains for many centuries God had a plan both in their bondage and in their deliverance. Whenever a people group is held in prescribed boundaries or any type of involuntary captivity, either because of their own sin or because of the wickedness of an outside force or nation, it's the means by which God develops within them a cry to be free. This cry to be free is a cry to find, know and pursue the purposes of God for their lives. It is a deep desire to find, know and worship the true and living God. Jesus said in John 8:31, 36 *....and you shall know the truth and the truth shall make you free. If the son therefore shall make you free you shall be free indeed.* The cry to be free is actually the cry to know truth, which is found in the words of the Son of God, Jesus Christ.

Chapter 4

THE NEW WINESKIN OF 21ˢᵀ CENTURY MINISTRY

THE REVIVAL FIRES OF EARLY AFRICAN-AMERICAN MODERN PENTECOSTALISM

Hebrews 6:20. *"Whither the forerunner is for us entered, even Jesus, Made a high priest forever after the order of Melchizedek."*

The Forerunner ministry of Jesus Christ will be the foremost ministry operating in the Church before Jesus returns. The Body of Christ mostly relates the forerunner ministry with the ministry of John the Baptist, preparing the way for Jesus' first coming. However, before we can tap into the forerunner message of John the Baptist we're going to have to understand and begin to operate in the forerunner ministry of Jesus Christ. How will the Church arrive to the place of unity and fullness in the earth? Who will lead the way? Who will be forerunners that go before preparing the way for the coming of the Lord? Who was the first forerunner and what was his mission? Many believers are unaware that the ministry function of a forerunner is firstly a ministry of Jesus Christ, because they are not familiar with this ministry in connection with Jesus' ministry.

The forerunner ministry of Jesus Christ is firstly a priesthood ministry of Intercession that is for the purpose of contending for the fullness of what God has promised in the earth under a better covenant. The priesthood ministry that Jesus operated in, after the order of Melchizedek, is the key and first step to operating in the forerunner message of John the Baptist. Jesus was the great and ultimate forerunner, going before us as an intercessor, entering beyond the veil (Heb. 6:20) making a way for us to enter in also to a new covenant. Hebrews 4:14-16 explains Jesus' high priestly ministry as an intercessor to be our forerunner, making a way for us to enter in also beyond the veil, saying;

59

14. Seeing then that we have a great high priest, that is passed into the heavens, Jesus the Son of God, let us hold fast our profession. 15 For we have not an high

*priest which cannot be touched with the feeling of our infirmities; but was in all points tempted like as we are, yet without sin. **16 Let us therefore come boldly unto the throne of grace that we may obtain mercy and find grace to help in time of need.***

The Forerunner ministry of Jesus Christ is the ministry of Intercessory Prayer, coming boldly before the throne of God to intercede for mercy and grace to help in our time of need. This ministry is the priesthood ministry of the believer that each of us must enter into as intercessors to prepare the earth for the release of fullness. This ministry is the ministry of prayer that every believer is to be prepared and perfected to enter into, before they can go forth with the message and witness of Jesus Christ in the earth.

The Better Covenant of the Priesthood ministry of Prayer

Hebrews Chapters 5-8 speaks of a new and better covenant that Jesus has initiated through the forerunner ministry after the order of Melchizedek. The old order and covenant under the ministry of Aaron's priesthood was limited to a man that would be the only one that could come before the Lord for the people and offer up sacrifices for the people. These chapters and verses contrast the ministry after the Law and the priesthood of man under the Levitical order of Aaron, with the ministry after righteousness and peace of the priesthood after the order of Melchizedek which is an everlasting priesthood that is unlimited. It gives access for every man to come before God for themselves.

The New Covenant Ministry of the 21st Century Church

This contrast in Hebrews 5-8 represents the change in the New Testament church from the Old Covenant. In the 21st Century the church of Jesus Christ that returns to be a House of Prayer for all Nations (people) is going to have to come to the perfection of this

60

ministry understanding and revelation, to release the body to seek and hear from God for themselves. We're going to have to go from the one man show of the few that hear from God and speak what God is saying in the earth, to the many that pray and hear from God and pray what God is saying in the earth. The Church of the 21st century must go from the ministry of a man that keeps people coming to them, to the priesthood of the believer ministry of prayer and intercession that perfects the saints to seek God for themselves. This is the difference between the old order and the new order. Many in the 21st century Church are still under the old order of Moses' administration. This is how the people under the old order under the ministration of Moses and the Law related with God.

> *Deu 5:24 And ye said, Behold, the LORD our God hath shewed us his glory and his greatness, and we have heard his voice out of the midst of the fire: we have seen this day that God doth talk with man, and he liveth. 25 Now therefore why should we die? for this great fire will consume us: if we hear the voice of the LORD our God any more, then we shall die. 26 For who is there of all flesh, that hath heard the voice of the living God speaking out of the midst of the fire, as we have, and lived? 27 Go thou near and hear all that the LORD our God shall say: and speak thou unto us all that the LORD our God shall speak unto thee; and we will hear it, and do it.*

Under this ministration the people expected only Moses to hear from God and come back and tell them what God was saying. They were unwilling to engage God's heart with the life necessary to have access into the presence of God and not be consumed. So, because of this unwillingness to live a life of holiness necessary to come into the presence of the Lord, they summonsed Moses and told him to do it for them and come back and tell them what God said. And they would do whatever the Lord said. However, that was a deception of understanding of how God's order works. If you will not seek God for yourself, you will not have the power to obey what God says within yourself. A personal relationship with God is what empowers us to keep the laws of God from our heart. Because of this lack of a personal relationship with God they had a propensity to fall short of God's laws and commands. There was a need for a new priesthood ministry after a new order, where the laws would be written on their hearts from God, not a man on tables of stone. Hebrews 5-8 contrasts the two priesthood ministries that would be established, one on the First Covenant and the other on the New Covenant. Chapter 5 of Hebrews speaks of the priesthood ministry of Aaron and the calling of priests under the Levitical law.

> *Heb 5:1 For every high priest taken from among men is ordained for men in things pertaining to God, that he may offer both gifts and sacrifices for sins:*

Chapter 6 begins speaking of the priesthood ministry of Melchizedek, after righteousness and peace and the eternal calling after an endless life that Jesus assumed as a forerunner in order to bring us into a better covenant. Chapter 7 speaks of how much better Melchizedek's priesthood ministry is than Aaron's priesthood ministry.

> *Heb 7:4 Now consider how great this man was, unto whom even the patriarch Abraham gave the tenth of the spoils. :5 And verily they that are of the sons of Levi, who receive the office of the priesthood, have a commandment to take tithes of the people according to the law, that is, of their brethren, though they come out of the loins of Abraham: 6 But he whose descent is not counted from them received tithes of Abraham, and blessed him that had the promises. 7 And without all contradiction the less is blessed of the better.*

Chapter 8 speaks of the better covenant of Jesus writing his laws on our hearts and minds and every man knowing the Lord, not having to have someone teach us to know the Lord.

> *Heb 8:7 For if that first covenant had been faultless, then should no place have been sought for the second. 8*

> *For finding fault with them, he saith, Behold, the days come, saith the Lord, when I will make a new covenant with the house of Israel and with the house of Judah: 9 Not according to the covenant that I made with their fathers in the day when I took them by the hand to lead them out of the land of Egypt; because they continued not in my covenant, and I regarded them not, saith the Lord.*

This greater covenant and ministry of the Melchizedek priesthood is a ministry of the priesthood of the believer, not a one-man priesthood of the first covenant ministry, nor a small group of special prayer warriors Interceding as the intercessory prayer ministry in a church. No, God is raising up every believer to fulfill this end-time New covenant ministry. In the latter days of the church in the earth Apostolic Pastors, evangelists and teachers that are not intercessors will not lead God's church. The end-time church will not be led by preachers or teachers but by Intercessors, those that recognize that their first and foremost ministry is the intercessory ministry of a priest after the order of Melchizedek. This is what this forerunner ministry is all about – Intercession that prepares the way for heaven to come to earth. *"Whither the forerunner is for us entered, even Jesus, Made a high priest forever after the order of Melchizedek."*(Heb 6:20)

The Forerunner calling of John was preceded by the Priesthood Ministry of Zacharias

Just as John's father Zacharias was a priest after the order of Aaron who prayed in the temple day and night, God is raising up the day and night 24/7 prayer movement in the earth. Zacharias, in the presence of God saw an angel that announced the coming of the miracle child whose name would be called John, so also in the end-times we're going to need to step into the priestly ministry of Jesus, after the order of Melchizedek. This ministry will enable us to receive the message from the Angel that will bring forth the message and miracle of forerunner messengers, preparing the way of the Lord.

Luk 1:5 There was in the days of Herod, the king of Judaea, a certain priest named Zacharias, of the course of Abia: and his wife was of the daughters of Aaron, and her name was Elisabeth. 6 And they were both righteous before God, walking in all the commandments and

ordinances of the Lord blameless. 7 And they had no child, because that Elisabeth was barren, and they both were now well stricken in years.

Luk 1:8 And it came to pass, that while he executed the priest's office before God in the order of his course, 9 According to the custom of the priest's office, his lot was to burn incense when he went into the temple of the Lord. 10 And the whole multitude of the people were praying without at the time of incense.

Luk 1:11 And there appeared unto him an angel of the Lord standing on the right side of the altar of incense. 12 And when Zacharias saw him, he was troubled, and fear fell upon him. 13 But the angel said unto him, Fear not, Zacharias: for thy prayer is heard; and thy wife Elisabeth shall bear thee a son, and thou shall call his name John. Luk 1:14 And thou shall have joy and gladness; and many shall rejoice at his birth.

15 For he shall be great in the sight of the Lord and shall drink neither wine nor strong drink; and he shall be filled with the Holy Ghost, even from his mother's womb.

Luk 1:16 And many of the children of Israel shall he turn to the Lord their God. 17 And he shall go before him in the spirit and power of Elias, to turn the hearts of the fathers to the children, and the disobedient to the wisdom of the just; to make ready a people prepared for the Lord.

The Forerunner calling birthed by the Miracle of Intercession

John's forerunner calling was birthed by the miracle of intercession. Zacharias, the intercessory priest and his wife Elisabeth had been interceding for many years to have a child. Luke explicitly states that John was born in answer to the prayers of his priestly father Zacharias, and mother Elisabeth while he was doing his priestly duties. Luke 1:13 says – *for thy prayer is heard; and thy wife Elisabeth shall bear thee a son, and thou shall call his name John.* As we approach the second coming of Christ, John's forerunner message through the church at the end of the age – *Repent for the Kingdom of Heaven is at Hand* - is going to need to be birthed in the place of intercession once again. Jesus' forerunner ministry after the order of Melchizedek - intercession, is what will release us to know and proclaim the end-time revelation of Jesus Christ and his forerunner message to the final generation.

Jesus is our great High Priest after the order of Melchizedek. And it's this forerunner ministry of Intercession, together with the forerunner message of Jesus and John the Baptist preparing the way of the Lord, that's going to go before the second coming of Jesus Christ. Forerunners must prioritize the Intercessory Prayer ministry of Jesus Christ, (*Which results in the ministry of reconciliation, calling man back to God, man back to one another, as well as calling heaven back to earth.*) over the preaching and teaching ministries of the coming of the Lord in the body of Christ. In our end-time churches, to adequately prepare the way for the Lord we must pray before we say, we must beseech before we preach, and we must intercede before we precede. Jesus said, *My House shall be called a House of Prayer*, not a house of preaching.

For fullness to be released to and through the church, this intercessory forerunner ministry of Jesus Christ, after the order of Melchizedek is going to have to arise in the church. When it does, the church will not only come into the unity of the faith, but she will discover and fulfill the work of her ministry leading the church to fullness, and the coming of the Lord. For the church to come to fullness she's going to first have to come into the unity of the faith. The unity of the faith is connected to a specific and particular ministry that

Ephesians 4:12 refers to as, **"the work of the ministry"** saying, *And he gave some, apostles; and some, prophets; and some, evangelists; and some, pastors and teachers; For the perfecting of the saints, **for the work of the ministry**, for the edifying of the body of Christ.*

The Work of the Ministry – Intercession unto Unity & Fullness

2nd Co 5:18 says, and all things are of God, who hath reconciled us to himself by Jesus Christ, and hath given to us the ministry of reconciliation; But what is this work of the ministry? What is this work supposed to build the body up to? This work of the ministry is supposed to build the body of Christ up until unity is not only possible or probable, but it is unavoidable. When we come into the unity of the faith, meaning every member, people group and nationality is in their place of leadership within His body, we will attain unto fullness, coming to the measure of the stature of the fullness of Christ, to receive all that God said we would have, to do all that God said we would do.

God wants to raise up forerunner messengers from the nations of Africa because of their original alliance with Israel in the formation of the nation of Israel. However, in order for forerunner messengers to be raised up from the African nations to lead the body of Christ into fullness there must be intercession that goes forth unto the purpose of unity. Unity won't just happen, unity must be interceded for. Many nationalities and ethnicities have been separated and segregated from one another for so long that there have been walls built up that have kept these ethnicities divided. Injustices and offenses have developed. Bitterness and distrust have developed. Fears and stereotypes have developed that seem insurmountable. However, as the body of Christ is matured for the work of the ministry and is built up as a body, we will come to the work of our ministry and we will begin praying for the release of the unity of the spirit, the unity of the brethren, and the unity of the faith in that order. Unity must begin in the Spirit, and then must progress to the unity of the brethren, which is the coming together of brethren by the spirit. When this happens, we will end in the unity of the faith. If unity does not begin with the Spirit it will never end in the unity of the faith, which is all people, races, and nationalities coming together in the body of Christ.

Notice I did not say the spirit of unity. This puts unity before the spirit and has all religions coming together keeping their false messiahs and various ways of finding God. This is a man-u-factored unity, but the unity of the spirit will end in the unity of the faith, being joined together by Christ Jesus. This is what will release the commanded blessing in the earth.

> *Psa 133:1-3 Behold, how good and how pleasant it is for brethren to dwell together in unity! 2 It is like the precious ointment upon the head, that ran down upon the beard, even Aaron's beard: that went down to the skirts of his garments; 3 As the dew of Hermon, and as the dew that descended upon the mountains of Zion: for there the LORD commanded the blessing, even life for evermore.*

It is interesting to note that for unity to come within the brethren the ointment or anointing had to run down the beard of Aaron the Priest, not Moses the deliverer. The anointing and commanded blessing that comes as result of unity begins with the intercession of the priestly order. There won't be unity, nor will there be blessing until there is priestly intercession for the release of the unity of the Spirit.

In order for African and European relationships to be healed, or Chinese and Japanese, or North Korean and South Korean, or Indian and American, or Indian and Pakistani, or any other people groups that are separated and divided along racial, ethnic lines, the body of Christ must come to the work of the ministry of Intercession unto unity. The offenses that have kept us divided and segregated are insurmountable without the ministry of Intercession. Revelation and wisdom that will release the hope of His calling for each nation will come through the priestly ministry of intercession. We must move into the ministry of reconciliation through the ministry of intercession that will bring about the fullness of the Gentiles.

A New Ministry Paradigm for the Release of Unity and Fullness

In order to reach this place of unity where we arrive to fullness we're going to need a whole new ministry paradigm. We're going to need a whole new ministry model. In the latter part of the 20th century the model the church tapped into significantly increased our ability to hold more wine in our wineskins. We we're able to go from a model that would minister to hundreds, to a model that would reach thousands, tens of thousands, and even hundreds of thousands. This model brought in the age of the Mega-church, where thousands in a congregation became a common-place, the norm and the standard by which we measured success in church growth. However, it didn't completely fulfill the total purpose of the work of the ministry of bringing the body to the unity of the faith.... etc., etc. of Ephesians 4:12-14. In that model we we're able to tap into the realization of the need for the restoration of the Five-fold ministry gifts in the church as recorded in Ephesians 4:11,12 - *for the perfecting of the saints for the work of the ministry*, but in most cases, we didn't tap into what that work was and what that work was unto. We came to the revelation of the church being built upon more than just the Pastors, but upon the Apostles and Prophets, Jesus Christ being the chief cornerstone. We began to embrace the Apostolic and Prophetic gifts, along with the gifts of the Pastor, teacher, and Evangelists. But often we failed to recognize what these ministry gifts being restored actually pointed to.

The 5-fold Ministry Gifts are to unite the Nations

The restoration of the gifts was meant to produce the unity of the faith, bringing all nations together in one body, the body of Christ. However, much of the time the body of Christ focused on these gifts from a fad approach. We approached these gifts from a stand-point of going after what was the latest in-thing in Christendom. We went after the gifts based on which gift is hot right now, or which gift is glamorous, or would bring us more engagements or influence. However, we failed to focus on these gifts from a true ministry and restoration approach of the gifts for the perfecting of the saints until we all come to the unity of faith.

Everybody seemed to want to be an Apostle or a Prophet. Many began attaching the title "Apostle" or "Prophet" before their name to identify themselves with this new ministry emphasis in the body. However, the true test of these gifts should have been how much healing, forgiveness and reconciliation among the races was being produced through the grace upon the lives of those operating in those gifts. It's not what you call yourself that makes you what you are, but it's what God calls you that makes you what are, and what fruit is produced. It's who God says you are that's most important in accomplishing a task in life, not what you call yourself, or what people say you are. Eventually who you think or say you are has to translate into the hope of God's calling for your life in order for your life to be productive.

What I recognized about Paul in his writings to the churches is that his Apostolic identification never preceded his name, but always followed his name and servant-hood calling to his churches. As in the opening of Romans 1:1; *"PAUL, a servant of Christ Jesus, called to be an apostle and set apart for the gospel of God."* He mentioned his name, his servant hood position to Jesus and His church first and foremost. Then he mentions the ministry gift he operated in. Why is this? Because who you are is always more important than what you do. His name was who he was. His function (an Apostle) was what he did. However, in the latter part of the 20th century and on into the 21st century it became a fad, as well as a badge of honor, importance, and even superiority to be called a five-fold ministry gift, and especially an Apostle, or a Prophet.

As we've come from the 20th century to the 21st century, many of our churches are still divided along ethnic and racial lines, and many in the church are stuck where God used to be, doing what God did, not what God is doing. Many are failing to realize that there's more to being a minister or ministry gift than a title or how many degrees you have, or how many people are in your church. Not realizing what the gifts are really unto in the 21st century the church has continued doing ministry for the sake of being seen or for the sake of being large, or from a fad approach of wanting to keep up with the times. All the while the church has become further divided, restless, bored and unfulfilled, dissatisfied with what we've come to know as the church.

The Greater Ministry Gift – The Forerunner Ministry of Intercession

The reason for this continued division, restlessness and boredom in the church is because we're missing something. That which we are missing has many thousands of believers exiting our sanctuaries and church services in this century as fast as they filed into them at the end

of the last century. What we're missing is the fact that there's more to the five-fold ministry gift restoration than just name calling, honor or positioning for great ministry. There's more to the five-fold ministry than more ministry responsibility or impact. There's a greater ministry assignment and ministry model that Jesus is releasing in the earth through his church for the fulfillment of all God called us to be. This release is so that we might do all God has called us to do. This ministry assignment or the actual work of the ministry is greater than and more important than the actual ministry gifts. Many in the church have failed to discern the shift, the change of emphasis and focus that is taking place. *For this cause many are weak, sick and many even sleep, not discerning the body of Christ.* (I Cor. 11:30)

Many in the church act as if they've obtained the fullness and come to the completeness of all Jesus had for us as a body in the earth when they acknowledged and received the baptism in the Holy Ghost. Or when they received their Doctorate degrees in Seminary, many leaders act as if they received the totality of ministry attainment and fulfillment. Others act as if when they received the revelation of the five-fold ministry gifts and began to embrace the Apostolic gifting and titles that they reached the pinnacle of the callings of God. Many in the church believe that the Apostle is the highest attainment of ministry in service to the Lord in his church. Many in the 20th century church wrongly received a hierarchical approach to the five-fold ministry gifts that had the Apostle at the top of the totem pole and the teacher at the bottom.

Many leaders failed to realize what ministry was supposed to look like and what it was supposed to accomplish after the five-fold ministry gifts perfected the saints for the work of the ministry. That ministry, if we were to really discover what we were being perfected for, is actually the greater ministry, *the ministry of intercession unto reconciliation*.

70

This is the ministry the saints are being perfected for. This is the great final ministry, the ministry of intercessory prayer, not the Apostle or any of the other ministry gifts. These offices will one day pass away. But the ministry of intercession is an eternal ministry. Jesus ever lives to make intercession for his saints. Yes, there's one last great ministry and move of the spirit coming after the restoration of the ministry gifts that Jesus has for his end time church at the end of the age.

It's the ministry that is unto the unity of the faith, THE MINISTRY OF INTERCESSION UNTO RECONCILIATION AND FULLNESS. It's a ministry gift that will be greater than the restoration of the ministry of Apostle, or Prophet, greater than the ministry of the Evangelists, or the Pastor, Teacher. The ministry we are being perfected for is a prayer ministry of intercession that will release reconciliation and fullness in the earth, raising up end-time messengers to proclaim the end of the age and prepare the way for the coming of the Lord. This is what happened in the early 20th century with the Azusa Street mission in Los Angeles California.

The Beginnings of the Great Pentecostal Movement of the 20th Century and Racial Reconciliation

What happened at Azusa Street has fascinated church historians for decades and has yet to be fully understood and explained. For over three years, the Azusa Street "Apostolic Faith Mission" conducted three services a day, seven days a week, where thousands of seekers received the tongues baptism. Word of the revival was spread abroad through The Apostolic Faith, a paper that Seymour sent free of charge to some 50,000 subscribers. From Azusa Street Pentecostalism spread rapidly around the world and began its advance toward becoming a major force in Christendom.

The Azusa Street movement seems to have been a merger of white American holiness religion with worship styles derived from the African-American Christian tradition which had developed since the days of chattel slavery in the South.

71

The expressive worship and praise at Azusa Street, which included shouting and dancing, had been common among Appalachian whites as well as Southern blacks. The admixture of tongues and other charisms with black music and worship styles created a new and indigenous form of Pentecostalism that was to prove extremely attractive to disinherited and deprived people, both in America and other nations of the world. American Pentecostal pioneers who received tongues at Azusa Street went back to their homes to spread the movement among their own people, at times against great opposition.

One of the first was Gaston Barnabas Cashwell of North Carolina, who spoke in tongues in 1906. His six-month preaching tour of the South in 1907 resulted in major inroads among southern holiness folk. Under his ministry, Cashwell saw several holiness denominations swept into the new movement, including the Church of God (Cleveland, Tennessee), the Pentecostal Holiness Church, the Fire-Baptized Holiness Church, and the Pentecostal Free-Will Baptist Church. Other Pentecostal pioneers who had been Methodists were Charles Fox Parham, the formulator of the "initial evidence" theology; J.H. King of the Pentecostal Holiness Church, who led his denomination into the Pentecostal movement in 1907-08; and Thomas Ball Barratt, the father of European Pentecostalism. All these men retained most of the Wesleyan teaching on entire sanctification as a part of their theological systems. Their position was that a sanctified "clean heart" was a necessary prerequisite to the baptism in the Holy Spirit as evidenced by speaking in tongues.

Other early Pentecostal pioneers from non-Methodist backgrounds accepted the premise of second blessing holiness prior to becoming Pentecostals. For the most part, they were as much immersed in holiness experience and theology as their Methodist brothers. These included C. H. Mason (Baptist), of the Church of God in Christ, A.J. Tomlinson (Quaker), of the Church of God (Cleveland, Tennessee), B.H. Irwin (Baptist) of the Fire-Baptized Holiness Church, and N.J. Holmes (Presbyterian) of the Tabernacle Pentecostal Church. In the light of the foregoing information, it would not be an overstatement to say that Pentecostalism, at least in America, was born in a holiness cradle.

72

It was not until 1906, however, that Pentecostalism achieved worldwide attention through the Azusa Street revival in Los Angeles led by the African-American preacher William Joseph Seymour. He learned about the tongues-attested baptism in a Bible school that Parham conducted in Houston, Texas in 1905. Invited to pastor a black holiness church in Los Angeles in 1906, Seymour opened the historic meeting in April 1906 in a former African Methodist Episcopal (AME) church building at 312 Azusa Street in downtown Los Angeles.

A Testimony of the beginnings of the Church of God in Christ & Founder Bishop C.H. Mason. Also, in 1906, Charles Harrison Mason journeyed to Azusa Street and returned to Memphis, Tennessee to spread the Pentecostal fire in the Church of God in Christ. Mason and the church he founded were made up of African-Americans only one generation removed from slavery. (The parents of both Seymour and Mason had been born as southern slaves). Although tongues caused a split in the church in 1907, the Church of God in Christ experienced such explosive growth that by 1993, it was by far the largest Pentecostal denomination in North America, claiming some 5,500,000 members in 15,300 local churches. Another Azusa pilgrim was William H. Durham of Chicago. After receiving his tongues experience at Azusa Street in 1907, he returned to Chicago, where he led thousands of mid-western Americans and Canadians into the Pentecostal movement.

His "finished work" theology of gradual progressive sanctification, which he announced in 1910, led to the formation of the Assemblies of God in 1914. Since many white pastors had formerly been part of Mason's church, the beginnings of the Assemblies of God were also partially a racial separate on. In time the Assemblies of God church was destined to become the largest Pentecostal denominational church in the world, claiming by 1993 over 2,000,000 members in the U.S. and some 25,000,000 adherents in 150 nations of the world. In this revival that broke out in Los Angeles, California on a "Street" called Azusa Street and conducted by the anointed evangelist W. J. Seymour, Bishop Mason, was baptized in the Holy
Spirit.

Elder Mason came back to Memphis, Tennessee sharing his experience and teaching this New Testament doctrine which would help others experience a deeper holy life. Also, he began to establish churches, the name of which was revealed to him several years before the Azusa Street Revival. The name that God revealed to him for this organization was the "Church of God in Christ", which because of his anointed ministry and vision, has become the 5th largest Black Pentecostal organization in the world and the 5th largest denomination in the United States. One of the churches that was established by Bishop Mason was in Norfolk, Virginia in 1906 where a great revival took place. Bishop Mason preached in the street at the Ferry Terminal on Commercial Place where over 6000 people received salvation. Out of this revival the Mother Church of God in Christ, 744 Goff Street, Norfolk, VA was born.

After the death of Bishop Mason in 1961, the Church was renamed the C. H. Mason Memorial Church of God in Christ by Bishop D. Lawrence William who, because of his love and respect for the founder, felt that a memorial of lasting memory to the life of Bishop Mason should be established.

In addition to the ministers who received their Pentecostal experience at Azusa Street, there were thousands of others who were indirectly influenced by the revival in Los Angeles. Among these was Thomas Ball Barratt of Norway, a Methodist pastor later to be known as the Pentecostal apostle to northern and western Europe. In addition to the ministers who received their Pentecostal experience at Azusa Street, there were thousands of others who were indirectly influenced by the revival in Los Angeles. Among these was Thomas Ball Barratt of Norway, a Methodist pastor later to be known as the Pentecostal apostle to northern and western Europe. From Chicago, through the influence of William Durham, the movement spread quickly to Italy and South America. African Pentecostalism owed its origins to the work of John Graham Lake (1870-1935), who began his ministry as a Methodist preacher but who later prospered in the business world as an insurance executive.

In summary, all these movements, both Pentecostal and charismatic, have come to constitute a major force in Christendom throughout the world with explosive growth rates not seen before in modern times. By 1990, The Pentecostals and their charismatic brothers and sisters in the mainline Protestant and Catholic churches were turning their attention toward world evangelization. Only time will reveal the ultimate results of this movement which has greatly impacted the world during the Twentieth Century.

CHAPTER 5

THE COMING FORERUNNER MINISTRY OF JESUS CHRIST AFTER THE ORDER OF MELCHIZIDEK

Hebrews 6:20 says, "Whither the forerunner is for us entered, even Jesus, made a high priest for ever after the order of Melchizedek."

As a 23-year-old bible college student I was taken from my cultural and religious expression in my African-American church upbringing and sent by God into another church cultural, racial and spiritual setting to bring God's expression of His house of prayer for all nations to that spiritual community. At the end of the age God is going to be raising up many forerunners from the continent of Africa, and from the African Diaspora to come out of their cultural and religious surroundings to lead God's house to reconciliation and fullness. A forerunner speaks of one who prepares a people for the coming of the Lord. It also speaks of a person that is to go before as a model or a foretaste of what's coming, someone that goes first, with inside information on what is coming. A forerunner is also one that leads others into his current place and position, preparing the way for others to come.

Jesus – Our Ultimate Forerunner

The book of Hebrews first mentions the word "forerunner" connecting it with Jesus Christ, relating this ministry to what's coming to every believer, the High priestly intercessory ministry of Jesus Christ after the order of Melchizedek. Hebrews 6:20 says, "Whither the forerunner is for us entered, even Jesus, made a high priest for ever after the order of Melchizedek." In relation to the return of Jesus to the earth at his second coming, this aspect of the forerunner ministry of high priestly intercession after the order of Melchizedek is to be the ministry that is to go before the coming together of all races in His house of prayer, as well as the coming of the Lord. This ministry will lead the earth into the way, the truth, and the life of Jesus Christ's eternal calling - *Intercession and Reconciliation*. Jesus ever lives to make intercession for those who come to God by Him. The restoration of this ministry of intercessory high priestly prayer is instrumental. At the end of the age it will help return God's church to her original and eternal identity as a house of prayer for all nations. First the Lord will raise up the forerunner ministry of intercessors, high priests after the order of Melchizedek, as He restores His church to be a House of Prayer for all nations. Then He will raise up forerunner messengers, after the order of John the Baptist and send them forth from the place of prayer into the nations to prepare the way for His second coming.

Many races and people groups within the body of Christ are sensing that the church is coming into this new expression of a House of prayer for all nations. Many believe this expression of the Church is to play a vital role in the preparation of the coming of the Lord. However, we should also be aware that someone is going to have to go before the process of this coming expression in prayer and fasting. We must be aware that the intercessory, high priestly ministry of *THE FORERUNNER* after the order of Melchizedek will lead the way for the church to raise up and release forerunner messengers from all the nations of the world to bring the church to reconciliation and fullness at the end of the age. This is what this book is all about, the Forerunner ministry of Jesus Christ and its role in releasing forerunner messengers out of Africa and the nations of the world to lead the church to reconciliation and fullness.

The Forerunner Ministry of Jesus Christ after the Order of Melchizedek

In the reconciliation of the nations in His house of prayer, the Forerunner intercessory ministry of Jesus Christ is the last, most significant ministry calling related to the end times within the Church of Jesus Christ. It is the most significant calling related to the uniting of the nations and the coming of the Lord of all of the ministry gifts and callings within the body of Christ. It's this ministry that will return God's house to being the House of Prayer. The personage of Melchizedek in scripture represents the ultimate work of reconciliation in heaven and earth. When Melchizedek comes on the scene in scripture he speaks of the Most High God being possessor of Heaven and earth when Abram met him after the defeat of the 5 Kings in Genesis 14.

Gen 14:19 and he blessed him, and said, blessed be Abram of the most high God, possessor of heaven and earth:

The Hebrew word for "possessor" is the word "kanor" which means redeemer, restorer, to reconcile or to recover. It seems clear through this blessing that Melchizedek released to Abraham, He had as a part of his ministry of righteousness and peace the mandate to release the vision of the reconciling and rejoining of heaven back to earth to the man Abraham. He introduced to Abraham the God most High, *POSSESSOR (RECOVER, RECONCILER) OF HEAVEN AND EARTH.* In the beginning heaven and earth were made to be one. Genesis 1 says, "*In the beginning God created the heavens and the earth.*" This denotes the union of heaven and earth. This was God's original intent for the earth, to be one with Heaven. When God made man, he was also made from heaven and earth united in one, when he made man of the dust of the earth and breathed into him the breath of life (*Heaven*). However, because of sin, heaven and earth, as well as man and God were separated from each other. Heaven and earth was separated by the firmament, which is where Satan and his principalities now dwell. God and man were separated by sin, which is what Satan brought when he deceived Eve. At the return of Jesus to set up his kingdom in the earth, he will manifest the abolishing of the enmity between God and man which was abolished in his flesh on the cross, and he will once again rejoin heaven and earth and all things in heaven and earth in one, the body of Christ.

Eph 1:10 That in the dispensation of the fullness of times he might gather together in one all things in Christ, both which are in heaven, and which are on earth; even in him:

I believe Melchizedek's appearance on the scene in Genesis 14:18 foretold what was to come for Jesus and His church's forerunner ministry declaring and releasing the vision of the LORD, possessor, redeemer or reconciler of heaven and earth. This ministry of reconciliation from Melchizedek is the main ministry that Jesus came to fulfill.

> *2Co 5:19 To wit, that God was in Christ, reconciling the world unto himself, not imputing their trespasses unto them; and hath committed unto us the word of reconciliation.*

There are many functions of ministry that Jesus undertook while on the earth. He operated as an Apostle, he operated as a Prophet, as a Pastor, he operated as a teacher and as an evangelist. However, of all those ministry offices the greatest ministry function that Jesus operated in while in the earth, and the ministry that he still functions in while seated at the right hand of the father, is the forerunner ministry office of a High Priest, an intercessor, ever living to make intercession for the unity of his saints in the earth. As a forerunner, Jesus was leading us into our eternal ministry as an intercessor. This is our eternal ministry. This is our eternal ministry calling and function, intercession unto reconciliation. We see Jesus' transition into the fullness of this ministry function at the end of his time here on earth, moving into its' fullness at the end of his life on the earth in John 17. At the conclusion of the last supper with His disciples, Jesus prepared to enter into the fullness of this end-time forerunner ministry when he prays his High priestly prayer that he prayed for his disciples to be one with one another, with him and with the father.

The Greater Glory of an Intercessor of Reconciliation

Jesus, after preparing his disciples to become Apostles – *sent ones to minister to His bride* - he then asked the Father to glorify him with the glory he had from the beginning. He called what he was called to do as a great High priest and intercessor, *"the glory which he had from the beginning."* This is the glory of the forerunner intercessory ministry of Jesus Christ, a High Priest after the order of Melchizedek. Being glorified in that same manner that Jesus was at the end of his life and ministry is what God is getting ready to release now to His bride.

That Glory is one of the things that this ministry function of a forerunner is all about – *Intercession unto Reconciliation, Oneness and Fullness*. In that respect Jesus was the ultimate Forerunner, preparing the way for our end-time ministry that would bring the church into unity and a new age of kings and priests in the earth.

This ministry that Jesus went before and made way for all believers to enter into is the ministry that the saints are being perfected to enter into at the end of the age. The forerunner ministry of intercession is what's going to bring the saints into the unity of the faith. It's this ministry that's going to cause the nations from Noah's three sons, from which all nations originate from, to come together, shoulder to shoulder, Ham, Shem, and Japheth all together in one holy earthly trinity of nations as it is heaven within the Godhead. This ministry that the saints are to be perfected to enter into is what's going to position the body of Christ to arrive to the measure of the stature of the fullness of Christ. Without the forerunner intercessory ministry of Jesus Christ being released to the body we will never come into unity, we will never come to fullness and we will remain splintered, segregated and separated from God and man in the earth. This forerunner ministry is the ministry of Jesus Christ. The Book of Hebrews is the only place in scripture that the actual word "Forerunner" (in the KJV) is mentioned. And it's mentioned concerning Jesus, saying, *"Whither the forerunner is for us entered, even Jesus, Made a high priest forever after the order of Melchizedek."*

The Forerunner Ministry of Jesus Christ and Melchizedek

In understanding the forerunner ministry of Jesus Christ, the connection between Jesus, His forerunner ministry and the priest hood of Melchizedek holds a vital key in the end-time church understanding, receiving and walking in her end-time calling as forerunners in the earth. When the end-time generation understands the connection between the forerunner ministry of Jesus and the priesthood of Melchizedek this generation will tap into her mission in picking up the baton of this forerunner ministry to usher back into the earth Jesus, His ministry, and His Kingdom, which is a kingdom of Priests and Kings ruling and reigning forever, also after the order of Melchizedek." In the proceeding pages and chapters of this book we will seek to answer some questions concerning the Melchizedek priesthood, which I believe will bring the reader to a greater understanding of the forerunner ministry and how we are all to fulfill this end-time calling through this ministry right before Jesus returns. Melchizedek's ministry is significant in relation to the end-times because at the end of the age Jesus is releasing understanding of mysteries that I believe deal primarily with the personage of Melchizedek and his ministry through His end-time church, that have not been able to be understood or tapped into until *"NOW."*

> *Col 1:25 Whereof I am made a minister, according to the dispensation of God which is given to me for you, to fulfill the word of God. 26 Even the mystery which hath been hid from ages and from generations, but NOW is made manifest to his saints:*

The ministry and personage of Melchizedek has definitely been a mystery. Scripture says concerning Melchizedek that his ministry is hard to understand but for those that are of full age. I believe the church at the end of the age will reach full age, or maturity. This statement from scripture is saying that it will only be understood by those that have been perfected to do the work of this ministry order at the end of the age. But it also says that there's much that can be said about this priesthood ministry of Melchizedek. However, there are many things that can't be revealed until we have been matured, or perfected to enter into the operation or function of that revelation. Hebrews 5 says concerning the ministry of Melchizedek;

> *"And having been perfected (speaking of Jesus) He became the author of eternal salvation to all who obey Him, called by God as High Priest according to the order of Melchizedek, OF WHOM WE HAVE MUCH TO SAY, AND HARD TO EXPLAIN, since you have become dull of hearing. For though by this time you ought to be teachers, you need someone to teach you again the first principles of the oracles of God; and you have come to need milk and not solid food. For everyone who*

partakes only of milk is unskilled in the word of righteousness, for he is a babe. BUT SOLID FOOD BELONGS TO THOSE WHO ARE OF FULL AGE....

I believe the ministry model embraced in the 20th century by the larger part of the body of Christ of the five-fold ministry gifts, for perfecting the saints, for the work of the ministry has been steadily maturing us and positioning us to answer these hard questions about the ministry order of Melchizedek. I believe the body of Christ is finally ready to enter into her time of maturity or perfection, to embrace her final and eternal ministry calling and assignment as priests, interceding after a new ministry order that will unite all things, both nationalities and ethnicities in the earth, and all things in heaven in one body, the Body of Christ.

Ephesians 4:11, 12 says, *And he gave some to be apostles, prophets, some, evangelists, and some pastors and teachers, for the equipping of the saints for the work of the ministry, for the edifying of the body of Christ, till we all come to the unity of the faith and the knowledge of the Son of God, to a PERFECT MAN, TO THE MEASURE OF THE STATURE OF **THE FULLNESS OF CHRIST**; that we should no longer be children, tossed to and fro and carried about with every wind of doctrine, by the trickery of men, in the cunning craftiness of deceitful plotting, but speaking the truth in love, may grow up in all things into him who is the head, even Christ.......*

I believe that the body of Christ is being positioned to contend for fullness. This fullness has been promised her, but is connected to her coming into her maturity for the work of the ministry that will bring her to unity so that she will come to the measure of the stature of the fullness of Christ. I believe that we are at the precipice of coming into that maturity and ministry here at the end of the age. And in that, I believe we are ready to tap into what we've been being prepared for in over 2000 years of the existence of the church in the earth.

How Will We Get There from Here?

In order to tap into this ministry calling I believe that there are 5 Questions that we must grapple with concerning Melchizedek in relation to *the ministry of the forerunner* in the body of Christ. In asking and attempting to answer these five questions of the Melchizedek priesthood we might not all see the same thing or come to the same conclusion as this book will attempt to answer concerning this man, who he is and where he came from. But I believe we will definitely see that through this man's forerunner ministry and his ministry order that God has more for us than we've ever imagined, and we've settled for so much less. So, I believe we must begin to grapple with these questions if we are to understand and enter into our end-time forerunner ministry of intercession unto reconciliation and fullness. These 5 questions are:

1. Who was Melchizedek?"
2. Why was Jesus made a high priest for ever after the order of Melchizedek?
3. What was Melchizedek's purpose in the coming forth of the Great Forerunner Jesus Christ?
4. Where was Melchizedek's kingdom, and what did it represent?
5. When Melchizedek visited Abraham what was the effect of this visit on the land and the people of the land and their descendants?

These are some of the questions that I believe are vitally important in discussing what I believe is one of the most vital subjects related to the end-times - *The Ministry of the Forerunner after the order of Melchizedek*. Jesus was the ultimate Forerunner. He was the firstborn of every creature; he is the head of the body, the church. He was the firstborn from the dead. He is head of all principalities. He was the firstborn among many brethren, and he came after the order of Melchizedek. This Ministry of the Forerunner was the ministry Christ assumed when he came into earth, and it is the ministry that will usher him back into the earth.

CHAPTER 6

JESUS, THE FORERRUNER, SAID I AM THE WAY

John 14:6 *"I am the Way, the Truth and the Life."*

JESUS CHRIST was and is forever THE FORERUNNER. He said in John 14:6, *"I am the way,"* but to what? What was Jesus referring to when he said I am the way? Thomas had just asked, "Show us the father," Jesus first replied by saying when you've seen me you've seen the father. He then replied by saying I am the way to the father. What Jesus was emphasizing to his disciples from this verse is that the way to access the father is found through three simple truths made clear by Jesus' statement, *"I am the Way, the Truth and the Life."*

1. Jesus came first to show us the way to access the father through his forerunner ministry of going beyond the veil, tearing down the middle wall of partition, to give us access to a relationship with our heavenly father. This would cause us to see him for ourselves within ourselves.
2. He secondly came to lead us to the truth of who the father was,
3. And lastly, He came to lead us into this way of access as an eternal lifestyle. *I am the Way, the Truth, and the Life.*

Only the one who has gone ahead of us can show us the way. He came first to make a way for us to return to fullness, to access heaven and bring heaven to earth. I believe we've yet to scratch the surface in the church on what this way is that Jesus came to show us. We've known and stated correctly that Jesus is the way, but because we have known very little about the truth of who Jesus is and all that he represents and exemplifies to the believer, we've not been able to adequately articulate or walk out the way or ministry of Jesus Christ. If Jesus is the way, the truth and life, the believer that walks in this way should naturally go forth as a FORERUNNER, leading people to a

85

relationship with Jesus with little to no effort because our encounter with others is preceded by our encounter with Jesus through intercessory prayer. It should be second nature. When we come to the understanding of Jesus Christ and the ministry of the forerunner we will lead people to the way that will prepare the people of the earth for the coming of the kingdom of God, and our eternal identity with him as Kings, and Priests.

Concerning his forerunner ministry In John 14:1 Jesus said;

> *"Let not your heart be troubled; you believe in God, believe also in me. In My father's house are many mansions; if it were not so, I would have told you. I go to prepare a place for you. And if I go and prepare a place for you, I will come again and receive you to myself; that where I am, there you may be also. And where I go you know, and way you know'*

> *Hebrews 6:19-20 "This hope we have as an anchor of the soul, both sure and steadfast, and which enters the Presence behind the veil, where the forerunner has entered for us, even Jesus, having become High Priest forever according to the order of Melchizedek.*

This is what Jesus was doing when He went to prepare a place for us; He was operating in this forerunner ministry. He was going before us to prepare the way for us to follow him. This is what Jesus was speaking of when he told his disciples, *"Where I am, there you may be also,"* and *"Where I go you know and the way you know."* He was speaking of going behind the veil to open up the way for all humanity to have access to the father as priests, just as he had. He was going before us as a FORERUNNER to make way for us to fulfill our ministry as kings and priests in the earth.

Prepared for the Priesthood

This is the ministry that all humanity must prepare to enter into at the end of the age. Jesus' return marks the beginning of eternal access to the father in the earth through the priesthood ministry of Jesus Christ after the order of Melchizedek, as heaven comes to earth. It is the ministry of intercession that we are being matured and perfected to enter by the spirit of God and the ministry gifts in his body. I Peter 2:9 foretells of our eternal calling saying; *"But you are chosen people," a royal priesthood," a holy nation, a people belonging to God, that we may declare the praises of him who called you out of darkness into his wonderful light.*

Hebrews 4:14 introduces us to our eternal calling and to Jesus Christ as the forerunner to that calling by saying;

> *Therefore, since we have a great high priest who has gone through the heavens, Jesus the Son of God, let us hold firmly to the faith we profess. For we do not have a high priest who is unable to sympathize with our weaknesses, but we have one who has been tempted in every way, just as we are yet without sin. LET US THEN APPROACH THE THRONE OF GRACE WITH CONFIDENCE, SO THAT WE MAY RECEIVE MERCY AND FIND GRACE TO HELP US IN OUR TIME OF NEED.*

Hebrews 5:1 then introduces us to the order and process of the high priest selection made in the earth under the law.

> *For every high priest taken from among men is ordained for men in things pertaining to God, that he may offer both gifts and sacrifices for sins: (Heb. 5:1)*

Then it goes on into the high priestly selection of Jesus made in heaven by God under the order of Melchizedek.

> *And no man takes this honor unto himself, but he that is called of God, as was Aaron. So also, Christ glorified not*
>
> *himself to be made a high priest; but he that said unto him, thou art my Son, today have I begotten thee. As he*

> *says also in another place, Thou art a priest for ever*
> *after the order of Melchizedek. (Heb. 5:4-6)*

Hebrews 5:4-6 tells us that under the selection made by God in heaven that the qualification for those that are called to be high priests under the order of Melchizedek is that you are begotten of God as sons of God. In other words, when we become sons of God, it's for the purpose of our high priestly calling to become intercessors after a new order. When we're born again, begotten of God we become sons of God and are to be perfected or matured to fulfill our priestly responsibilities as intercessors. Even as Jesus was chosen by God the father in Hebrews 5:6, saying unto him, thou are my son, Today, I have begotten thee. And I am your father, and in another place, you are a priest forever after the order of Melchizedek.

Our Primary calling with the Forerunner Ministry

What the book of Hebrews is telling us is that when we come to the measure of the stature of the fullness Christ as sons of God, our primary calling and responsibility in the earth as sons is to be High priests, intercessors contending for the fullness of heaven and earth being joined together in one. Hebrews 5:9-13 goes on to tell us that everything we are to receive as believers from the Holy Spirit, and from the five-fold ministry gifts in the church from the time of our new birth until our positioning to receive our inheritance as sons is for the purpose of perfecting us and maturing us for this Melchizedek order of our priestly calling.

> *Heb 5:9-13 And being made perfect, he became the*
> *author of eternal salvation unto all them that obey him;*
> *10 called of God a high priest after the order of*
> *Melchizedek. 11 Of whom we have many things to say,*
> *and hard to be uttered, seeing ye are dull of hearing. 12*
> *For when the time ye ought to be teachers, ye have*
> *need that one teach you again which be the first*
> *principles of the oracles of God; and are become such as*
> *have need of milk, and not of strong meat. 13 For every*

one that uses milk is unskillful in the word of righteousness: for he is a babe.

Are we on Milk or Meat in the Church?

Hebrews 5:11 says, *there is much to say about this, but it is hard to explain because you are slow to learn*. It goes on to say, that by this time you ought to be teachers, you need someone to teach you the elementary truths of God's word all over again. You need milk, not solid food! That solid food that is being spoken of here is the teaching and truth of the ministry of the Melchizedek priesthood, which all believers are to be prepared to enter into. But he tells them that they are not ready to receive that truth of this calling or enter into the purpose of this calling because they are dull of hearing. In other words, in our modern vernacular the Hebrew writer might had put it to the 21st century church like this, *"There's much to say about this subject of Melchizedek, and I would tell you more but you are too busy having Church to grasp the main purpose of these elementary principles that are supposed to bring you to the point of becoming the church.* Then Hebrews 6 goes on to tell us that we are to leave the elementary teachings about Christ and go on to maturity as to enter into the calling of the end-time forerunner ministry of the Melchizedek priesthood ministry.

Stuck on the Milk

The Hebrew writer is saying, instead of going on to be perfected you are continuing to hang out around the first principles of the doctrine of Christ. Hebrews 6:1-3 relates to us the profound truth of what the elementary principles of the milk of the doctrine of Christ are.

Heb 6:1 Wherefore leaving the doctrine of the first principles of Christ, let us press on unto perfection; not laying again a foundation of repentance from dead works, and of faith toward God, 2 of the teaching of baptisms, and of laying on of hands, and of resurrection of the dead, and of eternal judgment. 3 And this will we do, if God permit.

89

These verses are telling us that all of these elementary principles, which are; 1) Repentance 2) Faith 3) Baptisms, 4) laying on of hands, 5) the resurrection of the dead, and 6) eternal judgments, are all for the maturing of the believer to enter into her forerunner ministry of the priesthood after the Melchizedek order. However, this is where 95% of the modern churches have stopped. This is where 95 % of the Church is today, drinking from the milk of the first principles of the doctrine of Christ, as we teach on faith, lay hands on the sick, impart the gifts, preach and teach on baptisms and speak in tongues. All the while we are becoming more and more ineffective in our regions, reaching our world with the message of Jesus Christ. We are failing to go on from the milk of having Church on unto the meat of becoming the Church – A house of Prayer for all Nations. In other words, all the things in ministry in the church that we receive from the five-fold ministry gifts are perfecting us to be able to pray, to be intercessors, priests of the most-high God, interceding for heaven to come to earth – A House of Prayer for all nations. This is our highest and eternal calling. However, because we see these things we do in church as the end and not the means to the end of preparing us to enter into our priestly forerunner ministry, many in the church have become bored, apathetic and empty, frustrated with Church as usual. Why? Because any time we operate and function in things that were meant to be a means to an end as though they were the end we will soon become religious and/or get bored or burned out with Church.

In Danger of a Curse

Furthermore, Hebrews 6:8 even goes so far as to say that if we receive all of these first principles of the Doctrine of Christ without producing the fruit of maturing onto this forerunner ministry of intercession of bringing heaven to earth, our life in Christ is worthless and we are in danger of being cursed, and in the end our works being burned.

> *Heb 6:1 Therefore leaving the principles of the doctrine*
> *of Christ, let us go on unto perfection; not laying again*
> *the foundation of repentance from dead works, and of*

faith toward God, 2 Of the doctrine of baptisms, and of laying on of hands, and of resurrection of the dead, and of eternal judgment. 3 And this will we do, if God permit. 4 For it is impossible for those who were once enlightened, and have tasted of the heavenly gift, and were made partakers of the Holy Ghost, 5 And have tasted the good word of God, and the powers of the world to come, 6 If they shall fall away, to renew them again unto repentance; seeing they crucify to themselves the Son of God afresh, and put him to an open shame. 7 <u>For the earth which drinketh in the rain that cometh oft upon it, and bringeth forth herbs meet for them by whom it is dressed, receiveth blessing from God: 8 But that which beareth thorns and briers is rejected and is nigh unto cursing; whose end is to be burned. 9 But, beloved, we are persuaded better things of you,</u> and things that accompany salvation, though we thus speak.

As we go on unto perfection we will become High priests after the order of Melchizedek, and we will intercede for the release of Heaven to earth, and God to man and man to one another, releasing the commanded blessing in the earth. The book of Hebrews uniquely describes this forerunner ministry as a priesthood ministry of intercession, and the way of Jesus Christ for every believer to enter into. This was Jesus' eternal ministry that he came to prepare us for, which all humanity would operate and function in during the coming of the kingdom of God in the earth.

The Priestly Order of Melchizedek can be known

Melchizedek was a unique and little-known priesthood order, a man which fulfilled the office of king and priest during a time thousands of years before the kings of Israel and the Levitical priesthood, as a prefigure of what Christ would lead his body into. Melchizedek's priestly order is little known, not because there is not much said about Him, but because up to this time the body of Christ had not matured

91

spiritually enough to seek out the truth and understand what this man's ministry represented.

> Hebrews says, *this is because God chose him (Jesus) to be a high priest like Melchizedek.* **Much more could be said about this** *subject. But it is hard to explain, and all of you are slow to understand.* Heb. 5:10,11

If we're able to find out what that priesthood ministry consists of we will be on our way to determining what the forerunner ministry that Jesus Christ was and is - *the ministry of an eternal priest, an intercessor contending for the fullness of heaven and earth coming together in one -* and what it will take to bring this Forerunner ministry to the forefront in the end-times in order to bring back to the earth Jesus Christ. For Jesus to come back to the earth heaven must also come to the earth. In order for Jesus and heaven to come to the earth, the church must contend as intercessors for fullness. We must contend as priests for the joining together of heaven and earth.

What Jesus Received We Can Receive

This ministry of the Forerunner is the ministry of Jesus Christ that he assumed when he came into the earth. However, that ministry mantle, the Forerunner mantle was here before Jesus came into the earth, it was prefigured concerning him by this man named Melchizedek and released to Abraham. As a result, Jesus, the son of David, THE SON OF ABRAHAM, became the forerunner who entered the Most Holy Place because he received this priestly order from this man that was also a king and a priest called Melchizedek, from Abraham. Where did Melchizedek come from? Who was he? How did he become the prototype for the priesthood that Jesus would function under? These questions must be answered for this Forerunner ministry to once again come to the forefront and be offered back to Jesus for his second coming into the earth. It was the ministry of Melchizedek that prefigured Jesus to be THE FORERUNNER for all of humanity. Jesus could not have entered his priesthood ministry without Melchizedek's order because Jesus came not from the Levitical priesthood, but from the tribe of Judah. The Tribe of Judah were not priests, only the tribe of Levi.

CHAPTER 7

WHO IS MECHIZEDEK?

Heb 7:1 for this Melchizedek, king of Salem, priest of the most high God, who met Abraham returning from the slaughter of the kings, and blessed him; 2 to whom also Abraham gave a tenth part of all; first being by interpretation King of righteousness, and after that also King of Salem, which is, King of peace; 3 Without father, without mother, without descent, having neither beginning of days, nor end of life; but made like unto the Son of God; abideth a priest continually.

Hebrews 7:1 says Melchizedek was the king of Salem, the King of peace, King of Righteousness. All we know of him is recorded in Gen 14:18-20. He is subsequently mentioned only once in the Old Testament, in Psa 110:4. The typical significance of his history is set forth in detail in the Epistle to the Hebrews, Heb. 7. The apostle there points out the superiority of his priesthood to that of Aaron in these several respects,

(1.) Even Abraham paid him tithes;
(2.) He blessed Abraham;
(3.) He is the type of a Priest who lives forever;
(4.) Levi, yet unborn, paid him tithes in the person of Abraham;
(5.) The permanence of his priesthood in Christ implied the abrogation of the Levitical system;
(6.) He was made priest not without an oath; and
(7.) His priesthood can neither be transmitted nor interrupted by death: "this man, because he continues forever, hath an unchangeable priesthood."

The question as to who this mysterious personage was has given rise to a great deal of modern speculation. In attempting to address this subject in this chapter of who is Melchizedek is by no means a comprehensive attempt to definitively produce an answer set in stone.

You may or may not come to the same conclusion as this book concerning this man, who he is and where he came from. But I believe we will definitely see that through this man's forerunner ministry and his ministry order that God has more for us than we've ever imagined and that we've settled for so much less.

He comes before us in history in Genesis 14; in prophecy in Ps 110; in doctrine in Heb.7, and prefigures Christ's priesthood. Indeed, it seems, we are much in the dark about him. Some believe God has thought fit to leave us so, that this Melchizedek might be a livelier type of him whose generation none can declare. They say if men will not be satisfied with what is revealed, they must rove about in the dark in endless conjectures, some fancying him to have been an angel, others the Holy Ghost. I don't necessarily believe this. I believe God can shed light on our darkness and reveal the much which is said about Melchizedek in scripture. However, the opinions concerning him that are most popular and warrant our observation and maybe our consideration are these three:

Opinions Concerning Melchizedek

(1.) ***Therabbin, and most of the Jewish writers***, think he was Shem the son of Noah who was king and priest to their ancestors, after the manner of the other patriarchs; but it is not probable that he should thus change his name. Scripture does not call Melchizedek Shem, nor does it call Shem Melchizedek. The scripture calls Noah's son Shem, not Melchizedek. Therefore because Shem has a genealogy this man's description could not fit Shem. Shem has a Mother and Father listed in scripture for us to trace. Melchizedek is said to not have a traceable genealogy. So I'm not ready to call Melchizedek Shem.

(2.) ***Many Christian writers*** have thought him to be Jesus Christ himself, appearing by a special dispensation and privilege to Abraham in the flesh, and who was known to Abraham by the name Melchizedek, which agrees very well to Christ, and to what is said, Joh 8:56, Abraham saw his day and rejoiced. Much may be said for this opinion, and what is said in Heb 7:3 does not seem to agree with any mere man; but some say that it seems strange to make Christ a type of himself.

(3.) **The most general opinion** is that he was a Canaanite king, who reigned in Salem, and kept up religion and the worship of the true God; that he was raised to be a type of Christ and was honored by Abraham as such. We do read from scripture that when Abram arrived to the land and met Melchizedek scripture says "the Canaanite was in the land" (Gen 12:6).

Without Mother or Father

One of several things I believe the scripture is saying when it gives no genealogy of Melchizedek is that the Melchizedek order is above culture, time and nationality. It is without beginning of days or ending of life and anything earthly contradicts it. The Melchizedek order is a type of the Son of God, a priest without interruption, who abides eternally. It is a priesthood to which every believer is called, not on the basis of natural qualification, but in exact proportion as we are beyond time, culture and nationality, without mother or father or ancestry, without beginning of days or ending of life. It is priestly service performed in a continual flow, out from the throne of God, on the basis of the power of an endless and indestructible life.

Art Katz in his book, Apostolic Foundations says,

> *To come into this priesthood will be wrenching, because how will your father and mother like it? To renounce your physical identification will be like a slap in their face. You have to be cut off from those things that want to establish your identification in merely earthly terms. It is part of the price a believer must pay, and one that cannot be paid easily. "Who is My mother?" was Jesus' reply to being told that His mother*

and brothers were waiting outside. By an earthly evaluation that sounds cruel, but that is because we have not entered into His priestliness and have not understood the profound detachment that a priest must have from every fleshly connection here on earth. Ironically, we will never be a better son or daughter than when we will come to this priestly detachment, where we can put off whatever depth of sickly, soulish involvement of life there might yet be between parents and children.

In other words, we need to come to an identity beyond what we are in the earthly and natural way, which does not diffuse or eliminate our earthly heritages, male or female, Jew or Gentile. If that were the case Jesus would disassociate with his Jewish-ness as the coming King of the Jews and the nations of the world in Jerusalem. Those distinctions should not be abolished, but instead, something transcendent comes out of the union of these distinct entities that creates a "new man." It is a strange paradox of being a Jew or a Gentile, a male or female, and not annulling that obvious thing, but esteeming it as from God, who gave it for His own purposes. And yet, we should not celebrate it in a way that forms a membrane between ourselves and those who are not like us.

Wherever time, culture, ethnic, earthly and temporal factors are given the pre-eminent emphasis, consciously or unconsciously, we move out of priest-liness, and we forfeit, therefore, the priestly ground and the power of its life. A priest is detached from racial, ethnic and cultural lines as well as from time and place. He is not at all influenced or limited by present, contemporary culture. Standing above it, he transcends it, and therefore he is relevant everywhere and at anytime. You are in the Melchizedek priesthood in exact proportion as you are abiding in the Son, no more and no less. It has nothing to do with natural factors, but only with resurrection life, a life offered in sacrifice and raised up in glory. We are brought to a transcendent place of identification with Him by which every natural, racial, religious, ethnic and other distinction is transcended.

> *And this clearer still, if another priest arises according to the likeness of Melchizedek, who has become such not on the basis of a law of physical requirement, but according to the power of an indestructible life. Heb. 7:15, 16*

So Was He a Man or God

I can see aspects of this priesthood that would seem to point to Melchizedek being a man, and there are scriptures that would seem to attribute Melchizedek being God in the flesh – *A Theophany*. I don't believe Melchizedek being man or God is the question for this study on the forerunner ministry of Jesus Christ. I believe the greater question should be what was the extent of Melchizedek's ministry? What was His influence on the land and/or the people of that region where this encounter with Abraham took place?

In my opinion I believe that there's enough evidence to justify the belief that Melchizedek was a Theophany of God, and there's enough evidence for him being a Canaanite King in the land. However, whether he was a Theophany of God or a Canaanite King, the bigger question is *"what was the extent of His Influence in the land, and to the people of the land?"* If he was a Canaanite King what kind of Kingdom did he produce? First let's speak of how he could have been a Theophany of God. One of the founding leaders of IHOP, Kirk Bennett shared with me that In Genesis 14:18 Melchizedek appears to release a vision of fullness to Abraham, the one whose seed would join the earthly family of God – *natural Israel*, with the spiritual family of God – *the gentile nations in the earth that confessed Jesus Christ.* Genesis 15:1 speaks of God visiting Abraham in a vision to give him the blessing of the promised seed, right after Melchizedek visited Abraham to bless him and come into covenant with him. Genesis 15:1 says;

> *After these things the word of the LORD came unto Abram in a vision, saying, Fear not, Abram: I am thy shield, and thy exceeding great reward.*

This verse is connected to the verse detailing the visitation with Abraham by Melchizedek in Genesis 14:19. Remember, there were no chapter divisions when the bible was originally written. After Abraham's visit by Melchizedek in Genesis 14, then Genesis 15:1 says; *after these things THE WORD OF THE LORD came unto Abram in a vision. How does the word come in a vision, except it be in the flesh?* If Melchizedek was the vision of God's word to Abraham, then it is very possible that Melchizedek was the Word made flesh. John 1:1, 14 *says, In the beginning was the word, and the word was with God and the word was God…. And the word was made flesh and dwelt among us.*

Melchizedek as a Man in the earth

I also believe that those that say Melchizedek could have been an earthly man have several bases for their stance. In my study, I have studied how Melchizedek could have been a man in the earth. The first bases for Melchizedek being a man's not deep theological conjecture or reasoning, but simply the word of God. *(Hebrews 2:17, Hebrews 5:1, Hebrews 7:1-4,)*

> Hebrews 5:1 says, *EVERY High Priest is selected from among MEN and is appointed to represent them in matters related to God, to offer gifts and sacrifices for sins. (KJV)*

The words that sticks out in this verse are the words "EVERY" and "MEN". The word "Every" is an all-inclusive word that covers ALL. The subject matter is High Priests, saying that every High Priest is selected from among MEN. Hebrews 7:1 call Melchizedek *priest of the most high God.* Genesis 14:18 calls Melchizedek *priest of the most High God.* In Hebrews 2:17 it says concerning Jesus, since the children have flesh and blood, he too shared in their humanity so that by his death he might destroy him who holds the power of death-that is the devil… For this reason, he had to be made like his brothers in "EVERY" way in order

100

that he might become a merciful and faithful high priest in service to God. There's that word *"every"* again, speaking of Jesus becoming a high priest in service to God. Hebrews 7:3 says that Melchizedek was made like the Son of God. To be like the son of God he had to; #1 be born of a woman. To be like the Son of God; #2 he had to be selected from among men as a high priest. The Second reason that Melchizedek could have been a man in the earth is because the bible says he was a man in Hebrews 7:4 *saying, "NOW CONSIDER HOW GREAT THIS MAN WAS" unto whom even the patriarch Abraham gave the tenth of the spoils.* (KJV)

The Melchizedek Ministry of Peace on Earth

Heb 7:1 For this Melchizedek, king of Salem, priest of the most-high God, who met Abraham returning from the slaughter of the kings, and blessed him; 2 To whom also Abraham gave a tenth part of all; first being by interpretation King of righteousness, and after that also King of Salem, which is, King of peace;

If he was a man, attributing Melchizedek to be a King and of having a kingdom of righteousness and peace would be describing Melchizedek's ministry in the earth of righteousness and peace. This would mean he first was a King ordained by God to release into the earth the vision of fullness and the message and ministry of a coming peace and righteousness to the earth by the joining of heaven and earth in one – Jesus Christ, through this man's intercessory priestly ministry. The word "peace" in the Hebrew text is the word eirēnē *(i-rah'-nay) which is* probably from a primary verb εἴρω eirō which means (to *join*); *peace* (literally or figuratively); by implication *prosperity:* - one, peace, quietness, rest, + set at one again.

As I stated in Chapter 8, Melchizedek speaks of the Most High God being possessor of Heaven and earth when Abram met him after the defeat of the 5 Kings in Genesis 14.

> *Gen 14:19 and he blessed him, and said, Blessed be Abram of the most high God, possessor of heaven and earth:*

The Hebrew word for "possessor" is the word "kanor" which means redeemer, restorer, or to reconcile or recover. It seems clear through this blessing that Melchizedek had as a part of his ministry of righteousness and peace the mandate to release the vision of the restoring and rejoining of heaven and earth to the man Abraham. In the beginning, heaven and earth were made to be one. Genesis 1 says, "*In the beginning God created the heavens and the earth.*" This denotes the union of heaven and earth. This was God's original intent for the earth, to be one with Heaven. When God made man he was also made from heaven and earth united in one, when he made man of the dust of the earth and breathed into him the breath of life (*Heaven*). However, because of sin, heaven and earth, as well as man and God were separated. Heaven and earth were separated by the firmament, which is where Satan and his principalities now dwell. God and man were separated by sin, which is what Satan brought when he deceived Eve, and Adam and Eve sinned. At the return of Jesus to set up his kingdom in the earth, he will manifest the abolishing of the enmity between God and man which was abolished in his flesh on the cross, and he will once again rejoin heaven and earth and all things in heaven and earth in one, the body of Christ.

> *Eph 1:10 That in the dispensation of the fullness of times he might gather together in one all things in Christ, both which are in heaven, and which are on earth; even in him:*

I believe Melchizedek's appearance on the scene in Genesis 14:18 foretold what was to come for Jesus and His church's forerunner ministry declaring and releasing the vision of the LORD, possessor, or reconciler of heaven and earth. I believe Melchizedek ushers Abraham into this vision of fullness in the Genesis 15:1 encounter, causing Abraham to seek after a city whose builder and maker was God. In other words, from the time Abraham was encountered by Melchizedek he went seeking after a Heavenly City. We know much later in scripture that he was seeking after the New Jerusalem, a city coming down out of heaven to earth from God. This is what the Priesthood ministry of the forerunner after the order of Melchizedek is to be interceding for – heaven on earth, or fullness. Genesis 15:1-21 is where humanity, through Abraham, is promised the fullness of God, which is fulfilled in Abraham's seed – Jesus Christ. This is the reason Jesus tells us to pray in Matt 6:10, *Our Father which art in heaven, hallowed be thy name, thy Kingdom come, thy will be done, in earth, as it is in Heaven.*

Melchizedek's ministry of Fullness foretells of the Earthly and Heavenly in One

Regardless of whether he was man or God it is clear that Melchizedek, as a King of a righteous Kingdom, whether in heaven or in the earth, foretold of the coming kingdom of God to the earth. It is easy to see for those familiar with what the scriptures say about the kingdom of God, that His kingdom would be known and identified in a time to come as the Kingdom of God. The Kingdom of God is the only Kingdom that can produce a King of righteousness. That King of righteousness is none other than Jesus Christ. Matt 6:33 says, seek ye first the Kingdom of God and his righteousness. The book of Romans 14:17 say, the Kingdom of God is not meat or drink, but it is said to be *Righteousness, Peace and Joy in the Holy Ghost*. Two of the three designations attributed to the Kingdom of God were also attributed to this King Melchizedek. Therefore, Melchizedek's appearance would introduce the first indication that there would be a coming ministry that would be for the intercession of the release of the Kingdom of God in the earth. Even if Melchizedek was not a Canaanite King, or even if he was not in the land before he met Abraham, there's no doubt that Melchizedek's encounter with Abraham caused Abraham to go throughout the land, not only seeking a city from heaven coming to earth, but talking about and preaching about what he was seeking to the people of the land, the Canaanites, and all the sons of Ham, in the land. (Jebusites, Hivites, Hittites, etc,) I believe that all these inhabitants were influenced by this vision, visitation and/or ministry of Melchizedek, either directly or indirectly through Abraham.

103

I believe that the priesthood after the order of Melchizedek is a priesthood of fullness, for the ushering of heaven coming to earth, that the body of Christ will assume at the end of the age, as we are established in our eternal identity as the House of Prayer for all nations.

All nations will be led back to this priesthood ministry after the order of Melchizedek by forerunners that arise with this ministry of intercession in the last days. It would be this intercession that would have in view the dynamic convergence of heaven and earth as the Apostle Paul prophesied in Ephesians 1:10. The centerpiece of God's eternal purpose is for Jesus to come back to fully establish His Kingdom rule over all the earth as He joins the heavenly and earthly realms together. God's purpose has always been for God and His people to live together in this way. This is the interpretive key to understanding the End-times. Without this foundational revelation, confusion is inevitable when studying the book of Hebrews and the subject of Melchizedek

> Eph 1-9-10 *having made known to us the mystery of His will, according to His good pleasure which He purposed in Himself, that in the dispensation of fullness of the times He might gather together in one all things in Christ, both which are in heaven and which are on earth – Him."*

The Preaching of the Coming Christ in the Earth

I believe Melchizedek not only prefigured Christ, but I believe either he or Abraham preached and foretold about the Christ, the coming Messiah through Abraham's seed. I believe Melchizedek's ministry was that of a forerunner responsible for releasing and foretelling of the coming King and his righteous kingdom that would bring peace to the earth. We know that peace won't come to the earth until heaven and earth are joined together in Christ. So when Melchizedek visited Abraham, his very presence was preaching the peace of the kingdom he represented. His very presence was preaching, a Savior is coming, that is both heavenly and earthly, which is both man and God, which will set up His kingdom in the earth. Melchizedek's very appearance to Abraham preached about a savior that would die for the sins of the

104

whole world. I believe Melchizedek contended for the fullness of God in the earth, the joining together of heaven and earth in one region, one locale, and in one city. I believe Melchizedek preached about a city whose builder and maker was God, which would come down out of heaven. This is the ministry he was releasing to Abraham. His ministry was a ministry of fullness.

The Release of the Forerunner Ministry of Melchizedek to Jesus

This Melchizedek was made like unto the Son of God a forerunner of the priesthood of the believer in the earth through Jesus Christ. Meaning he was the prototype or Forerunner of what Jesus would become and reveal for the believer to walk in. He was the forerunner of the order that Jesus would establish in the earth, an unending priesthood that would be established for eternity, which would have no end. Jesus received this ministry of a forerunner and an eternal priesthood after the order of Melchizedek when Melchizedek blessed Abraham, who had the promised seed in his loins. Abraham was being called to cut covenant with this King Melchizedek, and to receive his Kingdom as the prototype of the kingdom that would be established by the promised seed of Abraham, Jesus Christ, son of David, Son of Abraham. This forerunner ministry of Melchizedek was an eternal priesthood that would enable Jesus to transcend the earthly law and priesthood of Aaron and go beyond the veil to save them to the uttermost that come unto God by him, seeing he ever lives to make intercession for them. Such an high priest became us, who is holy, harmless, undefiled, separate from sinners, and made higher than the heavens; Who needs not daily, as those high priests, to offer up sacrifice, first for his own sins, and then for the people's: for this he did once, when he offered up himself. For the law makes men high priests which have infirmity; but the word of the oath, which was since the law, makes the Son, who is consecrated for evermore. This is the ministry that was given Jesus, while he was in the loins of Abraham, by this Melchizedek that he might be a forerunner into the holiest of all in the Kingdom of God to be an eternal intercessor for those that would come after him, being King of kings, and Lord of lords.

The *Forerunner Ministry* as related to the Melchizedek priesthood is the ministry of Jesus Christ that will be released to the end-time church for the purpose of ushering Jesus Christ and his kingdom of Kings and Priests back into the earth. The end-time generation will go before and prepare the way for the Lord to return to set up this kingdom on the earth. The end-time generation will be the last generation of one age and the first ones leading all of humanity into the new age.

The Forerunner Ministry – Contending for the fullness of Heaven Coming to Earth

Therefore, the church picking up the forerunner ministry of Jesus Christ will be necessary not only to prepare the way of the Lord, but also to prepare a people for the way of the Lord. The forerunner ministry is the ministry of intercession as a High Priest contending for the fullness of Heaven coming to earth. Jesus Christ came as the great forerunner announcing and preparing His church for the coming Kingdom of God. The last generation will come as forerunners releasing that kingdom order into the earth. Jesus Christ came as a forerunner after the order of Melchizedek, preparing the way for humanity to be and do what God created us to do. The last generation will come as forerunners releasing humanity into the fullness of that calling.

The Influence of Melchizedek on the People of the Land

If Melchizedek was not a man that lived in the land where he met Abraham this man's message and ministry in the land still had the potential to cause the people of that region to be affected in some way. If his appearance was a divine encounter to Abraham, at the very least, through Abraham's witness, this encounter would affect the whole land of Canaan and all the people of that land. As a result of this ministry and message of Melchizedek they would all begin to seek after and contend for fullness, the coming together of heaven and earth, a city whose builder and maker was God. The people of the region that Melchizedek was in when he visited Abraham would be seekers after the heavenly realm, the spiritual realm along with Abraham. They would begin to seek after a city from heaven. In determining Melchizedek's influence on the people of that land, at the very least they were influenced by Melchizedek's encounter with Abraham as Abraham would no doubt go forth speaking of the encounter he had with this King-Priest of righteousness and peace.

Chapter 8

THE LAND OF CANAAN AND ITS PEOPLE

Gen 9:18 And Ham is the father of Canaan.

Where was Canaan and who were the people of Canaan? Why were the people of Canaan driven out of the land? Why did God tell the Israelites to destroy the Canaanites? Canaan is located in the geographical location known today as Jerusalem. It was the place that God established as the region from which heaven would come to earth at the time of the fullness of the restoration and reconciliation of heaven and earth at the end of the age. This is the place and region where Melchizedek met Abraham at the return of the slaughter of the kings in Genesis 14. In this encounter Melchizedek met Abraham and cut covenant with him for the purposes of releasing Heaven back into the earth as well as for the purposes of releasing God's son into the earth. Melchizedek released this vision to Abraham of the fullness of heaven coming back to earth when he said in *Gen 14:19 And he blessed him, and said, Blessed be Abram of the most high God, possessor of heaven and earth:*

It has been established that the word possessor is translated "recover" or "redeemer." Melchizedek was actually coming into covenant with Abraham for the release of the vision of the fullness of heaven and earth and all that is in the earth being restored to oneness in the King of the ages, Jesus Christ. It has already been established that as a result of this encounter Abraham went forth within the land of Canaan, waiting for and seeking after a city whose builder and maker was God, where heaven and earth would be united as one again. *Heb 11:9 By faith he sojourned in the land of promise, as in a strange country, dwelling in tabernacles with Isaac and Jacob, the heirs with him of the same promise: 10 For he looked for a city which hath foundations, whose builder and maker is God.*

The coming together of the earthly land of promise and the heavenly Jerusalem was God's original intention when he created the heavens and the earth, but because of sin, Heaven and earth were separated by the firmament, along with the separation of man and God by sin. At this encounter Melchizedek cut covenant with Abraham to give God access back into the earth at the spot where this covenant was cut. You could say that there was an open heaven over this region of land to which God's blessing would be released on the land and the people of the land as result of Melchizedek's appearance in Genesis 14:18.

Melchizedek's Priesthood Ministry and the Size of the Fruit of the Land of Canaan

This land where Melchizedek met Abraham was being inhabited at this time by the Canaanites. This encounter with the priest of the Most High God and His ministry in the earth at this encounter undoubtedly left a major impartation in that geographical region of the earth. It is recorded concerning this land and the fruit of this land when the children of Israel came into this promised piece of property in Numbers 13:23-27; *And they came unto the brook of Eshcol, and cut down from thence a branch with one cluster of grapes, and they bare it between two upon a staff; and they brought of the pomegranates, and of the figs. 24 The place was called the brook Eshcol, because of the cluster of grapes which the children of Israel cut down from thence. Num 13:25-27 and they returned from searching of the land after forty days. 26 And they went and came to Moses, and to Aaron, and to all the congregation of the children of Israel, unto the wilderness of Paran, to Kadesh; and brought back word unto them, and unto all the congregation, and shewed them the fruit of the land. 27 And they told him, and said, we came unto the land whither thou sentest us, and surely it floweth with milk and honey; and this is the fruit of it.*

I believe the prosperity and supernatural size of the fruit of the land of Canaan was directly related to the intercessory ministry of the Priest of the Most High God, Melchizedek, King of Salem, King of Peace and righteousness. Whether Melchizedek was the word made flesh or not,

110

it is certainly evidenced by the land that something supernatural happened to that region as a result of his ministry. We do know that his righteous kingdom and priesthood ministry of interceding for heaven to come to earth was having a direct result on the agriculture of the land.

Melchizedek's Priesthood Ministry and the Size of the people of the Land of Canaan

Not only did this priesthood ministry of this man have direct result on the agriculture of the land but it had a direct result on the people of the land. Numbers 13:28 says; *Nevertheless, the people be strong that dwell in the land, and the cities are walled, and very great: and moreover, we saw the children of Anak there. 29 The Amalekites dwell in the land of the south: and the Hittites, and the Jebusites, and the Amorites, dwell in the mountains: and the Canaanites dwell by the sea, and by the coast of Jordan.* Not only were the fruit supernatural in size, but the people were supernatural in size. They were strong, very great and giants were in the land. *Num 13:33 And there we saw the giants, the sons of Anak, which come of the giants: and we were in our own sight as grasshoppers, and so we were in their sight.* This was no ordinary piece of land, nor was the people of Canaan an ordinary people. I believe that could have been a direct result of this priestly King, Melchizedek and his ministry of interceding for heaven to come to earth.

Did Melchizedek's Ministry Influence the people of the Land

Could it be that during Melchizedek's time in the land that the people of Melchizedek's time that heard his message of righteousness, peace and fullness would prematurely seek after this fullness outside of the due order? Melchizedek, being the prefiguring of Christ, represented the coming of a savior of righteousness to humanity which would die for the sins of the world. His very ministry prophesied about the coming Messiah. If those that heard his message and received his ministry and sought to mix this ministry with the false gods and worship

111

of their idols, this would explain the spirituality with perversion that would pervade the land of Canaan. Seeking to mix this ministry that Christ would bring at the end of the age with their false gods, I believe this could be a reason this people would end up in a perversion of the ministry Melchizedek's appearance to Abraham prophesied about. If Abraham went through the land seeking this heavenly city and testifying about his encounter with this God-man this could have begun a mixed pursuit after the time, the place and man that would one day reign there in the age to come.

The Perversion of the Land of Canaan

It was recorded that the inhabitants of this land ended up sacrificing their children to their gods. Could this have been as a perversion of the Son who would come from heaven who would sacrifice his life for the sins of the world? It was recorded Nimrod the son of Cush, a brother to Canaan, attempted to build a city joining the earth with heaven, the tower Babel. Could this have been a perversion of the city Melchizedek's priesthood ministry would represent and seek to establish in the earth? It was recorded that the people of this land was involved in other spiritual perversions like witchcraft and necromancer. Could they have been trying to mix the ministry of the heavenly realm with their false indigenous religions, seeking after the fullness of the heavenly and earthly realm that only Christ could bring? 1 Corinthian 12:1 speaks of the danger of entering into the spirit world without Jesus being Lord, and the results of this perversion being heathen, idol worship. *1Co 12:1 says, Now concerning spiritual gifts, brethren, I would not have you ignorant. Ye know that ye were Gentiles, carried away unto these dumb idols, even as ye were led. Wherefore I give you to understand, that no man speaking by the Spirit of God calls Jesus accursed: and that no man can say that Jesus is the Lord, but by the Holy Ghost.* It takes Jesus being Lord of your life, to enter into the spirit realm and not be overrun by satanic forces of darkness. It takes Jesus being our Head to not be carried away with spiritual ignorance and end up in Idolatry and witchcraft.

Who were the Canaanites

Who were the Canaanites? Where was their Kingdom? And why was Abraham being given the mantle and scepter of this ministry of Melchizedek on their land? The answers to these two questions will give to us the key to unlocking the forerunner mantle and calling to the end-time generation.

Canaan was the fourth son of Ham, one of the three sons of Noah. From Ham came four main races; Cush (Ethiopia), Mizraim (Egypt), Phut (Nubia), and Canaan (originally before Abraham extending from Hamath in the North to Gaza in the South.), comprising six chief tribes, the Hittites, Hivites, Amorites, Jebusites, Perizzites, and Girgashites; to which the Canaanites (in the narrow sense) being added make up the mystic number seven. Ten are specified in Gen 15:19-21, including some on East of Jordan and South of Palestine. The four Hamitic races occupied a continuous tract comprising the Nile valley, Palestine, South Arabia, Babylonia, and Kissia. The Phoenicians were Semitic (from Shem), but the Canaanites preceded them in Palestine and Lower Syria.

Canaan became the father of Sidon his firstborn, Heth (the Hittites). The Jebusites, the Amorites, the Girgasites, the Hivites, the Arkites, the Sinites. The Arvites, the Zemarites and the Hamathites. Afterward the families of the Canaanites spread abroad. And the territory of the Canaanites extended from Sidon as one goes to Gerar as far as Gaza, and as one goes to Sodom, Gomorrah, Admah, and Zeboim, as far as Lasha. These are the sons of Ham by their families, their languages, their lands and their nations. The Canaanites represented a mixture of the perversion of the priesthood of their indigenous religions and child sacrifices with that which would come from the priesthood of Melchizedek, joining the spiritual realm with the natural realm. This ritual of child sacrifices is still a prevalent spirit predominant in the earth today with the culture of abortion in our nation and in the earth. This is why we must stand against the spirit of Abortion in the African-American community. I believe this is one of the main things that caused the first inhabitants of the promise land to be driven out of the land. This is the spirit that caused the Canaanites to be destroyed by God. And at the end of the age Zechariah says concerning the Canaanites; *Zec 14:21 Yea, every pot in Jerusalem and in Judah shall be holiness unto the LORD of hosts: and all they that sacrifice shall come and take of them, and seethe therein: and in that day there shall be no more the Canaanite in the house of the LORD of hosts.*

The Forerunner Ministry of the First Inhabitants of Jerusalem

The stories of the Bible took place in and around this land that we now call the Middle East, and people moved on and off its stage based on their relationship with the nations of ancient Israel and Judah. Consequently, the vast majority of the world's ethnic and racial groups are not specifically identified. But of those who are identified the most there in bible times seem to be represented in those we would now call of African descent. There is a strong tradition that some of the descendants of Noah through his son Ham were burned skinned because of their proximity to the sun. Ham had a son named Cush, which means "black" in Hebrew. Cush is the most common term designating color in reference to persons, people or lands used in the Bible. It's used 58 times in the King James Version. The Greek and Latin word is Ethiopia. In classical literature, Greek and Roman authors describe Ethiopians as dark skinned. Archaeology has found these people to be dark skinned. In the book of Jeremiah, the question is asked, "Can the Ethiopian change his skin?

Genesis 10:6-20 describes the descendants of Ham as being located in North Africa, Central Africa and in parts of southern Asia. Psalm 105:23 mentions the "land of Ham" in Egypt, and Psalm 78:51 connects the "tents of Ham" with Egypt. In Genesis 10, Nimrod, son of Cush (whose name means "black"), founded a civilization in Mesopotamia. In Genesis 11, Abraham was from Ur of the Chaldeans, a land whose earliest inhabitants included dark skinned people. The people of the

114

region where Abraham came from can be proven historically and archaeologically to have been intermixed racially. So it is possible that Abraham and those who traveled with him could have been racially mixed. When I travelled to Israel with a group of 30 African-American Pastors in May of 2011, through the agency *AIPAC – American, Israeli, Public, Affairs, Committee,* we were introduced to our tour guide for the immigrant absorption center. This is where Ethiopian Jewish immigrants that are brought over from Ethiopia lived while they are acclimated to the Israeli culture. As we were having a question and answer session, one of the African-American Pastors asked this Ethiopian Jewish immigrant how she knew she was Jewish, because in America, he said, we've thought Jews were white-skinned people. Her response startled our African-American Pastors group. She said she had never seen a white Jew, or never knew a white Jew existed until her family was brought to Israel with the Ethiopian Exodus of Ethiopian Jews beginning in the 1990's. She said, her family for generations had always dreamed of going to Israel, for centuries and centuries, it was passed down to them through their Jewish customs, - *NEXT YEAR IN JERUSALEM.*

When they finally came to the land they were very surprised to see white-skinned people who claimed to be Jewish. They had never personally seen white people and they had never seen white Jews. She then commenced to prove through scripture and through geographical and patriarchal names seen in scripture located in Africa, how Abraham, Isaac, and Jacob were definitely, in her peoples' minds, Black-skinned as Jews. It was an eye-opening biblical exegesis and presentation that she gave to prove that she, being an Ethiopian Jew, was most definitely Jewish, and cast doubt on whether or not those of European descent were Jews. We left that Absorption center with an eye-opening education in Ethiopian Jewish-ness. Genesis 14 tells how Abraham's experiences in Canaan and Egypt brought him and his family into areas inhabited by peoples who were very likely dark skinned. Both archaeological evidence and the account in 1 Chronicles 4 tell us that the land of Canaan was inhabited by the descendants of Ham.

Further black presence can be found in the accounts of Hagar the Egyptian, Ishmael and his Egyptian wife, and Ishmael's sons, especially Kedar. The Kedarites are mentioned many times in Isaiah, Jeremiah, Ezekiel and Nehemiah, and the word kedar means "blackness." Still further evidence of black presence in the patriarchal period appears with Joseph's experiences in Egypt. Joseph married an Egyptian woman, Asenath, who was descended from Mizraim, which made her Hamitic. Thus there is a strong possibility that Asenath was dark skinned. She was the mother of Ephraim and Manasseh.

Ham – means, Hot, dark, colored, swarthy. Ham was the youngest son of Noah and father of Canaan and founder of many peoples. (Gen. 5:32; 6:10; 7:13; 9:18, 22; Ps. 78:51) The Hamite races, were originally the most brilliant and enlightened races made up of (Egypt, Babylon, Ethiopia, and Canaan), They had the greatest tendency toward the spirit realm and things supernatural, as well as a great tendency to degenerate towards idolatry, spiritual perversion and humanism, because they were so enlightened they would become most disinclined to the true religion of Jehovah God, the great preserver of men. In consequence of the improper conduct of Ham when Noah was drunk, the heart of his father was set against him. The indignation of Noah found expression in the thrice repeated curse upon Canaan, one of Ham's sons Gen.9:25-27). Ham himself suffered in failing to receive the blessing pronounced on his brothers, Shem and Japheth. The peoples polluted by Ham's sin (Gen 10:15-19) inhabited the land later promised to Abraham's seed; thus the curse of servitude was fulfilled in Joshua's conquest of the Canaanites, when he made them hewers of wood and drawers of water (Joshua 9:23,27).

Africa is not cursed because of Ham's sin

It should be noted here however, that the writer doesn't believe that today there is a curse on African people as related to this act of Noah and Ham in Genesis 8. It should also be noted that God did not curse Ham or Canaan, Noah cursed Canaan. But concerning God's action towards Ham, Genesis 9:1 says, *God Blessed Noah and his three sons.* So I ask which one is greater, God's blessing or Noah's curse. I would say God's Blessing is greater than Noah's curse. In addition, it should be noted that a curse of man was said to last 3 to 4 generations at the most. So, Noah's curse of Canaan cannot be used to justify or validate the modern Slave trade of the middle Ages or the subjugation of Caucasians over Africans.

The Hebrew word for Ham means "hot" and is surely prophetic of the climates that have created the darkness of the skin of those of African descent, and the dark complexions of other peoples from the same stock. Egypt is called "the land of Ham" (Ps.105:23) and the Egyptian word for "Ham" is Kem, meaning black and warm. From whom we have the Egyptians, Africans, Babylonians, Philistines and Canaanites. Biblical figures, such as the Queen of Sheba, Moses' Cushite wife Zipporah, Prophet Jeremiah's right-hand man Ebedmelech, and Sarah's Egyptian handmaiden Hagar, are among the many royal Black personalities mentioned in the Bible. **CUSH** – means Black or an Ethiopian. 1. Eldest son of Ham and grandson of Noah and founder of a tribal family (Gen 10:6-8; Chron.1:8-10). Also name of the land where the Cushites dwelt (Isa. 11:11; 18: **CUSHI** - 1 The messenger who brought news to David concerning Absalom's defeat (II Sam. 18:21-32) 2 An ancestor of Jehudi who lived in Jerermiah's time (Jer. 36:14) 3. The father of Zephaniah the prophet who lived in the time of Josiah, king of Judah (Zeph.1:1)

Nimrod, the First Mighty Man in the Earth.

The bible states Nimrod was the first mighty man in the earth. NIMROD means - valiant, strong or He that rules. Nimrod was a son of Cush, son of Ham. Nimrod was a mighty hunter and a potent monarch whose land bore his name (Gen 10:8, 9; I Chron. 1:10; Micah 5:6) Gen.10:8 Cush was the father of Nimrod; he was the first to be a mighty man on the earth. He was a mighty hunter before the Lord; therefore, it is said Like Nimrod, a mighty hunter before the Lord. The Beginning of His kingdom was Babel, Erech, Accad, and Calneh, in the land of Shinar (in Babylonia). Out of the land he (Nimrod) went forth into Assyria and built Nineveh, Rehoboth-Ir, Calah, and esen, which is between Ninevah and Calah; all these (suburbs combined to form) the great city. And Egypt (Mizraim) became the father of Ludim, Anamim, Lehabim, Naphtuhim. Pathrusim, Casluhim. (from whom came the philistines), and Caphtorim.

The Tower of Babel

Gen 11:1-9 says, and the whole earth was of one language and of one accent on one mode of expression. And as they journeyed eastward they found a plain (valley) in the land of Shinar, and they settled and dwelt there. And they said one to another, come, let us make bricks and burn them thoroughly. So they had brick for stone, and slime for mortar. And they said Come, let us build us a city and a tower whose top reaches into the sky, and let us make a name for ourselves, lest we be scattered over the whole earth. And the Lord came down to see the city and the tower which the sons of men built. And the Lord said, behold, they are one language; and this is only the beginning of what they will do, and now nothing they have imagined they can do will be impossible for them.... Therefore the name of it was called Babel, because there that Lord confounded the language of all the earth; and from that place the Lord scattered them abroad upon the face of the earth.

118

Nimrod, the son of Cush was responsible for the building of this tower. And as we know this endeavor was not the will of God for the people of this time. As a result, God had to come down and scatter them by confounding their languages to thwart this work and disperse them across the earth. But it should be noted that if Africans and African-Americans are descendents of Cush/Ham then it is a part of the original inheritance and DNA of this people group to be a people that are ONE and capable of working together as ONE, not only amongst ourselves but with other ethnicities, to bring about whatever our minds can imagine. When this people group fully returns to God through Christ and receives the power of the Holy Ghost to unite us again, as on the day of Pentecost, this people group will be a great asset to the nations of the world and the mission of the coming Kingdom of God in the earth.

The Table of Hametic Nations

Hametic Line:

Ancestry	Nation	Notes
Cush	Ethiopia	
Mezraim	Egyptian	
Put (Phut or Punt)	Libya	
Canaan	Canaanites only one of Ham's sons w/o	
a homeland		
Seba	Sudan (Sabeans)	
Heth	Hittites	
Ham	American Indian Mongoloids	

These were the Inhabitants of the land Canaan and the regions surrounding this plot of land during the first 2000 years in the earth. It is safe to say that Canaan, as well as several of the sons of Ham, from which Canaan descended, settled somewhere in the continent of Africa.

With that being the case this group of people were not only the first to inhabit this land that would later be promised to Abraham's descendants, known as the land of Israel, the Holy City, but this people group would be the first to be availed to the ministry of Melchizedek. At the very least through Abraham, who lived in the land for many years seeking after that city whose builder and maker was God. I believe this particular seek after a holy city, and after a divine visitation of God's son in the earth was put into the first inhabitants of the promise land, those descendants from Noah's son Ham. I believe that this particular inclination towards spirituality, though perverted in the land during this time, was left in the people of this land that later migrated south to Egypt, and Ethiopia, in what we know to be on the continent of Africa.

This spirituality, I believe, is at the root and a part of the DNA of those of African Descent and any people whose heritage goes back to the first inhabitants of the promise land. As a result of this kingly, priesthood ministry of Melchizedek, or at the very least, this visitation of Melchizedek in the land with Abraham, the people of the land were strong and very great and giants were in the land. This even speaks to some of the characteristic traits of black people recorded of the land of Cush in Isaiah 18:2, 3. The Prophet Isaiah says, *Woe to the land whirring with wings which is beyond the rivers of Cush or Ethiopia, which sends ambassadors by the Nile, even in vessels of papyrus upon the waters! Go ye swift messengers, to a nation tall and polished, to a people terrible from their beginning. (feared and dreaded near and far), nation strong and victorious, whose land and rivers divide!* This certainly would explain the strong and athletic physical attributes that enhanced the value of Africans to the slave trade of the 15th-19th centuries, and even speaks to some of the characteristic traits of black people today. This ministry of Melchizedek or His encounter with Abraham is what very well could have been at the root of these physical characteristics of this people from this land, as well as many of the perverted spiritual practices in the land of Africa over the generations that are still prevalent to this day. However, Jesus Christ is the answer to the search for true spirituality. He is the only way to access the heavens to pray for this heavenly realm to encounter the earth realm for the consummation of the Kingdom of God being established in the earth, and he is the fulfillment of the purpose of the Priesthood ministry of righteousness and peace of Melchizedek that every believer in Christ has access to.

The Melchizedek Priesthood is the priesthood for every believer in Christ. It is the Priesthood that will bring Jesus back to the earth. Because this is the priesthood that Jesus came as a forerunner to lead us into, it is the priesthood that the church must enter into in order to bring heaven to earth. Jesus came to lead us into this new and living way to God. He came to bring us into a new ministry that would be our eternal identity and calling. Upon forerunners out of Africa and the lands where those of Hametic descent originally inhabited in Canaan is a priestly anointing to enter into the realm of the spirit with ease. There's a natural priesthood inclination within those that have roots back to the time of the land before Israel possessed the promise of this land through Abraham. There's a natural inclination to the things of the spirit. People groups all over the world call it different things in different regions. In America it is said that African-Americans have SOUL. This is stated for the innate propensity for expressing the fullness of their inner selves in the arts and worship. Much of this worship and expression in the arts is often misplaced and not used for the worship of Jehovah. However, this is a part of the nature of the African that goes back to the first two thousand years of man in the earth, when that part of the earth was unlocked and opened up during the priesthood ministry of Melchizedek.

I believe that this spirituality of the African people and those of African descent is what is going to lead forth in worship through this people group at the end of the age. God is going to use this people group to lead the nations of the world into this priesthood ministry that accesses the heavens and joins the spirit realm with the earth realm and usher's heaven to earth. God is going to use this people group to release a level of power in the earth like was seen of Moses in Egypt (Africa) when God came down with power to deliver his people from Egyptian bondage. Make no mistake this ministry is not a matter of color of skin but a matter of proximity to the original release of this spirit and ministry. This Priesthood ministry of Melchizedek is a ministry that goes beyond color, race, creed or culture.

This ministry of Melchizedek is Spirit. It is a ministry of fullness that will transcend all races, all cultures, and all generations, into eternity to fulfill our eternal and everlasting calling to worship and intercede for the joining of heaven and earth, God and man in the New Jerusalem.

Chapter 9

THE COMING REVIVAL OF FORERUNNERS OUT OF THE CONTINENT OF AFRICA

Zeph 3:10"From beyond the rivers of Cush my worshipers—including my dispersed people—will present offerings to me (ISV)

We can see the mind of God in this intention of God for the original forerunners amongst the nations from the three sons of Noah, even after the day of Pentecost when the Holy Spirit was poured out in Jerusalem. Initially the spirit was poured out on Jews from every nation that had gathered at Jerusalem. However, I don't believe that it is a coincidence that the first Gentile nation to receive the message of Christ as Messiah after the Holy Spirit fell on Jerusalem on the day of Pentecost was The Ethiopian Eunuch, an offspring from Ham (Acts 8:26-36). As forerunners to the nations in the beginning with the great civilizations of Egypt and Babylon, Ethiopia, this people group from Ham were singled out by God through Phillip and brought into the middle of what God was doing by the power of the Holy Ghost from the day of Pentecost.

Act 8:26-36 And the angel of the Lord spake unto Philip, saying, Arise, and go toward the south unto the way that goeth down from Jerusalem unto Gaza, which is desert. 27 And he arose and went: and, behold, a man of Ethiopia, an eunuch of great authority under Candace queen of the Ethiopians, who had the charge of all her treasure, and had come to Jerusalem for to worship; 34 And the eunuch answered Philip, and said, I pray thee, of whom speaks the prophet this? of himself, or of some other man? 35 Then Philip opened his mouth, and began at the same scripture, and preached unto him Jesus. 36 And as they went on their way, they came unto a certain water: and the eunuch said, See, here is water; what doth hinder me to be baptized?

Remember the Gentile nations were not formally given access to the preaching and receiving of the gospel until Acts 10, when Peter went down to Cornelius' house after Cornelius had a vision and sent his servants to Peter to ask him to come to His house to preach the gospel message of Salvation through Jesus Christ. It wasn't until this account that Peter realized that God intended for the Gospel to be preached to all nations, including the Gentiles. However, the Ethiopian Eunuch had already heard and received the message of Salvation through Jesus Christ in Acts 8, years before Peter unlocked salvation for the Gentiles. And history tells us that this Ethiopian convert went back to his nation and evangelized Ethiopia with the message of Salvation. So much so that Ethiopia from that time to this has been a Christian nation. With this being the mind of God for God to make nations from Ham forerunners, since Ham, through Nimrod was the first son to attempt to reign in the earth back at the beginning of civilization, subjugating the other brothers under his rule, I believe those from the sons of Ham should be the first to serve the purposes of God in humbling themselves to the other two sons to bring about a reconciliation and unity within the nations of the earth. Look at what the bible says about how this son from Cush, son of Ham, went forth to rule first in the earth in Genesis 10. It says Nimrod the son of Cush, (*from whence it is believed that those from Africa descended*) was the first mighty man in the earth. (Gen 10:6-9)

> *Gen 10:6 and the sons of Ham; Cush, and Mizraim, and Phut, and Canaan. 7 And the sons of Cush; Seba, and Havilah, and Sabtah, and Raamah, and Sabtecha: and the sons of Raamah; Sheba, and Dedan. 8 **And Cush begat Nimrod: he began to be a mighty one in the earth.***

> *Gen 10:9 He was a mighty hunter before the LORD: wherefore it is said, Even as Nimrod the mighty hunter before the LORD. 10 **And the beginning of his kingdom was Babel,** and Erech, and Accad, and Calneh, in the land of Shinar.*

Man's day of subjugation, division, strife, competition, and segregation began after the scattering of the nations after Nimrod, the son of Cush attempted to build the Tower of Babel. However, at Pentecost it was the beginning of the end of that scattering as God brought all nations to Jerusalem as he poured out his spirit on all flesh. Consequently, as the Church comes to her day of maturation and perfection, man's day of division, disunity and subjugation is coming to a close in His House of Prayer. God's day of unity, power, provision, and purpose is coming forth as he makes us joyful in His house of prayer. The Churches day of coming forth out of the tomb of separation, strife, segregation is upon us and God's day of glory is going to manifest through this resurrected, glorified church. The purpose of the three sons of Noah and the knowledge and fulfillment of their purpose as related to the plan of God for the entire earth is the basis of mankind's dominion in the earth. In addition to this, it's our power to remain in unity throughout the nations of the world to fulfill all of the will of God in the earth, preparing the way for the coming of the Lord. The remainder of this book is about how those from the African Continent and the African Diaspora will be restored to their place of leadership significance in the trinity of nations in His House of Prayer, and how they will help lead the church to fullness in the earth, standing shoulder to shoulder with the other two sons of Noah to fulfill the High Priestly Forerunner ministry of Jesus Christ after the order of Melchizedek at the end of the age.

Forerunners to the Promised Land

In addition to this, at the end of the first 2000 years of the reign of Noah's youngest son Ham, God sent a righteous King called Melchizedek from the land of Canaan - *the fourth son of Ham* - which had been living in the geographical region known today as the Holy Land. Melchizedek met Abraham in this land on the way back from the slaughter of the kings of Chedorlaomer. From this divine encounter there was a blessing released to Abraham, and this writer believes, a mantle released of authority in the earth to receive this land from this King Melchizedek. Abraham was given the promise to have authority over that land called Canaan for the second two thousand years of attempted dominion, as well as for the promise of the eternal inheritance of the land to prepare it for the coming Messiah's eternal rule. This encounter began the 2000 year reign of the descendents from Shem in the earth, as Abraham cut covenant with this King of righteousness and peace in the land of Canaan in Genesis 14:18.

> *Gen 14:18 And Melchizedek king of Salem brought forth bread and wine: and he was the priest of the most high God. 19 And he blessed him, and said, Blessed be Abram of the most high God, possessor of heaven and earth: 20 And blessed be the most high God, which hath delivered thine enemies into thy hand. And he gave him tithes of all.*

This encounter took place in the land of Canaan, the fourth son of Ham. It was this transference from a visitation from a righteous King in the land of one of Ham's descendants that released the promise of blessing and divine inheritance to Abraham. After Abraham met this King Melchizedek in Genesis 15:1-21 the scripture tells us what the covenant entailed. Abraham was promised a son and the Land that the descendents from Ham had been in possession of.

> *Genesis 15:4-21 And, behold, the word of the LORD came unto him, saying, This shall not be thine heir; but he that shall come forth out of thine own bowels shall be thine heir. 5 And he brought him forth abroad, and said, Look now toward heaven, and tell the stars, if thou be able to number them: and he said unto him, So shall thy seed be. 6 And he believed in the LORD; and he counted it to him for righteousness.*

> *Gen 15:13 And he said unto Abram, Know of a surety that thy seed shall be a stranger in a land that is not theirs, and shall serve them; and they shall afflict them four hundred years; 14 And also that nation, whom they*

shall serve, will I judge: and afterward shall they come out with great substance.

Gen 15:16 But in the fourth generation they shall come hither again: for the iniquity of the Amorites is not yet full.

Gen 15:17 And it came to pass, that, when the sun went down, and it was dark, behold a smoking furnace, and a burning lamp that passed between those pieces. 18 In the same day the LORD made a covenant with Abram, saying, Unto thy seed have I given this land, from the river of Egypt unto the great river, the river Euphrates:

Gen 15:19 The Kenites, and the Kenizzites, and the Kadmonites, 20. And the Hittites, and the Perizzites, and the Rephaims, 21. And the Amorites, and the Canaanites, and the Girgashites, and the Jebusites.

When it was time for this promise to come forth the next son from Noah, Shem, was ready to come to the forefront in the earth. God's chosen people Israel began to be positioned to be brought forth to fulfill the promise given to Abraham that his seed would be a great and mighty nation. When the fulfillment of the promise was near, the Lord sent a 17 year old boy named Joseph from Canaan and from His people in the promise land into slavery in a land called Egypt. At the time Egypt was the greatest civilization in the earth. Joseph was sent as a slave, but he eventually would arise to second in command to the Pharaoh, King of Egypt, and would preserve His nation and the Egyptian nation during the time of a great national and world famine. He would also oversee the birthing forth of the nation of Israel as a people. He was sent ahead into that country as a forerunner, to help preserve his people and the people of the world from the coming world famine.

Israel is birthed out of Africa

This people that God chose to use in Egypt, in the region which we know today to be on the continent of Africa, became the womb to birth forth His chosen people Israel. This people from the African Continent in Egypt provided a haven for the Sons of Jacob during the greatest time of tribulation and famine the world had ever known up to that time. These people would be identified today as Africans, from what the bible calls the land of Ham. As we stated in Chapter 2, they would be identified as Africans, not because of the color of their skin but because of the geographical region they were from. The color of the skin is not what makes you an inheritor of a particular people group, but the patriarchal-geographical heritage from whence men are from. In the original formation of the nations those from Egypt came from Ham. And the Hamites were forerunners, going before the birthing of God's chosen people, preparing the way of the Lord. As stated in earlier chapters, a forerunner speaks of a person that is to go before, or one that goes first. A forerunner is one that leads others into his current place and position.

The writer believes that in the formation of the nation of Israel this particular group of people in Egypt, those from the land of Ham, went before Israel as forerunners to be a covering and a place of refuge for them.

A Continent of Refuge for God's Chosen People

I believe at the end of the age this group of people from the African continent will be restored once again to the forerunner spirit and ministry of Jesus Christ. This people and this continent will once again become a place of refuge for Israel and be instrumental in ushering the body of Christ and Israel into the time of fullness for the preservation of all mankind at the time of the greatest tribulation known in the history of humanity. This truth is not only depicted of this nation on the continent of Africa in the Old Testament but also in the New Testament. Matthew 2 speaks of this reality when the angel visited another Joseph, Mary's espoused husband, in a dream to warn him to take the child to Egypt to hide him from Herod's attempt to kill Jesus at his birth.

> *Mat 2:12 And being warned of God in a dream that they should not return to Herod, they departed into their own country another way. 13 And when they were departed, behold, the angel of the Lord appeared to Joseph in a dream, saying, Arise, and take the young child and his mother, and flee into Egypt, and be thou there until I*

> *bring thee word: for Herod will seek the young child to destroy him. 14 When he arose, he took the young child and his mother by night, and departed into Egypt:* .

I believe this speaks of what God will do even at the end of the age through those on the African Continent, not just Egypt, but throughout east and central Africa, to preserve God's chosen people during times of extreme persecution and tribulation. God will once again, as he did with Jacob's son, Joseph in the beginning, and as he did with Jesus, send His people to Africa to be preserved from the persecution of the modern-day Herod, the end-time Anti-Christ.

The First to Enslave and the First to Save

In the Old Testament in the nation of Egypt through the forerunner ministry of Jacob's son Joseph, the people of God were favored, nurtured, prospered and grew and finally out of fear, enslaved. Nevertheless, in this context in Egypt, the nation of Israel came forth in a strange land and language, until they became so great that the next generation from Joseph feared that this people were multiplying faster and greater than the native people of the land, to which they began to afflict them and enslave them. Once God had completed the process of preserving and bringing forth through adversity his chosen people, after they had endured over 400 years of slavery and persecution, God brought them out with a mighty right hand. I believe that there is a connection here between Jews and those of African descent. I don't believe that it was just a coincidence, that Africans in the middle-ages we're also in slavery in the America's and Europe for the exact same time frame of 400 years.

Is it possible that because we enslaved Israel in the first two-thousand-year period for 400 years, that we were enslaved for 400 years in the third two-thousand-year period as a consequence? Whatever the connection, and I do believe there is one, I believe that God's purposes for slavery in a foreign land of the Israelites – *to raise up a people to worship the true and living God as their deliverer from Egypt* - and God's purposes for slavery of the African Nations in the middle ages were the same. God uses slavery and adversity, persecution and affliction to form and raise up a people that will call upon his name and serve him as deliverer, savior and God almighty.

Through the slavery of Joseph in Egypt, God positioned his people to be protected during the famine that came to the world. And through the slavery of Africans all over the world during the middle-ages God is going to position this people to protect his chosen people again at the end of the age. God used a people on the continent of Africa, in Egypt, to be the womb to form and birth forth the nation of Israel. The writer believes at the end of the age, as a result of persecution and affliction, God is going to again raise up out of the continent of Africa and out of the African Diaspora a people of worship with a unique ministry to preserve and bring forth His Church and Israel during the unique dynamics of the end-times. African heritage knows the recent experience of world-wide persecution, hatred and domination. Africa knows what it means for her land to be robbed, stripped and the people of the land left on the side of the road for dead.

In the account in Luke 10:30 of the Good Samaritan, this man stopped by the road side to pour in the oil and the wine into the certain man who had been beaten, stripped and left for dead, because he was, no doubt, touched with the feelings of his infirmities, being a mistreated Samaritan himself. I believe Africans will respond with the same compassion when the nations of the world begin to persecute, strip, wound and leave God's chosen people half dead on the side of the road during the unique dynamics at the end of the age.

It's interesting to note that when Joseph went into slavery in Egypt, it was his brothers who sold him into slavery. Also, when Africans went into slavery to the European-American slave trade of the 1400's -1800's they were also sold into slavery, in most cases, by their brothers. I believe from that time of suffering in slavery God is going to raise up Africans, and the African Diaspora as end-time worshippers, that will be instrumental in leading the church and Israel into Fullness, until, as Romans 11 says, *"The fullness of the Gentiles is come and all of Israel is saved."* This is what the ministry of the forerunner is unto – Fullness.

And it will be actualized completely at the end of the age through the coming forth of this ministry led by those from the sons of Ham, the original forerunners in the first two thousand years. The ministry of this people group is paramount to the coming forth of the church of the end-times into the fullness of the Gentiles and the salvation of Israel. Romans 11:25, 26 says

> *For I would not, brethren, that ye should be ignorant of this mystery, lest ye should be wise in your own conceits; that blindness in part is happened to Israel, until **the fullness of the Gentiles** be come in. And so all Israel shall be saved: as it is written, There shall come out of Zion the Deliverer, and shall turn away ungodliness from Jacob:*

The Fullness of the Gentiles–The Full Anointing coming on the United Church

The fullness of the Gentiles speaks of the full anointing that will come upon the church as she comes into the unity of the faith, causing all nationalities, ethnicities and people groups to come together in one body, the body of Christ to fulfill the purpose of the nations of preparing the earth for the coming of the Lord. During this move of the spirit, there will not be a Black Church, a White Church, an Asian Church, Hispanic Church, or a Gentile Church. We will just be the Church, His house of Prayer for all Nations. This coming together of all people groups to the unity of the faith will come about by the understanding of the mutual need for dependency of each people group on the other to endure the unique dynamics of the end-times and accomplish the purpose of God for each nationality in the earth. In short, we will understand that we need one another. Each people group will have a particular emphasis and tow-post – *position of opportunity* - which will bring the body of Christ to fullness during the most tumultuous times the earth has ever seen.

Eyes to See and Ears to Hear

One of the purposes of the descendents from the sons of Ham being restored to a place of primary leadership at the end of the age is found in Numbers 10:29-32

> *29 And Moses said unto Hobab, the son of Raguel the Midianite, Moses' father in law, We are journeying unto the place of which the LORD said, I will give it you: come thou with us, and we will do thee good: for the LORD hath spoken good concerning Israel. 30 And he said unto him, I will not go; but I will depart to mine own land, and to my kindred. 31 And he said, Leave us not, I pray thee; forasmuch as thou knows how we are to encamp in the wilderness, and thou mayest be to us instead of eyes.*

Hobab, son of Raguel the Midianite was from the sons of Ham. What Moses was saying concerning Hobab is that he knew the wilderness. He knew the wilderness life. He knew how to maneuver around barrenness, around the animals in the wilderness. He knew how and where to encamp in the wilderness. In essence he knew how to live in tight and dangerous times. I believe this same designation applies to the sons of Ham even today. I believe the sons of Ham are the eyes of the body of Christ today. Mainly because with all the wilderness experiences, with barrenness, lack and suffering that Africans and the Diaspora have been through over the years, centuries and millennia's, I believe that once again God is going to use the descendents from the sons of Ham to lead the body of Christ and Israel at the end of the age, as we maneuver through the unique dynamics surrounding the coming of the Lord. I believe these descendents will be instrumental in the coming forth of many of the prophetic prayers, messages, songs, and worship that will be released from the throne during these unique times to release grace and supplication in the earth for Israel to see Yeshua as their Messiah. Africans/Diaspora know how to pray under duress. Africans/Diaspora know how to pray in times of distress and persecution, when an oppressor is threatening our lives. Africans/Diaspora know how to pray when all we have is God.

As we come upon some of the most tumultuous times our world has ever seen at the end of the age, our leadership is going to be defined by what we've already been through in slavery and the 400 years of suffering and oppression. What we've been through is preparation for what we're coming to at the end of the age. God is going to begin to speak to leaders in the body of Christ, his church, to invite the sons of Ham, those from Africa, *TO COME GO WITH US.* I believe he's releasing his spirit upon this people group to rise up to a place of leadership, to be the eyes in the body, to be forerunners going before with a unique prophetic, prayer, worship, intercessory ministry and message to help lead a company of forerunners to and through the wilderness of the last days to the coming of the Lord to set up His kingdom in the earth. During these times Africans and the African Diaspora are going to have to resist the response of HOBAB in Numbers 10:32 - *I WILL NOT GO; BUT I WILL DEPART TO MINE OWN LAND, AND TO MY OWN KINDRED.*

Get thee out of thy Country and from thy Kindred

Just like Abraham in Genesis 12:1-3, and just like Joseph in Genesis 37, many have had to leave their own land and kindred to help fulfill the prophetic destiny of other nations. And many more will begin leaving Africa to be dispersed among the nations of the world to help lead prayer and worship movements all over the world to preserve the Church and Israel at the time of the end. When we think about the fact that we were taken from our land in Slavery, and held down in our land in Colonialism, we must know that this was preparation for leadership at the end of the age, when persecution and suffering will once again be prevalent as the end-time world leaders attempt to persecute Jews and Christians. We must also remember that God will often times take a people from their land to make of them a great nation. Just as it was with Abraham, who also had to leave his native land to become a great nation, Africans and the Diaspora must be willing to be missionaries to the nations of the world. The land of Canaan wasn't Abraham's native land, nor was the Israelites Abraham's father's people. Abraham's people were from the Ur of Chaldees, but God called him to leave his native land, and the people of His father to become a great and mighty nation, that in him all the families of the earth would be blessed.

> *Gen 12:1 -3 Now the LORD had said unto Abram, Get thee out of thy country, and from thy kindred, and from thy father's house, unto a land that I will shew thee: 2 And I will make of thee a great nation, and I will bless thee, and make thy name great; and thou shall be a blessing: 3 And I will bless them that bless thee, and curse him that curses thee: and in thee shall all families of the earth be blessed.*

In order for the Church to come to fullness every tribe, nation and tongue is going to have to recognize the need to come together in unity for the preservation and blessing of other nations and lands, and specifically the nation of Israel. Even if it was necessary that Africans had to be taken from their own land into slavery in foreign lands we must know that God had a plan beyond the plans of man. Just as Joseph, when he came into Egypt as a slave to bless Egypt, God wanted to send those of African Descent to the nations of the world to preserve the nations and be eyes to maneuver the nations through the unique dynamics at the end of the age, to be a blessing to these nations.

Prayer for the Peace of Jerusalem Is the Key to National Blessing

Just as in Egypt with God raising up Joseph to be Prime minister of Egypt, he has a purpose in raising up those from the descendents of Ham to help lead at the end of the age. We see this trend in the earth with the sons of Ham taking their place of leadership in the nations, with the U.N. in Kofi Annan, as General Secretary from 1997-2006 and Barack Obama, the President of the USA from 2008-2012. We must see what God is seeing and doing and specifically see that at the end of the age, the key to securing the blessing of God on oppressed third world nations on the continent of Africa is for these nations to be positioned to be a blessing to the nation of Israel. *Gen 12:3 says, I will bless them that bless thee, and curse them that curse thee. And in thee all the families of the earth shall be blessed.* As the nations in Africa begin to Bless Israel by praying for the peace of Jerusalem, and as they open their borders to be cities of refuge for persecuted Jews, God will bless this continent again, just as he did when Joseph and his father's house were protected and provided for in Egypt during the famine in Genesis 42.

The Key to the blessing of the continent of Africa and her people is prayer for the peace of Jerusalem and protection for Jews during times of persecution. This is why I believe the United States of America is blessed. Because in 1950 after World War II millions of Jews were finally given the access they were denied 8 or 10 years previous at the dawn of WWII. However, after WWII, when the immigration laws were loosened to let Jews into our continental borders, the US economy begin to soar, as God opened up the windows of heaven and began to pour out a blessing on the nation where his chosen people began to flood into. And we have been the most blessed nation on the earth every since. God is all about bringing all nations together for His purposes concerning Israel and His Church. Just like in the days of Joseph, God is able to cause an evil deed like slavery done by your brothers to turn to work for good - His and yours.

Slavery – The Positioning of Forerunners in the Nations of the Earth

Through Slavery God was positioning forerunners in the nations of the earth for the full expression of His house of prayer for all nations, and for the preservation of His church and Israel at the time of the end of the age. This was one of the things God was working out of the enslavement of Africans in the middle-ages - *divine positioning for unity and fullness.* Slavery was not good, but it worked for good. Romans 8:28 says, *And we know that all things work for Good....to them who are called according to His purpose.* Slavery, in the middle ages of the

African nations accomplished the departing from our own land and kindred to come together with other nations to position this people to fulfill their end-time destiny as forerunners to preserve the nations of the earth and lead them to the fullness of their callings and destinies in the earth. As was stated earlier, many times when God calls a man or a nation he will call them out of their own lands or familiar surroundings to a foreign land to become a great nation that leads the nations of the earth into the worship of the God of the whole earth. I believe God is again releasing His spirit to prophetically call forth this unique group of end-time forerunners out of Africa and the African Diaspora to arise shine with light in the time of gross darkness, to take their place of leadership in His body, shoulder to shoulder with the nations of the world, to lead the church to fullness. I believe that Zephaniah 3:8, 9 speaks of what God will do to cause His church to come together into the unity of the faith for this purpose. Zephaniah 3:8, 9 says,

> *Therefore, wait for Me, says the Lord, for the day I rise up to the prey; for My judgment is to gather the nations, for Me to assemble the kingdoms, to pour on them My fury, all My hot anger. For all the earth shall be burned up with the fire of My jealousy. For then I will give to the people a pure language, to call all of them upon the name of Lord, to serve Him shoulder to shoulder. From beyond the rivers of Ethiopia, My worshipers, the daughter of My scattered ones, shall bring My offering.*

This specific people group, anointed by God, and coming forth through the end-time church in the earth will be acknowledged, encouraged and appointed to take a place of primary leadership shoulder to shoulder with the other two sons of Noah, from which all nations have come, Ham, Shem and Japheth. However, before divine positioning comes judgment always comes first. Even in the last days, right before the coming the Lord, before the offering up of the Lord's people and the scattering of Jews to places on the continent of Africa, there will come a shaking to this continent, and to the nations of the world. We have seen the beginnings of this in North Africa over the last few months of the year as this book is being written, but we will see a whole lot more of the fire of the Lord's jealousy before he makes Africa a place of refuge for His chosen people. This specific people group, together with the other two sons of Noah, will help preserve the nation of Israel and lead the body of Christ into fullness.

The Purpose of the Raising up of a Modern Day Joseph – President Obama's calling

Barack Obama becoming President of the United States, in a country in which his ancestors were slaves, and where he was subject to discrimination and racism, is a testament to the Justice of God. Psalm 19, says, His Judgments are true and righteous altogether. However, in addition to this, if we follow the pattern of Joseph's rise from slavery to Prime Minister of Egypt, it's very possible that his presidency signals a *coming shaking in the nations*! This is what Joseph's rise from slavery to the Prime Minister of Egypt indicated, with the interpreting of Pharaoh's dream of the coming world famine. It's very possible that His presidency was to be a sign of a coming world economic, financial shaking, to which God wants to preserve his people. Right before President Obama took office in 2008 the US economy collapsed with the stock market crash of the fall of 2008, and the house market collapse of that same year.

Anytime an oppressed people are raised up and brought to a place of prominence in the earth I believe it's the hand of God at work. I believe that this should signal a time for His people to begin seeking him in prayer for national wisdom and worship, as well as God's provision and protection for coming times of affliction, persecution and famine. God raises up an oppressed people because that people are more bound to acknowledge His hand in raising them up out of the hard times, and will seek him and his wisdom in governing the people in mercy. He also raises them up because they should know how to lead during times of shaking, having been born into hard times and passed safely through the shaking with the help of the Lord throughout their lives. This people are versed in living during hard times, enabling them to lead with an upward gaze when hard times come. Therefore, God raised up Joseph in Egypt, because Joseph had learned in the midst of adversity and affliction to serve others by interpreting dreams from the Lord, and now he would lead the King of Egypt into the wisdom of God to preserve the nation and the world. This is why God raised up David to be king of

Israel after Saul, Because David had learned to worship and love the Lord his God with all His heart, mind and soul and he knew he would lead from that place of Love & worship. This may very well be what Barack Obama's raising up is supposed to signal. This is what the body of Christ should begin to pray for President Obama, that he would acknowledge God as the one who placed him in this office as President of the United States, and leader of the free world, and that he would seek God's wisdom for the preservation of this nation and the nations of the world during the present and coming economic shaking. One thing is certain; African-Americans, Africans, and African Diaspora people everywhere should acknowledge and worship the God of Justice that is able to make everything work for our good as he takes the oppressed from the pit to the palace, from slavery to a place of leadership in the earth.

Chapter 10

THE COMING REVIVAL OF FIRE

Luk 3:16 John answered, saying unto them all, I indeed baptize you with water; but one mightier than I cometh, the latchet of whose shoes I am not worthy to unloose: he shall baptize you with the Holy Ghost and with fire:

There is one more revival coming to the earth through the church. And I believe that this revival is going to be a revival of fire.

God is going to once again speak to us out of the fire.
God is going to once again show us his glory out of the fire
God is going to once again show us his greatness out of the fire
God is going to once again show us he lives out of the fire

We have arrived at the time and season in the earth and the church for the last revival and restoration of the church the world will see before the coming of Christ. We have come to THE DAY OF THE REVIVAL OF FIRE in the church. And this revival is going to burn up every work that is not of God and purge and reveal the hearts of men.

1Co 3:13 Every man's work shall be made manifest: for the day shall declare it, because it shall be revealed by fire; and the fire shall try every man's work of what sort it is. 14 If any man's work abides which he hath built thereupon, he shall receive a reward. 15 If any man's work shall be burned, he shall suffer loss: but he himself shall be saved; yet so as by fire

The last great revival of note that ushered the church into the 20th century was the Azusa Street revival. This revival released the fullness of the Holy Ghost back into the church and the earth. As a result, the 20th century was the greatest century of progress, ingenuity and knowledge that we had ever seen in all the previous 19 centuries combined.

As we've come into the 21st century the revival that God is releasing in the church and the earth is the revival of the baptism with fire.

Luk 3:16 John answered, saying unto them all, I indeed baptize you with water; but one mightier than I cometh, the latchet of whose shoes I am not worthy to unloose: he shall baptize you with the Holy Ghost and with fire:

When we talk about the baptism in the Holy Ghost most people in Christendom today can define and describe its' purposes in the believer. Most of the past century, from the Azusa outpouring on, we received extensive revelation on the functions and purposes of the Holy Ghost. Many have come to the knowledge of the truth concerning the accompaniment of the unknown tongues in the baptism of the Holy Ghost. Many have come to the knowledge of the truth of the gifts of the spirit in the Holy Ghost, the word of wisdom, the word of Knowledge, the discerning of spirits, the gifts of Healing, the gift of faith, the working of miracles, the gift of tongues, the interpretation of tongues, and prophecy. The Baptism of the Holy Ghost has, by in large, been completely restored to the body of Christ in the earth. Its' restoration began in the 20th century at Azusa street in Los Angeles California in 1906. And for the next 94 years of the 2th century God unfolded, unveiled and revealed himself in the person of the Holy Ghost.

A New Thing in a New Century

In the 21st century God is doing a New Thing. Isaiah 43:18, 19 says, remember not the former things, neither consider the things of old, Behold I do a New thing, now it shall spring forth. In this New Century God is going to bring forth a new thing in the Church, and the next and last restoration movement of the church is going to culminate in the restoration of the baptism with fire, with God unfolding, unveiling and revealing himself through the manifestation of the sons of God.

As a result of this revival of fire and the manifestation of sons of God, it's going to be the greatest century of progress relationally, as far as, ethnic, nation and racial reconciliation, peace, prosperity, and the love of God and man, we've seen since the days of Adam. Dr. Martin Luther King stated back in the 1960's that through our ingenuity and great inventions of the 20th century, like the telephone, the radio, television computers, as well as the Jet Airplane, we've made our world a neighborhood. Now through love, understanding and goodwill, and I would like to interject, the heart of God, we must make our world a brotherhood. To make the world a brotherhood man's heart needs to be transformed to the heart of God. This is what's coming in the 21st century with the revival of the fire baptism that's coming to the church and the earth in 21st century. The baptism of fire is what purifies and purges man's selfish heart, sinful attitudes, and motives, enabling man to receive the heart of God. This is what is coming in this millennium. Through the restoration of the baptism of Fire and the manifestation of the sons of God in the earth, we're going to see a coming together in the earth of God and man, bringing a uniting of all races, tribes and ethnicities that will enable man to accomplish all of the will of God for the earth.

The Baptism with Fire Revelation Restored

If I were to ask what the baptism of the Holy Ghost was most people in the church would be able to tell me, even if they had differing views on its manifestations or evidences. Most people could tell me that it involved the speaking of tongues (unknown tongue). But if I were to ask, "Who can tell what the baptism in fire is?" Most people would not be able to say. This is because we have not seen the restoration of the fire baptism returned to the body. We have thought that the Holy Ghost baptism and the fire baptism were one in the same.

Another Baptism

Luke 3:15, 16 and as the people were in expectation, and all men mused in their hearts of John, whether he were Christ, or not; john answered, saying unto them all, i indeed baptize you with water; but one mightier than i cometh, the latchet of whose shoes i am not worthy to unloose: he shall baptize you with the HOLY GHOST and with FIRE

141

He Shall Baptize You With

While the baptism with the Holy Ghost has been widely recognized and regarded as part and parcel of the Pentecostal outpour, the baptism with fire has been overlooked and lightly regarded as just a part of the baptism with the Holy Ghost. While it is a part of the spirits work in the believer, it is also a baptism distinct and separate from the baptism with the Holy Ghost. "He shall baptize you with the Holy Ghost and with fire. The baptism with the Holy Ghost is one function of the spirits working in the believer, and the baptism with fire is another function of the spirits working in the believer. The key word in this verse is "with." It is stated twice, "he shall baptize you with... and with..." denoting two baptisms.

We know from the past century's restoration of the truth of the baptism with the Holy Ghost, that the holy ghost deals with leading the believer into all truth, which is Jesus. (John 16:13 howbeit when he, the spirit of truth, is come he will guide you into all truth.) What then is it that the baptism with fire deals with? What is the function of the baptism with fire? What are the major attributes of the baptism with fire? Why have we not seen more of the baptism with fire, with its' evidences and manifestations in the life of the believer in the modern church. Why have we not made a smoother transition from the baptism with the Holy Ghost to the baptism with fire before now? These are some the findings that this century's believers are going to come to know and receive. This is the next revival that is coming in the earth through the church.

Why Are We Stuck on The Holy Ghost Baptism?

Let's begin by answering the last question first. "Why have we not made a smoother transition from the baptism with the Holy Ghost to the baptism with fire before now?" Firstly, man tends to camp out around a movement of god's spirit and make a shrine around it. We tend to want to worship the move rather than the mover. We forget that god moves at one point to get you to the next point. It is not God's desire for man to become content or satisfied with what we've seen of god. God is always ready to reveal himself in new

142

dimensions and new ways. Man, however is bent towards his religious works and ritualistic ways.

So, when man received the baptism with the Holy Ghost his natural tendency was to make a religion out of it and build a memorial unto god. We have treated the baptism with the Holy Ghost as the end of our experience with god. However, the baptism with the Holy Ghost is the doorway to another level, and another baptism, called the baptism with fire.

Because we have thought that the Holy Ghost is the zenith of the spirits working in us we have become stuck in Pentecostal religion, centered around talking in tongues. But beginning in 2011 the fire baptism is being restored to the church and is going to become as commonplace as the previous century's baptism with the Holy Ghost. This is where God is taking his people in 2011. This will make the 21st century the century of the manifestation of the sons of God and birth a revival of prayer in the church that will usher in faith into the earth and the coming of the King of kings, Jesus Christ.

Rediscovering the purpose of the baptism with the Holy Ghosts

We've lost the purpose of the Holy Ghost baptism because we've thought that this was all there was to the spirits working in the believer. However, the Holy Ghost baptism should usher the believer into the fire baptism. How is this accomplished? Firstly, we must rediscover, and take back from religion, prayer in the Holy Ghost. The baptism with the Holy Ghost comes to give you power through prayer to make you a witness of the resurrection of Jesus Christ. With the Holy Ghost baptism, we receive our prayer language. He that believes shall speak with new tongues. (Mark 16:16) however, we became so enamored with the phenomenon of speaking in other tongues that we stopped there and made a religion out of the experience instead of letting it take us to the next level in God. We wore it as badge of our spirituality rather than as an instrument of the spirits working in us.

143

From the Holy Ghost baptism to the Fire Baptism

We must rediscover that we don't speak in tongues to speak in tongues to say we speak with tongues. We speak in tongues to speak god's word with the understanding. I Corinthians 14:14,15 for if I pray in an unknown tongue, my spirit prays, but my understanding is unfruitful. What is it then? I will pray with the spirit, and I will pray with the understanding also. The purpose of prayer in the spirit is simply, prayer with the understanding.

Prayer in The Spirit Leads Us To The Word

When we pray with the spirit, the spirit leads us to the prayer answer in the word. Once God's spirit leads us to the word, it's that word that we speak by the inspiration of the spirit that brings life, or that brings manifestation. It's the word of God, that is our prayer answer. It's the word of God we should be seeking from prayer in the spirit. This word is what brings direction, wisdom, sanctification, purification and yes, manifestation.

The Word Is for Meditation

Once we get the word on our situation from the Holy Ghost, the next thing we should do in prayer in meditation. Psalm 39:3 *David said, my heart was hot within me, while I was musing, (meditating) the fire burned; then spake I with my tongue.* Meditation of the word that the spirit has revealed is the stairway up to the fire baptism. To meditate is to mutter or confess. Once prayer in the spirit leads you to the word you must then begin to pray with the understanding the word of God. Confession should be birthed from prayer in the spirit, not our heads, or mental reasoning. Genesis 1:1-3 when God created the heavens and the earth before he ever said one word, #1 *the spirit of God moved upon the face of waters (word).* #2 *and God said; and said, and said, and said, 11 times in chapter 1 until he saw in verse* 31. The words from the spirit, that we meditate on, is what leads us to the manifestation of the Word.

144

Meditation leads to the fire

Psalm 39:3 David said, my heart was hot within me, while I was musing, (meditating) the fire burned; then spake I with my tongue. When we begin to speak that word that has been revealed by the spirit of God through prayer in the spirit, the word begins to have his free course in the believer. II Thessalonians 3:1 finally, brethren, pray for us, that the word of the Lord may have free course, and be glorified, even as it is with you. The word has a course that it takes in you as you meditate on it, before it takes you through to the manifestation. This course goes through dedication, sanctification, purification on unto manifestation. The manifestation comes after the fire purges out everything that is contrary to the word. The manifestation comes after the fire purges out everything that would hinder the word from manifesting.

When we speak the revealed word, it begins to work on us until we are cleansed from everything that is not like God. When that word is cleansing us, it is making way for God to flow through us freely and uninhibited. This is what leads us to the fire baptism. The fire baptism is initiated by the word that we speak from prayer in the spirit that begins to work on us and eventually through us. Fire deals with manifestation. Fire deals with purging and purifying. Fire deals with judgment. Fire deals with the consuming of a sacrifice. These will all be seen in the church and in the earth in 21st Century

What is the fire baptism? - It's another baptism distinct and separate from the water baptism and the Holy Ghost baptism – Luke 3-15

Luk 3:15 and as the people were in expectation and all men mused in their hearts of john whether he were the Christ, or not 16 john answered, saying unto them all, indeed baptize you with water; but one mightier than i cometh, the latchet of whose shoes I am not worthy to unloose: he shall baptize you with the Holy Ghost and with fire:

How do you receive the fire baptism? You must repent, be filled with the Holy Ghost and continue in the word of the Holy Ghost

145

What is the fire baptism for? Prayer/purging, purify, intercessory prayer – my house shall be called the house of prayer, boldness.

Luk 3:17 Whose fan is in his hand, and he will thoroughly purge his floor, and will gather the wheat into his garner but the chaff he will burn with fire unquenchable.

The Attributes of the Fire Baptism

The baptism with fire with all its' attributes and characteristics is what's going to be rediscovered in the 21st century, beginning in 2011. Now that we see how we go from the baptism with the Holy Ghost to the baptism with fire, what are the characteristics of the baptism with fire that will be synonymous beginning in 2011 and on into the 21st century? If tongues is what's synonymous with the baptism with the holy ghost, what is the outstanding attribute of the fire baptism? Both baptisms deal with our prayer life. The baptism with the Holy Ghost leads us from prayer in the spirit into prayer with the understanding. But the baptism with fire leads us from prayer with the understanding into intercessory prayer with groanings that cannot be uttered, praying for things we know not that we should pray for as we ought. Romans 8:22 shows us the end result of the baptism with fire. It begins by saying, for we know that the whole creation groans and travails in pain together until now. And not only they, but ourselves also, which have the first fruits of the spirit, even we ourselves groan within ourselves, waiting for the adoption, to wit the redemption of our body. 26. *Likewise the spirit also helps our infirmities: for we know not what we should pray for as we ought: but the spirit itself makes intercession for us with groanings which cannot be uttered. And he that searches the hearts knows what the mind of the spirit is, because he makes intercession for the saints according to the will of God.*

146

Attributes of the Holy Ghost baptism

Tongues (unknown)
Prayer in the spirit
Memorization and meditation
Gifts/fruit of the spirit

Attributes of the fire baptism

Groanings
Travail
Intercessory prayer
Manifestation of the sons of God

THE PURPOSE OF THE BAPTISM WITH FIRE

Act 1:4 and, being assembled together with them, commanded them that they should not depart from Jerusalem, but wait for the promise of the father, which, saith he, ye have heard of me. 5 for john truly baptized with water; but ye shall be baptized with the holy ghost not many days hence.

When you've gone through a period of waiting on the Lord for the promise of the father which he hath said, then you shall be baptized with water, the spirit and the fire for the promise to come through you to you. This promise will first manifest itself through you with power, signs, wonders and fruitfulness and multiplication of the nature and purposes of God. As a result of this season of birthing and the subsequent release of the promise of the fire baptism will see and increase and multiplication of the nature of God (love) in the earth, the people of god, and the works of God. The spirit of prayer will increase in the earth, the spirit of covenant and reconciliation will increase in the earth, the works of God will increase in the earth. There will be a proliferation of houses of prayer being raised up all over the earth. There will be the release of the true expression and purpose of the house of God; my house shall be called the house of prayer.

Act 1:7 and he said unto them, it is not for you to know the times or the seasons, which the father hath put in his own power. 8 but ye shall receive power, after that the holy ghost is come upon you: and ye shall be witnesses unto me both in Jerusalem, and in all Judaea, and in Samaria, and unto the uttermost part of the earth.

The promise of the father which he hath said unto you is manifested by the power of the spirit that he releases through you to be a witness of his death burial and resurrection when you wait on him to receive the water, spirit, and fire.

Why didn't Jesus finish John's statement in Acts 1:5 that ye shall be baptized with the holy ghost and fire? He stopped short of saying ye shall be baptized with fire as is recorded in Matt 3:11, and Luke 3:16. Why is that? Because he was only going to release the baptism with the Holy Ghost for them to be witnesses in all of the world, but the fire baptism would be released to fulfill verse 6. The question they asked him, Lord wilt thou at this time restore again the kingdom to Israel? The Holy Ghost baptism is for the power to be a witness to the uttermost parts of the earth. The fire baptism is for the power to restore the kingdom to Israel in the end. The fire baptism is for the bringing back of the kingdom of God to the earth in Jerusalem, for king Jesus being enthroned as King of kings and Lord of Lords, and for the Jews receiving Jesus as their messiah.

Chapter 11

THE COMING END-TIME PRAYER AND WORSHIP MOVEMENT AND THE DAY OF THE LORD

25 Therefore He is also able to save to the uttermost those who come to God through Him, since He always (forever) lives to make intercession for them. (Heb. 7:25) Christ...at the right hand of God, who makes intercession for us. (Rom. 8:34)

In this chapter I would like to begin connecting the dots of this book and bringing to conclusion the convergence and synergy of the end-time purpose of Africa and those of African descent, together with the Forerunner ministry of Jesus Christ after the order of Melchizedek, and His house becoming a House of Prayer for all nations. We have established thus far that the House of Prayer for all Nations and the ministry of Jesus Christ after the order of Melchizedek is how God is going to reconcile the races together in Him, as well as reconcile Heaven and earth. We've also established that Melchizedek's blessing of Abraham came within the context of His encounter in the Land of Canaan, one of the sons of Ham. While Noah's three sons Ham, Shem and Japheth, were each operating in separate two-thousand-year time frames of attempted dominion over the earth, while holding the other two sons under their domination, God was actually preparing them to be reconciled within His house of prayer for all nations at the end of the age. We have also established that Noah's son Ham, from whence come those of African Descent, was an original forerunner to the ministry of reconciliation and fullness, being the first inhabitants of the promised-land where Melchizedek encountered Abraham to release unto him the inheritance and fullness of the ministry of reconciliation of heaven to earth and of man to God. At the end of the age as God once again raises up this forerunner High Priestly ministry after the order of Melchizedek, His house of prayer is going to be the vehicle by which He ushers back into the earth Jesus Christ to reign as King of the nations.

149

If His house is to be a House of Prayer for all nations and accomplish her end-time purpose, it's going to have to include all nationalities, and ethnicities from the three sons of Noah. If His house of Prayer for all nations is going to accomplish her end-time purpose of *"All Israel"* being saved and the reconciling of the world to God, Africans, and those of African descent are going to have to take their place of leadership as forerunners, alongside all the other nations in his house of prayer to serve Him shoulder to shoulder. (Zephaniah 3:10)

The Priesthood Ministry of Melchizedek and the Day of the Lord

The significance of the unveiling of the end-time intercessory priesthood ministry after the order of Melchizedek cannot be overstated. Melchizedek's ministry is an end-time messianic ministry calling. Psalm 110:1-7 gives David's Messianic prophetic utterance detailing the conversation between the Father and the Son in eternity past, with the father stating concerning His Son, that he had sworn and will not repent, *thou are a priest for ever after the order of Melchizedek.*

> *Psa, 110:1 The LORD said unto my Lord, Sit thou at my right hand, until I make thine enemies thy footstool. 2 The LORD shall send the rod of thy strength out of Zion: rule thou in the midst of thine enemies. 3 Thy people shall be willing in the day of thy power, in the beauties of holiness from the womb of the morning: thou hast the dew of thy youth. Psa. 110:4 The LORD hath sworn, and will not repent, Thou art a priest for ever after the order of Melchizedek. 5 The Lord at thy right hand shall strike through kings in the day of his wrath. 6 He shall judge among the heathen, he shall fill the places with the dead bodies; he shall wound the heads over many countries. 7 He shall drink of the brook in the way: therefore, shall he lift up the head.*

This prophetic utterance of the Melchizedek priesthood calling of Jesus Christ is set within the context in Psalm 110:7 of *the Day of the Lord*, which is called in this verse, the *"Day of His wrath."* This Day of the Lord is "one day" at the end of the age where human history will be transitioned to the millennial reign of Christ in the earth through His praying Church calling down the judgments on His enemies of the 7 seals, bowls and trumpets in the book of *"The Revelation of Jesus Christ."*

The Great and Terrible Day of the Lord

The Lord's Day is the day when the Lord will judge and cleanse the earth from sin and evil and release his spirit to gather his people together for the setting up of his kingdom on the earth. Malachi, Joel and the book of Acts calls this day, *"The Great and Terrible Day of the Lord."* It's followed by the question, *"Who shall be able to stand?"* This day is what the Apostle John was seeing and relaying in the book of the revelation. He says, *"I WAS IN THE SPIRIT ON THE LORDS DAY."* He was actually saying, *I was there in spirit.* In other words, *I saw it as if I was there.* But I was not there; I was there in the spirit, transported to the end of the age, and the Day of the Lord, by the spirit of God. John saw the day of the Lord at the end of the age, and in Revelation 1 he begins to describe a man (Jesus, the glorified Christ) and a message that was given him to write and speak to the church right before and during that day, preparing the church for that day of the Lord. It's this message that *"The book of the Revelation of Jesus Christ"* represents. Both the *"Great"* and the *"Terrible"* dimensions of the Day of the Lord will both increase dramatically the closer we get to the return of Jesus and will find their fullest expressions in the final 3 ½ years of natural human history.

GREAT DAY - The Day of the Lord will have "great" attributes and characteristics for those that respond to Him as He releases the greatest manifestation of His power in natural human history. He is going to change the understanding and expression of Christianity in the whole earth in one generation. It will be the greatest time for the church in history.

VERY TERRIBLE DAY - The day of the Lord will also be the most severe time of God's judgment ever on earth since the beginning of human history. (Rev. 6-20) It is this day that Psalm 110:1-7 is referring to when the Father says to the Son;

> *The LORD said unto my Lord, Sit thou at my right hand, until I make thine enemies thy footstool. 2 The LORD shall send the rod of thy strength out of Zion: rule thou in the midst of thine enemies......The Lord at thy right hand shall strike through kings in the day of his wrath. 6 He shall judge among the heathen, he shall fill the places with the dead bodies; he shall wound the heads over many countries.*

The Father's invitation to the son to *"Sit thou at my right hand, until I make thine enemies thy footstool,"* is an invitation to the place of intercession in the presence of the father. The place of intercession, as the Son is seated at the father's right hand until His enemies are His footstool, is also the position of the Church as His House of Prayer at the end of the age through this priesthood ministry of Jesus Christ after the order of Melchizedek.

> *Eph 2:6 And hath raised us up together, and made us sit together in heavenly places in Christ Jesus:*

The Importance of the Restoration of the Descendants of Ham At The End of the Age

The Melchizedek priesthood ministry of the Church being understood, embraced, and entered into at the end of the age is vital to the coming of the Day of the Lord. As was stated in Chapter 15, the Melchizedek appearance in the earth happened at the time of the Hametic reign of Canaan in the land of promise. During this time the Hamites were the predominant people group from Noah's three sons attempting to take dominion in the land of God, and in the earth. As the forerunners from the first 2000 year reign from the descendants of Ham are restored to their place of leadership in the body of Christ, and in the earth at large, God is positioning His body to enter into the

Melchizedek priesthood ministry of reconciliation and fullness of the heavens and the earth, along with the reconciliation of God to man, and man to one another to release the Day of the Lord judgments in the earth through His house of prayer. Africans, and all those of African Descent being restored to their place of leadership at the end of the age, is not only prophetic, it is strategic. It will signal the beginnings of the release of the Day of the Lord and the final end-time battle between the Kingdom of darkness and the Kingdom of Light.

The Purpose of the Prayer Movement

It is the eternal identity of the Church to be united in God's house for all nations that operates by prayer. *7 For My House shall be called a House of Prayer for all nations. (Isa. 56:7)* In Scripture, a person's "house" spoke of their family, resources and future inheritance. The highest identity of the redeemed throughout eternity is to be *"God's House"* or His Family that releases His resources into the natural realm by functioning as a *"House of Prayer"*. We were created to interact deeply with God's heart. God speaks and moves our heart. Then we speak and move His heart. The result is that God's resources are released into the earthly realm. His resources include wisdom (creative ideas), unity, money, impact, zeal for righteousness, etc. Our identity as sons of God and the Bride of Christ come together in being His Family or House. The Father has ordained that His family rule with Jesus through "intimacy based intercession". God opens doors of blessing and closes doors of oppression in response to our prayers. There are blessings that God has chosen to give, but only as His people rise up in the partnership of prayer.

> *18 The Lord will wait, that He may be gracious to you...19 He will be very gracious to you at the sound of your cry; when He hears it, He will answer you. (Isa. 30:18-19)*

153

God jealously protects His relationship with us by NOT releasing His resources until we speak to Him in prayer. We must offer specific prayers, not just think about our need with fear, frustration and desperation. He requires that we ask because it causes us to interact with His heart.

2 You do not have because you do not ask. (Jas 4:2)

The Father's resources are strategically withheld to "starve us out of prayerlessness". When the pain of lacking His resources is greater than our busyness then we pray. God knows that our greatness, satisfaction and security are only found in our interaction with His heart in prayer. God requires us to cooperate with Him in the grace of God. This is an expression of His desire for intimate partnership with us. **God will not do our part** and **we cannot do His part**. If we do not do our part then God withholds some of the help and blessing He would have given us. God has given us a dynamic role in determining some of the measure of the "quality of life." Prayer tells God what He tells us to tell Him. Many consider this to be too simple and weak to do since everyone can do it. God releases His power in a way that we cannot boast (1 Cor. 1:31). Intercession causes us to internalize God's Word by saying it back to Him many times. Each time we say what God says, it marks our spirit and changes us. Like a computer program may be changed by rewriting each line of code, our inner man is renewed by multitudes of prayers. Intercession draws us in intimacy with His heart while it unifies and transforms us.

Jesus Governs the Universe through His House of Prayer

The governmental center of the universe is the "Prayer Room" which includes all the prayers in heaven and on earth that converge in unity before the Throne. Corporate intercessory worship is the primary means God uses to release His power. It is the most powerful weapon that exists.

The **House of Prayer in any particular city** is the whole Church in this area (consisting of all the congregations). One particular Day & Night prayer ministry is **NOT** the House of Prayer in a city. It functions with others as a "gas station that squirts gasoline" on the prayer furnace of the Church of that particular city. Ministries with a heightened focus on prayer are only catalysts not the whole House of Prayer.

A New Thing in an Old System

Remember not the former things, neither consider the things of old, Behold I do a New Thing, Now it shall spring forth. Isaiah 43:19

In 1999 as I was praying about the direction of the church going into a new decade, century and millennium, God spoke to my heart and begin to relate to me His heart and vision for the 21st century church. He began to tell me about a church that I had no grid or paradigm for. He said, in the 21st century church is going to be opened like Wal-Mart, 24hrs a day. He said the church won't be known by its buildings or it's separate, distinct congregations, but that it would be known by the body of believers in whole cities. At the time I was a new Pastor, leading a traditional apostolic storefront Church of 150 people that my Father had started in 1986 in the inner-city of downtown Columbus Ohio. My father led that church for 11 years, when in 1997 he installed me as the Pastor and he became the overseer. From 1997 to 1998 we grew from about 35 people to about 150 people, which was a miracle for a traditional Apostolic Oneness Church. However, in 1999 God spoke a verse of Scripture into my heart from Isaiah 43:18,19 that says, *Remember not the former things, neither consider the things of old, Behold I do a New Thing, Now it shall spring forth.* Then he said these words to me. *Brondon, I'm doing a New Thing, but my Church keeps doing the same ole things.*

You must let go of the Old to see the New

I said, "God, tell me how to do this new thing and I'll do it." He said "You won't do it even if I told you!" You were a traditional church goer, who grew up from a traditional church boy, and you're now a traditional church preacher. What the church of this generation has shown you is what you're going to do, even if I tell you to do something different. In order for you to do something new you've got to SEE something new.

In order to see something new you've got to LET GO OF THE OLD...*Remember not the former things....BEHOLD, I do a New Thing...(Isa. 43:18,19)* After I made significant steps towards letting go of the old, which included resigning as the Pastor of my father's Church, he then begin to reveal to me the new. He then began to show me what His coming end-time church would look like. He said in the 21st century when my people begin praying again to build my church as opposed to just "saying" (preaching) or "paying" (giving) or "playing" (Having a good time in church) to build my church, they won't be able to build fast enough to contain those that are coming seeking my glory that will be poured out in the earth.

He said look around you and see if there's anything like that where you are - a place that's open whose gates are continually open. I looked around in my mind and thought for a while about the church and I couldn't come up with one church in my mind that had so many people coming that they could not shut their doors day or night. Then I thought about the marketplace wondering if there was anything like that anywhere in society in the earth, and I said, WAL-MART! Wal-Mart's open 24hours a day and they're one of the most prosperous businesses in the world. I said, Oh Okay Lord! This must be what Isaiah 60:11 speaks of, the end-time paradigm that will cause the people and the kings of the earth to bring the forces (wealth) of the gentiles to the light of the church; a 24/7 house of prayer. As I stated earlier, I had no grid or paradigm for this type of a church, a church of victory, of power and confrontation, a place where the nations would come to our light, and kings to the brightness of our rising, whose gates would not be shut day or night.

A Church Culture of Day & Night Prayer not just Prayer times

Initially upon receiving this revelation I thought that only a big church could hold this new wineskin of day and night prayer. I was soon enlightened that *THIS WAS NOT TRUE! You don't have to be a big church to hold this new wineskin, all you have to be is a willing church, willing to let go of the old to embrace the new. You don't even have to try to do prayer services 24hrs a day, seven days a week. All you have to do is be* willing to set up a time to pray at any time people can come together corporately, adding worship and music with adoration and Love to God into the corporate prayer gatherings. It's not one church location that God is requiring and calling to establish night and day prayer, it's the body of Christ in a particular region, world-wide.

A Change in the Understanding and Expression of Christianity in One Generation

God's not calling one people in one congregation to start a 24/7 house of prayer, as much as he is calling the body of Christ in a particular city or region throughout the nations to come together and begin praying night and day within their church, ministry expression. God is raising up His church to establish a culture of prayer that no matter where you would go, at whatever time in a 24hr period in the world, or in a given city or region, you could find a people calling on the name of the Lord. God wants his church in a particular city, nation and world to come together in such a way that they establish prayer watches, or prayer cultures where people are always praying and never fainting. In the day that Daniel speaks of in the end-times when Satan will attempt to wear out the saints, the church that is not praying will faint. A people that are not praying will give in to compromise and give up during times of extreme pressure and persecution. In the present prayer culture in the body of Christ in the earth you would be hard pressed to go into a city or a region and find a place or a people praying at any time of the day or night. Why? because there's not a prayer culture in the church of our generation. *BUT GOD IS CHANGING THE UNDERSTANDING AND EXPRESSION OF CHRISTIANITY IN ONE GENERATION.*

Since that time over twelve years ago, God has released a spirit of prayer into the earth and has begun raising up the prayer movement and prayer ministries all over the world that have begun to express this expression of night and day prayer in the earth. In Kansas City God even has raised up one of the first 24/7 Prayer & Worship ministry expressions in the earth – *The International House of Prayer – IHOP-K.C.* And it began the same year, 1999, which God began revealing to me this *"New Thing"* that was coming in the earth from Isaiah 60:1-11.

CHAPTER 12

THE URGENCY OF AFRICAN DESCENT LEADERSHIP AND ISRAEL AT THE END OF THE AGE

For then there will be great tribulation, such as has not been since the beginning of the world until this time, no, nor ever shall be. And unless those days were shortened, no flesh would be saved; but for the elect's sake those days will be shortened. – Matthew 24:21-22 NKJV

At the International House of Prayer in Kansas City God has spoken prophetically to our community that the black community must take their place in the end-time Prayer movement. Many leaders are feeling this prophetic urgency in the prayer movement. When we speak of the black community we must clearly include all African descent believers, both those in Africa and those throughout the earth due to the African Diaspora. Because I am an African-American residing in the United States of America, I have highlighted the experiences that have kept African-Americans for uniting within his house of prayer for all nations. However, the call to the African descent community to take leadership in the prayer movement is a global call because of the immensity of our role at the end of the age. Many in this international family of affection have taken up this intercessory burden. One such Caucasian leader at IHOP, Samuel Clough, recently shared this burden at one of our African-American Conferences. This chapter is dedicated to some of his thoughts and notes on this subject that he shared during this gathering. This prophetic urge must not be seen as a prophetic whisper, but as a prophetic shout coming from all the nations from the three sons of Noah, due to the urgency of the hour. It is critical that we understand that this is not a good idea or another man-made attempt at reconciliation.

This is a critical issue and there will be massive repercussions in the years ahead based on how we respond to this prompting of the Holy Spirit. We must respond both in the place of intercession and in action. While action is necessary, intercession is more necessary. We fail to intercede over this issue because we fail to understand how truly critical it is. Man-made attempts at superficially uniting the races have caused many to ignore the call to unity. We must understand that, in this hour, the call for black leadership in the prayer movement is not a fad, a trend, or another man-made attempt at reconciliation, it is critical once we understand the prophetic context that we are living in and the context in which the events at the end of the age will unfold.

Yet and still, the issue of African descent leadership in the prayer movement is not just an issue of racial unity, which is extremely precious to the Lord, but it has great eschatological significance. If we do not give ourselves to intercession and to action, whether you are of African descent or not, to see that believers of African descent are established in her place of leadership we are ignorant of the times in which we live and lack understanding of how our actions now will have massive repercussions as the end of the age unfolds with greater intensity.

The Origins of Racism in the Church

The racial separation in the church is a serious concern before the Lord regardless of the eschatological implications. As stated in Chapters 1 and 3 the conflict between Jew and Gentile is the origin of all racism, and from the beginning, the church was intended to be a miraculous demonstration of unity between the Jew and Gentile.

> *Behold, how good and how pleasant it is for brethren to dwell together in unity! – Psalm 133:1 NKJV*

> *...where there is neither Greek nor Jew, circumcised nor uncircumcised, barbarian, Scythian, slave nor free, but Christ is all and in all. – Colossians 3:11 NKJV*

> *There is neither Jew nor Greek, there is neither slave*
> *nor free, there is neither male nor female; for you are*
> *all one in Christ Jesus. – Galatians 3:28 NKJV*

One of the greatest blights on the church is the initial racial divide that occurred as the gentile community of believers outgrew the Jewish community of believers and began separating from them and persecuting them as early as the 3rd century. This racism had profound implications for the church. This separation is felt to this day in Jewish distrust of the very people that carry their own Scriptures. Beyond the blindness spoken of in the Scriptures, there is a resistance to Christians due to their experience of racism. Even Christian theology suffered tremendously from this divide as the gentile church divorced itself from the Jewish context of the Scripture and sought to synthesize the Scriptures with other philosophical ideas. While we want to examine the eschatological issues that surround African descent leadership in the prayer movement, we must acknowledge that the Lord truly desires unity in His church and our separation grieves His heart.

Because we are considering the prayer movement specifically in this chapter, we must understand why the prayer movement is exploding at this particular time in history. One of the reasons that the prayer movement is exploding now is that the prayer movement serves the purpose of unifying the church, laboring for revival, and demonstrating the worth of Jesus; however, that is not the primary reason for the unique night and day prayer movement that is spreading rapidly throughout the earth.

The night and day prayer movement specifically exists for Israel at the end of the age. The Scripture is very clear that night and day prayer will precede the end of the age. This contending prayer is Jesus' global welcoming party and will also be required for the events that befall Israel at the end of the age. Below is a list of scriptures that all tie prayer, worship and singing of the worth and beauty of the Lord, with Israel coming forth, and receiving their Messiah, Yeshua Hamishiach, at the end of the age.

> *O sing to the LORD a new song, For He has done*
> *wonderful things, His right hand and His holy arm have*

161

gained the victory for Him. The LORD has made known His salvation; He has revealed His righteousness in the sight of the nations. He has remembered His lovingkindness and His faithfulness to the house of Israel; All the ends of the earth have seen the salvation of our God. Shout joyfully to the LORD, all the earth; Break forth and sing for joy and sing praises. Sing praises to the LORD with the lyre, With the lyre and the sound of melody. With trumpets and the sound of the horn Shout joyfully before the King, the LORD. Let the sea roar and all it contains, The world and those who dwell in it. Let the rivers clap their hands, Let the mountains sing together for joy before the LORD, for <u>He is coming to judge the earth</u>; He will judge the world with righteousness And the peoples with equity. - Psalms 98:1–9 NAS95

<u>Sing</u> to the Lord a new song! <u>Sing</u> to the Lord, all the earth...<u>Worship</u> the Lord...<u>tremble before Him</u>, all the earth...For <u>He is coming to judge the earth</u>. (Ps. 96:1-13)

O people in Zion, inhabitants in Jerusalem, you will weep no longer. He will surely be gracious to you <u>at the sound of your cry</u>; when He hears it, He will answer you. - Isaiah 30:19 NAS95

<u>They shall lift up their voice, they shall sing</u>; for the majesty of the LORD...<u>glorify the LORD in the dawning light</u>, the name of the LORD God of Israel in the coastlands of the sea. <u>From the ends of the earth we have heard songs: "Glory to the righteous!"</u> (Isa. 24:14-16)

Listen! <u>Your watchmen lift up their voices</u>, They shout joyfully together; For they will see with their own eyes When the LORD restores Zion. - Isaiah 52:8 NAS95

Gather yourselves together, yes, gather, O nation without shame, Before the decree takes effect — The day passes like the chaff — Before the burning anger of the LORD comes upon you, Before the day of the LORD'S anger comes upon you. Seek the LORD, All you humble of the earth who have carried out His ordinances; Seek righteousness, seek humility. Perhaps you will be hidden in the day of the LORD'S anger. - Zephaniah 2:1–3 NAS95

I will pour out on the house of David and on the inhabitants of Jerusalem, the Spirit of grace and of supplication, so that they will look on Me whom they have pierced; and they will mourn for Him, as one mourns for an only son, and they will weep bitterly over Him like the bitter weeping over a firstborn. - Zechariah 12:10 NAS95

...now, will not God bring about justice for His elect who cry to Him day and night, and will He delay long over them? I tell you that He will bring about justice for them quickly. However, when the Son of Man comes, will He find faith on the earth [A people crying out day and night]? - Luke 18:7–8 NAS95

When He had taken the book, the four living creatures and the twenty-four elders fell down before the Lamb, each one holding a harp and golden bowls full of incense, which are the prayers of the saints...Another angel came and stood at the altar, holding a golden censer; and much incense was given to him, so that he might add it to the prayers of all the saints on the golden altar which was before the throne. And the smoke of the incense, with the prayers of the saints, went up before God out of the angel's hand. Then the angel took the censer and filled it with the fire of the altar, and threw it to the earth; and there followed peals of thunder and sounds and flashes of lightning

163

> and an earthquake...*The Spirit and the bride say,* *"Come."* And let the one who hears say, "Come." And let the one who is thirsty come; let the one who wishes take the water of life without cost. - Revelation 5:8; 8:3–5; 22:17 NAS95

The Scripture is particularly clear that night and day prayer exists for God's purposes in Jerusalem. Isaiah 62 is very clear about the connection of day and night prayer with the urgency in God's heart to see all His purposes regarding Israel and Jerusalem come to pass:

> *For Zion's sake I will not hold My peace, and for* *Jerusalem's sake I will not rest,* until her righteousness goes forth as brightness, and her salvation as a lamp that burns. – Isaiah 62:1

> I have set watchmen on your walls, O Jerusalem [for the cause of Jerusalem]; *they shall never hold their* *peace day or night.* You who make mention of the LORD, do not keep silent, and *give Him no rest till He* *establishes and till He makes Jerusalem a praise in the* *earth*. – Isaiah 62:6-7 NKJV

Jesus taught that justice would be established through a night and day prayer watch for vengeance against our adversary (speaking God's Word). Justice is God making wrong things right. Jesus is the ultimate social reformer. He was the first to connect justice (social reform and making wrong things right) to night and day prayer.

> 7 Shall God not avenge (bring about justice for, NAS) His elect who cry out day and night to Him? 8 I tell you that He will avenge (bring about justice to, NAS) them speedily. (Lk. 18:7-8)

164

Global Concerts of Prayer and African descent Worshippers at the End of the Age

Jesus comes back at the Second Coming in answer to global concerts of prayer and worship. The End-Time prayer movement in partnership with Jesus' heavenly intercession will release the Great Harvest, the Great Tribulation and even drive Satan "the usurper" off this planet (Rev. 20).

> *10 Sing to the LORD a new song, and His praise from the ends of the earth, you who go down to the sea...you coastlands and you inhabitants of them! 11 Let the wilderness and its cities lift up their voice...13 The Lord shall go forth like a mighty man (Second Coming); He shall stir up His zeal like a man of war...He shall prevail against His enemies. (Is 42:10-13)*

Contending day and night prayer, which includes day and night worship and singing is a part of the end of the age. As the earth groans, so too will the people of God in faith, corporately groan in prayer for His appearing. Not only is night and day prayer significant for Jesus' appearing, it is required because of the magnitude of the events that are going to befall Israel, and the entire globe, at the end of the age. Much of the church has little or no awareness of the magnitude of the trouble that is coming for Israel. Many assume that Israel's troubles are mostly over because they are back in the land. The reality is that Israel's troubles are only about to escalate. The terrors of the day ahead should cause us to have difficulty speaking about these things without weeping.

> *Alas! For <u>that day is great, so that none is like it</u>; and it is the time of Jacob's trouble... - Jeremiah 30:7*

Jeremiah 30-31 describes the time of Jacob's trouble, an unparalleled time of difficulty and suffering for Israel. Many assume this is past, when a careful study of Scripture reveals that the most terrifying days of Jewish suffering are in front of us.

Jewish suffering will not only affect Israel, but it will become an issue throughout the entire earth. The issue of Jerusalem will affect the entire earth as the Jews are persecuted and driven throughout the nations of the earth. Throughout the earth Jews will be on the run and in hiding. What was seen in Nazi Germany was a graphic illustration of what is coming again as the end time scenario unfolds.

> And it shall happen in that day that I will make Jerusalem *a very heavy stone for all peoples*... - *Zechariah 12:3 NKJV*

In the hour of their greatest suffering, God will be looking at the gentiles, the "wild olive branches that have been grafted in to the natural olive tree" to make provision for and suffer with the Jewish people in order to display His own unending love.

The Preparation of a People that Can Endure Crisis

As the hour of trial for the entire earth approaches, the church must be prepared to endure crisis and pressure unlike any point in human history.

> *For then there will be great tribulation, such as has not been since the beginning of the world until this time,* no, nor ever shall be. And unless those days were shortened, no flesh would be saved; but for the elect's sake those days will be shortened. – *Matthew 24:21-22 NKJV*

Since the prayer movement exists specifically for this time of great tribulation, and the many decades leading up to this time, as the pressure begins to build, the Lord will prepare a people for this hour of suffering that are capable of enduring with strength. Particularly in the preceding centuries, people of African descent throughout the earth have endured great suffering and great trial. Because of this suffering, they have a unique history that the entire church is going to need in the hour of suffering to come.

If the church is going to be prepared to endure the hour of suffering, it is critical that believers of African descent take a significant leadership role to begin to prepare the church at large to endure the type of suffering that believers of African descent have experienced over the last several centuries. The entire community of believers around the earth will soon experience the suffering that we endured simply because of skin color. The root of all racism is the divide between Jew and gentile. At the end of the age, this racism will come to its zenith. However, persecution will not be limited only to those that are Jewish by blood though they will take the brunt of the suffering. Those who join themselves to Jacob in that hour will endure the suffering as well.

The African people have uniquely experienced the suffering that comes from racism on a global level and therefore have a great understanding of the suffering that will come as anti-Semitism reaches its height in all of history. Believers of all backgrounds, who join themselves to the Jewish people in this hour of suffering, will begin to experience the full weight of suffering that comes from racism. In this hour, believers of African ancestry have been uniquely prepared to lead the church with strength. Because we have born the weight of suffering rooted in racism, we will be equipped to lead the entire church as it comes under the weight of racial suffering through faithfulness to the Jew.

This is the hour for believers of African descent to give the entire church strength to endure the persecution that is coming. If we do not take our place of leadership the entire church will be unequipped for the eschatological suffering that is coming.

There is a call to believers of African descent to receive the love and warmth of other areas of the church who are genuinely repentant towards the history of racism that has existed in many countries of the earth and was affected by many of our ancestors. Just as Jesus forgave those who persecuted Him, so too the believers of African descent must forgive so that we can take our rightful place of leadership across the entire church. There is a clear call to non-black believers to have genuine love and sympathy for the suffering that believers of African descent have endured. There is a tendency for non-black believers to over simplify the suffering endured by believers of African descent and the issues it has subsequently faced because of centuries of slavery. This over simplification creates a barrier that prevents the believers of African descent from coming into a place of leadership in the church. *Love must become the preeminent value of non-black believers towards their brothers and sisters of African descent.*

> *Though I speak with the tongues of men and of angels, but have not love, I have become a sounding brass or a clanging cymbal...Though I give my body to be burned, but have not love, it profits me nothing...the greatest of these is love. – I Corinthians 13:1, 3, 13 NKJV*

The African Witness and the Jews at the End of the Age

Even as believers of African descent are called to strengthen the entire community of believers at the end of the age, we are also uniquely called to minister to the Jew in the hour of suffering and trial. The African history of Diaspora, suffering, and slavery has uniquely prepared the black community to minister to Jews in flight at the end of the age. Our shared history of suffering will enable us to minister to the Jews in a unique way. God has uniquely prepared the black community to serve Jews in flight during their hour of crisis.

It is critical that believers of African descent do not see its suffering only through an Afro-centric lens. Yes, God cares about the unique suffering that believers of African descent have endured, but our community must see our own suffering as a unique preparation that allows us to minister at the end of the age in the way that others cannot. (This, of course, in no way justifies the suffering perpetrated on the African people, but rather it is God's glorious redemption of the wickedness we have endured.)

Believers of African descent will only find full healing from the suffering we have endured as we see the incredible gift we now have that will be required at the end of the age. Though there are real issues within our community that all believers should labor for, believers of African descent ourselves cannot allow our own suffering to cause us to lose sight of our call which extends far beyond our own community.

A primary tool of the enemy at the end of the age will be to make believers of African descent entirely self focused so that we cannot give our unique gift to the Jew and the church at the end of the age. The enemy knows how significant our role is to be and this is why he consistently wars against us coming into true freedom and releasing the power of our history of suffering to the church and, in a coming hour, to Jews in flight.

The Musical History of both people of African Descent and Jews

It cannot be overlooked that both the African people and the Jewish people are known as a musical people. Isaiah 24:14-16 is very clear that, at the end of the age, amidst all the destruction songs will be heard from the ends of the earth.

> From the end of the earth we have heard songs... -
> Isaiah 24:16 NKJV

As Jews are persecuted throughout the earth, the Lord will cause them to be sheltered by gentile believers who will be singing the very songs of Zion throughout the nations of the earth. In the very hour when the Jews feel least like singing, they will be sheltered by a singing people singing their own songs from the Scripture. This global singing will be a primary witness of Jesus to the Jews at the end of the age. The black community has a unique gift for song and for music. Not only does the Lord intend to use this gift to fill the earth with prayer and worship in preparation for the Lord's return, He also intends to use it to minister to the Jews at the end of the age.

Eschatological Urgency

We must always be clear that no one knows the day or the hour of Jesus return, but the Scripture is also clear that we will know the signs of the times as the end approaches. It is unbiblical to act as though we should not anticipate the end of the age or even watch for specific, biblical signs that the end is drawing near. The clear tone of Jesus' and Paul's writings is that we are actually in error when we do not recognize the times and seasons.

> *When you see all these things, know that it is near--at the doors! – Matthew 24:33 NKJV*

> *Watch therefore, for you do not know what hour your Lord is coming. Matthew 24:42 NKJV*

> *Now when these things begin to happen, look up and lift up your heads, because your redemption draws near. – Luke 21:28*

> *The Pharisees...came, and testing Him asked that He would show them a sign from heaven...Hypocrites! You know how to discern the face of the sky, but you cannot discern the signs of the times. - Matthew 16:1-4 NKJV*

> *Concerning the times and the seasons, brethren, you have no need that I should write to you...But you, brethren, are <u>not in darkness so that this Day should overtake you as a thief</u>...Therefore...<u>let us watch</u>. - 1 Thessalonians. 5:1-6 NKJV*

Virtually all of the church recognizes the significance of Israel's return to the land beginning in 1948 and their occupation of Jerusalem in 1967. After 2,000 years of absence from the land, this was a stunning development that shows us very clearly that we have entered a different prophetic season on God's timetable. While most of the church recognizes there is great significance to the state of Israel, most of the church is still ignorant of the fact that the current state of Israel is not the full fulfillment of God's promises to Israel and a great suffering exists between what exists now and what God will establish at Jesus' return. As we have already noted, the time of Jacob's trouble (Jeremiah 30-31) is still future and almost no one is preparing for it. The current state of Israel will not endure as it is and the Jewish people will experience another disastrous season of suffering that both the holocaust and the previous Diaspora were precursors to. While the understanding of Israel's future suffering has been considered by many to be a fringe idea in the last few decades, not only is the church not growing in understanding of the coming crisis but the actual events that must come before the crisis are beginning to occur with frightening speed. In the last twelve months, virtually every Arab state around Israel has become embroiled in revolution. While these revolutions are often presented as movements for democracy in the western media, everyone knows that the end of these revolutions will always be a strict Islamic government. Both of Israel's great allies in the region have suddenly shifted course in the last year. Turkey has gone from a quiet presence in the region that allied itself with U.S. interests to become very vocal against the state of Israel.

Egypt, a close ally of Israel, now exists without a real government and, barring miraculous intervention from the Lord, is set to transition to an aggressive Islamic government. Protests in the nation have included calls for a military march on Israel and an attack against the Israeli embassy. Both Turkey and Egypt are now quickly becoming allies united against the presence of Israel in the region. Other surrounding nations are also rapidly positioning themselves to participate in an attack against Israel. Iran has been very clear about its intentions to wipe Israel out of the land.

The Palestinians have repeatedly refused moderate land swap proposals and are instead pushing for an internationally recognized state that will be one step to their plan of annihilating Israel. Palestinians have been very clear about their refusal to recognize Israel as a legitimate nation. Smaller Arabic nations surrounding Israel are all in the midst of turbulence and revolution.

As the dust settles in each nation, it will be the radical Muslims who will be in charge of each nation. The current turbulence in the Middle East is very clearly setting up a situation where Israel is surrounded with a hostility that is far more overt than what it has experienced in the last 20 years. When Israel begins to be overrun by Arabic nations and Jews again flee into the nations of the earth, most of the church who will have no understanding of what is happening will retreat into fear and confusion. Many will even lose their faith and fall away entirely because of unbiblical ideas they had about Israel and the end of the age. We cannot know if these events are months, years, or decades away, but it is very clear that the Middle East is rapidly transforming to the point where the future suffering of Israel is no longer just an idea, but a reality. At this point, it only takes one nation to pull the trigger and a unified Arab coalition in the region could easily bump Israel right off the map. Very little remains, except for the actual military invasion, to setup the final scenario of Jewish suffering. This is no longer just a theological or eschatological idea for us to wrestle debate-it is reality on our evening news.

When we understand the reality of our condition, we should tremble at the lack of understanding and, even greater, the lack of day and night intercession for the issue of Jerusalem. In addition, it should fill our hearts with urgency for believers of African descent to take their place in the prayer movement. It is the enemy's scheme that believers of African descent do not come into their place so that Israel will not come into hers in the final suffering.

The black church and the Jewish predicament at the end of the age are intertwined and this is why the enemy wages such war against believers of African descent coming into a place of leadership in a unified praying church at the end of the age. If he can prevent believers of African descent from standing in our place and strengthening the church and ministering to the Jews at the end of the age, then he can affect far more damage in his rage against the church and the Jewish people.

The Assault Of Islam

Given the significance of the eschatological call on the African people, we would expect to see Satan raging against this call. I propose that the growth of Islam in the black community is one of Satan's primary schemes against the call of the African people at the end of the age. Islam has become the greatest religious assault on the African people in our generation. While Islam, by nature, seeks to dominate all nations, in our generation we can see a clear focus on the African people. In the west among the African Diaspora, Islam began to creep into the black community during the civil rights movement. While the growth of Islam in the black community began with non-orthodox forms of Islam such as the Nation of Islam, we are now seeing the growth of more orthodox forms of Islam such as Sunni Islam. In the United States, Islam is growing rapidly among the black community through conversion and black Muslims are becoming increasing involved in global Islamic issues, such as the Palestinian cause, rather than only in Afro-centric forms of Islam

While Afro-centric versions of Islam highlight black suffering, global Islam shifts the focus to the Jew as the cause of all suffering. By causing black converts to identify with the suffering of the Palestinians, the more orthodox forms of Islam now infiltrating the black community brings them directly into Islam's confrontation with the Jews. For the past several centuries, Islam has been entrenched in northern Africa due to Arabic influence while the south has been increasingly Christianized due to the labor of missionaries, the maturing of African churches, and the spread of the gospel.

Islam is no longer simply the religion of northern Africans. It is increasingly pushing south in a concentrated effort to consume all of Africa from Egypt to South Africa. There is now a brutal bloodline across Africa as Islam is violently pushing south across the continent. Christian communities in Africa south of the Sahara are now being terrorized and slaughtered by the same violent techniques Islam used to originally conquer Arabia. As Islam advances, it leaves behind a people locked in darkness. In addition, there are two significant theological and practical premises of Islam that are particularly relevant to the crisis that will enfold the earth at the end of the age. The book of Revelation introduces the end-time storyline in Revelation 1:1 by summarizing it as the "revelation of Jesus." Because Jesus is the centerpiece of the events at the end of the age, the most critical question on the earth as we approach the end of the age will be "Who is Jesus?"

Islam postures itself as if it honors Jesus while in reality it robs Him of His deity and creates a Jesus in its own image that is less than God and subservient to the prophet Mohammed. This redefinition of Jesus is at the heart of all antichrist religions, but Islam's posture of "honoring Jesus" helps it to appeal to the black community in America where the local church has been a prominent part of African-American culture. Islam seeks to tear down the true identity of Jesus and thereby enslave the African people to a false Jesus thereby preparing them to receive both the antichrist and the false prophet as the antichrist religion develops and emerges in the decades to come. Islam, at its heart, is an anti-Semitic movement. The oppression and slaughter of the Jews has been an intrinsic part of orthodox Islam from its origin. Islam is Satan's clear attempt to take the people who are called to be the Jews' chief

174

protector in the hour of trial and instead make them a chief enemy and executioner of the Jews. Islam is systematically training and preparing Africans, on a global level, to join the antichrist in the slaughter of the Jews at the end of the age.

The consequences of believers of African descent not coming into the fullness of their destiny are massive. The scenario in the Middle East should make us tremble with urgency. The events of the end, though they may take decades to unfold, are upon us and yet believers of African descent have still not been brought into their full place of leadership at the end of the age. The situation is not accidental, nor is it isolated. Let us labor with sobriety to see our community come into their fullness and to see other believers recognize the awesome responsibility that believers of African descent have in the events of the end of the age. Let us labor with great love to see the fullness of God's calling for believers of African descent come to pass.

CHAPTER 13

THE PURPOSE OF THE UNITY OF THE FAITH & NATIONS– *The Peace of Jerusalem*

Eph 4:13 Till we all come in the unity of the faith

The coming forth of those of African descent, as well as the body of Christ coming into the unity of the faith, or the ministry of reconciliation, will not only bring about the measure of the stature of the fullness of Christ, but it will be the predecessor to the coming of the Lord, the peace of Jerusalem, and a healing of a severed relationship that has been severed for over 3000 years between Jacob and Esau. This is what I believe unity and fullness within the body of Christ is unto - *the coming of the Lord to bring forth the peace of Jerusalem.*

The ministry of this African Descent people group is paramount to the coming forth of the Church of the end-times into the fullness of the Gentiles and the salvation of Israel. Romans 11:25, 26 says

> *For I would not, brethren, that ye should be ignorant of this mystery, lest ye should be wise in your own conceits; that blindness in part is happened to Israel, until **the fullness of the Gentiles** be come in. And so all Israel shall be saved: as it is written, there shall come out of Zion the Deliverer, and shall turn away ungodliness from Jacob:*

The Fullness of the Gentiles–The Full Anointing coming on the United Church

The fullness of the Gentiles speaks of the full anointing that will come upon the Church as she comes into the unity of the faith, causing all nationalities, ethnicities and people groups to come together in one body, the body of Christ to fulfill the purpose of the nations of preparing the earth for the coming of the Lord. During this move of the spirit, there will not be a Black Church, a White Church, an Asian Church,

177

Hispanic Church, or a Gentile Church. We will just be the Church, His house of Prayer for all Nations. This coming together of all people groups to the unity of the faith will come about by the understanding of the mutual need for dependency of each people group on the other to endure the persecution during the unique dynamics of the end-times and accomplish the purpose of God for each nationality in the earth. In short, we will understand that we need one another. Each people group will have a particular emphasis and tow-post – *position of opportunity* - which will bring the body of Christ to fullness during the most tumultuous times the earth has ever seen.

As a 23-year-old Bible College student God spoke audibly to me after reading Romans 10:1. Though I had never heard the audible voice of the Lord before, I could not deny what I was hearing. I heard the Holy Ghost say through Paul, *Brethren my heart's desire and prayer to God for Israel is that they might be saved*; I could not shake that voice in my spirit saying to me; "COME TO ME SON AND I'LL SHOW YOU MY HEART CONCERNING THE SALVATION OF MY PEOPLE ISRAEL AND THE WHOLE WORLD..." The more I read Romans 10 and 11 the clearer that voice in my spirit became. "COME TO ME SON AND I'LL SHOW YOU MY HEART CONCERNING THE SALVATION OF MY PEOPLE ISRAEL AND THE WHOLE WORLD." After much seeking concerning what God was inviting me to, I realized he was calling me to his Holy city Jerusalem, the place where His throne will be set in the millennial reign.

The Challenge of the Nations

In 1992 by a miraculous chain of events I left the country for the first time, as a 26-year-old Bible College student on a Holy Land pilgrimage, journeying from my father's African American storefront church in the inner-city of Columbus Ohio to my heavenly father's future home in the earth in Jerusalem Israel. While in Jerusalem on this Holy Land pilgrimage, God gave me a life time challenge that changed my life, in response to a question I asked him while standing on the balcony of the Jerusalem Hilton. I had been speaking with two Israelis. One was an Arab and one was a Jew, and both were conciliatory and amicable as they discussed the situation of land and peace, just wanting to live together in peace in the nation they both had been born in. After speaking to them both, I asked God in prayer, "What is the solution to this dilemma. What is the answer to the Jewish, Arab conflict in the Middle East?" "How is it possible for both brothers from Abraham to live together in harmony and peace in the Middle East?"

He didn't answer me right away but gave me a challenge first. He said, you go home and learn how to live together in God-ordained relationships as Husband with wife, black with white, rich with poor, Pentecostal with Baptist, etc, and you'll receive the solution to the Jewish, Arab dilemma. He said every ethnic, religious, sectarian, doctrinal, and racial conflict throughout the gentile nations of the world that ends in reconciliation through Christ Jesus are all meant to be the lights to bring about the coming of the Lord to bring forth the solution to peace, to bring forth PEACE IN THE MIDDLE EAST AND THE PEACE OF JERUSALEM.

The coming together, uniting and correct functioning of all marriages, Christian denominations, all races, in all nations as one in Christ Jesus are meant to be lights, sign posts and the forerunner to THE PEACE IN THE MIDDLE EAST COMING WHEN JESUS RETURNS. As the nations come together in Christ, the Church will shine the light of God's love for the reconciliation of the brothers from Abraham in the middle-east in Jerusalem and around the world. When the races at conflict in the nations of the world come together and live in peace and harmony through the acceptance of Christ and his principles as their answer, the answer to the middle-east dilemma will be witnessed by that people.

African & African-American Forerunners to peace in Jerusalem

This is where Africans and African-Americans have gone before the middle-east nations as forerunners having already dealt with race wars, racists' views and relations under slavery, colonialism and oppressive systems of segregation, discrimination and domination. At the end of the age I believe these nations from the continent of Africa and the African Diaspora will be challenged to lead the church and the nations of the world into reconciliation and forgiveness. Dr. Martin Luther King Jr. gave us a foretaste of the methods necessary for racial engagement during times of tense ethnic, racial strife and disengagement. Through

179

the response of the Agape Love of God, the principles of the sermon on the mount, through non-violent passive resistance and prayer in the midst of an unjust system of segregation and discrimination, Dr. Martin Luther King Jr. in the Civil Rights Struggle modeled a response to their oppressors in the mid 20th century that will be needed at the end of the age in the middle east. Nelson Mandela in South Africa and many of our nations on the continent of Africa in their fight for freedom and human dignity also modeled for the nations the same spiritual weapons for the initiation of the release of peace and reconciliation.

The Method of Prayer for Justice in the Earth

When we respond rightly to one another in Love, knowing that Justice comes from the Lord we will be positioned to receive the presence of true Justice in the earth, Jesus Christ. This doesn't abdicate our responsibility to petition the unjust Judge for Justice. It just requires that we prioritize day & night prayer for Justice over Justice that comes from God-ordained authority in the earth. There will be a fight for true Justice in the earth at the end of the age that only the ways and the principles of Jesus will be able to answer and respond to. Jesus tells the parable of the release of the Justice of the unjust judge in Luke 18:1-8 in relation to the prayer's of the end-time praying church. With the same energy that African-Americans exerted in going before unjust judges for Justice in the civil rights movement for our civil liberties in America, we are going to have to seek the Judge of heaven and earth for our spiritual inheritances and release of the Justice that only Jesus brings at the end of the age. This parable is one of the major signs of the coming of the Lord. It depicts what the church will look like at the end of the age praying for Jesus to give them speedy justice in the earth during the time of tribulation and persecution.

> *Luk 18:1 And he spake a parable unto them to this end, that men ought always to pray, and not to faint; 2 Saying, There was in a city a judge, which feared not God, neither regarded man: 3 And there was a widow in that city; and she came unto him, saying, Avenge me of mine adversary. 4 And he would not for a while: but afterward he said within himself, Though I fear not God,*

nor regard man; 5 Yet because this widow troubles me, I will avenge her, lest by her continual coming she weary me. 6 And the Lord said, Hear what the unjust judge saith. 7 And shall not God avenge his own elect, which cry day and night unto him, though he bears long with them? 8 I tell you that he will avenge them speedily. Nevertheless, when the Son of man cometh, shall he find faith on the earth?

At the end of the age Day and Night prayers for Justice is what is going to bring Jesus back to the earth. Jesus says when the Son of man comes back to the earth he will be looking for persistent faith, witnessed by day and night prayers for the release of Jesus to bring Justice in the earth. Day and Night prayer for Justice is what's going release the Judgments of the book of the Revelation on our adversaries at the end of the age. This is depicted beginning in Revelation 6-22 with the release of the end-time prayers of the saints in both heaven and earth, as the seal, trumpet and bowl Judgments are released from this book on the unjust Anti-Christ system at the end of the age. It's this pattern that Jesus testifies of in this parable, which will be seen in complete fulfillment at the end of the age. This was an aspect of the pattern and methods undertaken by Dr. King and the civil rights movement in their quest for civil Justice that began in the African-American Church, which began the release of civil Justice in America and around the world in the 20th century. Though there were differing methods employed by different groups during this movement that might have cluttered and attempted to shroud over the methods employed by Dr. King; in the end it was Dr. King's visionary leadership and principles of engagement that won out over an unjust system of racial discrimination. Dr. King often led prayer vigils in the churches before they would lead protest marches for the rights of African-Americans for freedom and Justice. He wrote during the Montgomery bus boycott in an Article called **Pray for Justice**. – *From the book A Testament of Hope, Harper Collins. p.84*

Even though convicted, we will not retaliate with hate, but will still stand in love in our hearts, and stand resisting injustice, with the same determination with which we started out. We need a great deal of encouragement in this

181

movement. Of course, one thing that we are depending on, from not only other communities but from our own community, is prayer. We ask people everywhere to pray that God will guide us, pray that justice will be done, and that righteousness will stand. And I think through these prayers we will be strengthened; it will make us feel the unity of the nation and the presence of Almighty God. For as we said all along, this is a spiritual movement.

While Martin Luther King and the civil rights movement was a forerunner of what is coming with their many prayer meetings, speeches, marches, and sit-ins, resisting unjust laws in a system of injustice towards African-Americans, it was not the complete fulfillment of this model coming at the end of age depicted in Luke 18:1-8. There is going to be a new form of resistance that arises from the end-time movement of day & night prayer and worship in the earth that will stand against an Anti-Christ, unjust, ungodly system. This end-time movement for Justice will highlight worship and Prayer as the primary means for the release of Justice. It is during this time that many African, African-American forerunners in the house of prayer for all nations are going to need to rise up as end-time resisters with the further wisdom from this blueprint for the release of Justice that comes only through day and night prayer in the Love of God. Dr. King and the civil rights movement gave us a foretaste of what's coming at the end of the age.

The Method of Unity for Justice in the Earth

Another one of the methods that was seen in the Civil rights movement that was a forerunner of what's coming at the end of the age was the coming together of the Church in the unity of the brethren as is seen in Psalm 133-1-3. *How Good and pleasant it is for brethren to dwell together in Unity.* Dr. King also commented on this in his article, An Experiment of Love;

One of the glories of the Montgomery movement was that Baptists, Methodists, Lutherans, Presbyterians, Episcopalians, Church of God in Christ, and others all came together with a willingness to transcend denominational lines. Although no Catholics priests were actively involved in the protest, many of their parishioners took part. All joined hands in the bond of Christian love. Thus the mass meetings accomplished on Monday and Thursday nights what the Christian Church had failed to accomplish on Sunday Mornings.

At the end of age as the Church begins to grapple with peace and reconciliation of all races in His house of prayer the forerunner to the peace and reconciliation of Jews in Jerusalem to Yeshua Hamishiach is the Church of Jesus Christ being reconciled to God and one another. The Church coming together to stand against the forces of darkness and the spirit of this age will be what gives us power in prayer to pray for the peace of Jerusalem. These two conjoined - persecution with the Jews, and prayer for the peace of Jerusalem - is what will be a witness for many Jews to turn to Jesus as their Messiah. We can't really pray for the peace of Jerusalem, which is reconciliation to God and man, until we are willing to suffer persecution and tribulation along with them and be completely reconciled to God and one another within his body.

The Method of Prayer for Unity, Justice and Peace for Jerusalem

Psalm 122:1-9 give us a pattern of focus in prayer as we pray for the peace of Jerusalem.

> *Psa 122:1 I was glad when they said unto me, Let us go into the house of the LORD. 2 Our feet shall stand within thy gates, O Jerusalem. 3 Jerusalem is builded as a city that is compact together: 4 Whither the tribes go up, the tribes of the LORD, unto the testimony of Israel, to give thanks unto the name of the LORD. 5 For there are set thrones of judgment, the thrones of the house of David. 6 Pray for the peace of Jerusalem: they shall prosper that love thee. 7 Peace be within thy walls, and prosperity within thy palaces. 8. For my brethren and companions' sakes, I will now say, Peace be within thee. 9 Because of the house of the LORD our God I will seek thy good.*

David shows us the pattern and process of Prayer for the Peace of Jerusalem in this Psalm. It should be noted right here that how we've interpreted this scripture has led many to pray wrong for Jerusalem. Most of the body of Christ has interpreted this section in verse 6. *"PRAY FOR THE PEACE OF JERUSALEM:"* **And if we do WE will prosper.** But this verse is actually telling us how to pray for Jerusalem, not the benefits of praying for Jerusalem. It says; *PRAY FOR THE PEACE OF JERUSALEM!* **And this is what should pray:** *LORD, PROSPER, OR SECURE, AND RECONCILE TO YOU, THOSE THAT LOVE YOU IN JERUSALEM.* The Hebrew word "Peace" in this verse means reconciliation and protection.

I don't believe Psalm 122 is speaking of praying for peace for All of Jerusalem, but only for those that love Him (Yeshua) in Jerusalem. He wouldn't be telling us to pray a blanket prayer against war or conflict (Peace) in Jerusalem, when we've already seen from scripture in chapter 14, that before the end of age there is going to be another epic conflict, shaking and scattering coming to the Jews in Israel, known in Jeremiah 30 as Jacob's trouble.

Again, if we read this chapter carefully, we see that God is telling us to pray for the security or prosperity of those that love Him in Jerusalem, after the beginning of the set times of Judgment from verse 5, that's coming to the House of David in the Holy City right before their Messiah returns. He begins Psalm 122:1 with describing their initial return to the land as being a time of ingathering to, and gladness in the House of the Lord. Then he goes on in verse 3 to describe the return of the tribes regular feast pilgrimages that will begin again to Jerusalem, journeying in each season – *Passover, Pentecost, and Tabernacles* – to give thanks to the Lord for their fruitful harvests, and for returning them back to the land. He then goes onto the subsequent time, in verse 5, of remaining Judgments that will happen within the gates of Jerusalem to the House of David, before the coming of their Mesisah, Yeshua Hamishach. Then verse 6 tells us how to pray for those in the land that love Yeshua, as the remaining and last Judgments come upon that land at the end of the age. The chapter ends with the results of their reconciliation to God (Yeshua Hamishach) and man, and the peace and prosperity that will happen within the gates of Jerusalem, and the whole world, as a result of their reconciliation to their Messiah, at the return of Yeshua.

The 6 Point Process to Prayer for Jerusalem from Psalm 122:1-9

1. *V. 1 Unity of all Nations, and Joy and gladness in His House of Prayer.* David said, *I was glad when they said unto me, let <u>US</u> go into the House of the Lord. Isaiah 56:7 says, Even them will I bring to my holy mountain, and make them joyful in my house of prayer: their burnt offerings and their sacrifices shall be accepted upon mine altar; for mine house shall be called an house of prayer for all nations.*

2. *V.2 Identification within the gates of Jerusalem of His House of Prayer. Our feet shall stand within thy gates O Jerusalem.*

3. *V. 3, 4 Yearly Feast pilgrimages to Jerusalem of the tribes of the Lord, to give thanks to the name of the Lord. Whither the tribes go up, the tribes of the LORD, unto the testimony of Israel, to give thanks unto the name of the LORD.*

4. *V. 5 A predetermined time of Judgment of the people of God in the Land of Jerusalem before peace. For there are set thrones of judgment, the thrones of the house of David.*

5. *V. 6, 7 Prayer for Peace (Safety and reconciliation to God and man) to come within the walls of the city during this Set time of Judgment coming to the people in the Land of Jerusalem. Pray for the peace of Jerusalem: Saying, May those who love you be Secure and saved (turned to God)*

6. *V. 6-8 World-wide Prosperity & Peace to come out of the peace (reconciliation to God and man) of*

185

> **Jerusalem.** *...they shall prosper that love thee. Peace be within thy walls, and prosperity within thy palaces. 8. For my brethren and companions' sakes, I will now say, Peace be within thee.* **9** *Because of the house of the LORD our God I will seek thy good.*

African-Americans and many nations within Africa can relate to the many struggles that have happened to the Jews over the years that are meant to be the forerunner to the peace of Jerusalem. Many of our persecutions, sufferings, battles for freedom for the right to be considered as human beings with equality in our history is meant to give us intercessory identification and grace to pray for the peace of Jerusalem at the end of the age. Just as during the civil rights movement, as the body of Christ comes together in unity to stand and resist at the end of age the onslaught of animosity and legislated persecution against the Jews; Africans, African-Americans and the Diaspora worldwide are going to be forerunners, leading the way to reconciliation, love and peace of Jerusalem in this colossal struggle in Jerusalem.

The Method of Christian Love & Non-Violent Resistance for Justice in the Earth

Just as during the Civil Rights movement there was a form of Non-violent resistance to an unjust evil system in Montgomery, Birmingham Alabama, and throughout the south, there will be another greater resistance movement that arises to an evil, unjust system at the end of the age, which will be arrayed against Jews and Christians. During this time God will raise up his house of prayer for all nations to stand against this system even as they stood against the system of injustice in the south and throughout America in the mid 20th century. God will once again raise up forerunners out of Africa, and the nations of the world to lead this resistance movement in his house of prayer. Dr. Martin Luther King Jr. as a forerunner of what's coming at the end of the age, showed us the weapons of our warfare in the Civil Rights movement, being Unity, Prayer, Non-Violent resistance with the Christian principles of Agape Love, which he stated is the most powerful creative force in the universe. Dr. King said, Agape Love is God's love for humanity. It does not just recognize value, but it creates it. Agape love imparts value by loving. He said the man who is loved by God has not value in himself; what gives him value is precisely the fact that God loves him. Agape Love is a willingness to go to any length, even to the laying down of one's life, to restore that value of God's love for all humanity in our community. As this resistance movement unfolded in Montgomery its weapons began to develop, almost accidently as Dr. King goes on to state in the rest of his article, An Experiment in Love.

> *It was Jesus of Nazareth that stirred the Negroes to protest with the creative weapon of Love. As the days unfolded, however, the inspiration of Mahatma Gandhi began to exert its influence. I had come to see early that the Christian doctrine of love operating through the Gandhian method of nonviolence was one of the most potent weapons available to the Negro in his struggle for freedom. About a week after the protest started, a white woman who understood and sympathized with the Negroes' efforts wrote a letter to the editor of the Montgomery Advertiser comparing the bus protest with the Gandhian movement in India. Miss Juliette Morgan, sensitive and frail, did not long survive the rejection and condemnation of the white community, but long after she died in the summer of 1957 the name Mahatma Gandhi was well known in Montgomery. People who had never heard of the little brown man of India were now saying his name with an air of familiarity. Nonviolent resistance had emerged as the technique of the movement, while love stood as the regulating ideal. In other words, Christ furnished the spirit, and motivation, and one of the methods of prayer, while Gandhi furnished one of the methods, called Non-violent resistance.*

Martin Luther King's Principles of Nonviolence and Passive Resistance used during the Civil Rights Era

The below Excerpts are taken from a Speech by Martin Luther King Jr. called An Experiment in Love – from the book a Testament of Hope, Harper Collins.

From the beginning a basic philosophy guided the movement. This guiding principle has since been referred to variously as nonviolent resistance, noncooperation, and passive resistance. But in the first days of the protest none of these expressions was mentioned: the phrase most often heard was "Christian Love." It was the Sermon on the Mount, rather than a doctrine of passive resistance, that initially inspired the African Americans of Montgomery to dignified social Action. It was Jesus of Nazareth that stirred African-Americans to protest with the creative weapon of love. In fact, when I became president of the Montgomery Improvement Association, I did not recognize that I was using nonviolent resistance. It was Reverend Glenn E. Smiley, a white minister and Bayard Rustin who were primarily responsible for convincing me that I should interpret the movement in the light of the principles and techniques of nonviolent resistance.

It's probably true that most of the resisters in the movement did not believe in nonviolence as a philosophy of life, but because of their confidence in their leaders and because non-violence was presented to them as a simple expression of Christianity in action, they were willing to use it as a technique. Admittedly, nonviolence in the truest sense is not a strategy that one uses simply because it is expedient at the moment; nonviolence is ultimately a way of life that men live by because of the sheer morality of its claim. But even granting this, willingness to use nonviolence as a technique is a step forward. For he who goes this far is more likely to adopt nonviolence later as a way of life.

Dr. King's Biblical Philosophy for Christian Non-Violent Resistance

As the movement developed Dr. King begin to have crystallized for him a philosophy of Christian resistance that he began to teach and model for those Christians that desired to become more active in resisting evil and injustice in society. Many hesitated on becoming a part of this movement against injustice until they were able to see the efficacy of Dr. Kings philosophy of resistance together with a scriptural responsibility to petition both unjust judges and the Judge of heaven and earth for Justice in the earth. Because we are citizens in two realms, the earthly and heavenly realm, Dr. King laid out the rules of engagement for both realms. Some of His rules of engagement are listed below.

1. It is the responsibility of just citizens of a democracy, a republic or a kingdom to break unjust laws to bring those laws to justice.

2. Just citizens that refuse to resist unjust laws for fear of reprisal, retribution or the threat of death will eventually become as unjust as the laws they tolerate.

3. Just citizens that break unjust laws that are punished with persecution, jail, execution or crucifixion will release the justice into that system to cause those laws to be changed. This is what the 3 Hebrews boys did in Babylon. This is what Daniel did. This is what Dr. Martin Luther king Jr. and the civil rights movement did. Most of all **this is what Jesus did**!

4. Many that interpret certain scriptures on the surface like *"render under Caesar what belongs to Caesar and render unto God what belongs to God"* would call this resistance of unjust laws unbiblical. But this verse is not speaking of acquiescence to unjust laws, but this verse is actually saying *"as long as the laws of Caesar (laws of the land) allow you to keep the laws of God, keep the laws of Caesar (the laws of the land) as a witness to Caesar of the God you serve."* But once the laws of Caesar (laws of the land) prohibit you from keeping the law of God, breaking the unjust law also becomes a witness of the God you serve, being a God of Truth and Justice. Jesus was actually saying with this principle of rendering unto Caesar, *"Wear the laws of the land loosely as your outer garment and the laws of God tightly as your under garment.*

5. The Christian doctrine of love is not sentimental and anemic. It's not passive, but aggressive and confrontational. God's love at its core is aggressive, confrontational and spiritually violent. And sometimes physically violent. Not physically violent in that it releases violence to the aggressor, but it is physically violent in that it is willing receive violence from the aggressor without retaliation to bring conviction to the conscience of the aggressor in the face of

189

6. injustice and confrontation of an unjust law. This is the Sermon on the Mount lifestyle of turning the other cheek, love your enemies, taking up your cross, and do good unto them the despitefully use you.

Unjust Laws and Non-violent Resistance

7. What is an unjust law? It's a law that prohibits and restricts the God given law of man's moral, ethical and human responsibility to worship and love the Lord their God with all their hearts, minds, soul and strength, and to love their neighbor as themselves. Any law that is immoral, unethical or illegal, transgressing man's love walk with God or man is an unjust law.

8. This principle of confronting an unjust law with breaking that law to expose it and bring it to justice was seen in the lives of:
    1. Shadrach, Meshach and Abednego vs. king Nebuchadnezzar; (Daniel 3)
    2. Daniel vs. King Darius; (Daniel 6)
    3. Jesus vs. The chief priests and officers of the Sanhedrin, (John 19:7) _The Jews answered Pilate, WE HAVE A LAW, AND BY OUR LAW HE OUGHT TO DIE._

Updating Outdated Laws

At the beginning of the civil rights movement with the bus boycott in Montgomery Alabama, it was not just a matter of breaking an unjust law, as much as it was a matter of breaking an outdated law that Montgomery had refused to update. Because no one had been willing to challenge their unwillingness to enact the updated law, what was outdated had not been updated. So the updated just law was actually being disregarded for the outdated unjust law in Montgomery Alabama in the desegregating of the buses in Montgomery. When Rosa parks sat down on the bus in Montgomery she was in the back section of the bus and was breaking no law by not getting up. That was the section where the blacks were designated to sit according to the segregation laws that had been in place since the 19th century with the Plessy doctrine of *"Separate but Equal"*. However, Montgomery had established a humiliating practice of requiring black passengers to get up when the bus got crowded. When Rosa Parks refused to move from her seat in the segregated section of the bus to give her seat to a white passenger she was arrested. This was an unjust law being challenged by a just citizen which exposed the unjust law to bring that law to justice.

This unjust law that was challenged by Rosa parks was not only unjust it was no longer constitutionally the law of the land. A year before in 1954, it had been challenged in a case of *"Brown vs. the Board of Education"* in little Rock Arkansas and it was found that the old unjust law of *"Separate but Equal"* in public accommodations was unconstitutional. It took government military escorts for the Little Rock eight to integrate Little Rock high school that year. By the time 1955 came around this unjust outdated law had yet to be challenged in public accommodations on the city buses of Montgomery Alabama, so Montgomery refused to update its unjust law. When Rosa parks challenged this unjust law she brought to light the injustice. And after a year of the African American community in Montgomery challenging this unjust law the decision was handed down from the Supreme Court of the United States of America that *"Separate but Equal"* in the Montgomery bus system was also unconstitutional and Montgomery was mandated to update and change that unjust law. That unjust and outdated law was brought to justice and brought up to date through a citizen of Montgomery breaking the unjust law to bring the law to justice.

Below are the scriptural references on the rights of just citizens to challenge unjust laws in Scripture. In the book of Acts with Paul and the Roman Judicial system, along with the scriptural accounts of the results of the 3 Hebrew boys, and Daniel standing against the King of Babylon, as well as the scriptural references to Jesus being judged with a death sentence for challenging unjust pharisaical laws. It is the responsibility of just citizens of a Democracy to challenge unjust laws. And in scripture Paul often stood against this and resisted the subjugation of his rights in dealing with the Romans, as not only a Jew, but a roman citizen.

Act 21:39 But Paul said, I am a man which am a Jew of Tarsus, a city in Cilicia, a citizen of no mean city: and, I

191

beseech thee, suffer me to speak unto the people. 40 And when he had given him license, Paul stood on the stairs, and beckoned with the hand unto the people.

Paul Brings To Light His Rights As A Roman Citizen That He Should Not Be Scourged, Uncondemned As A Citizen.

Act 22:25 And as they bound him with thongs, Paul said unto the centurion that stood by, Is it lawful for you to scourge a man that is a Roman citizen, and uncondemned? 26 When the centurion heard that, he went and told the chief captain, saying, take heed what thou doest: for this man is a Roman. 27 Then the chief captain came, and said unto him, Tell me, art thou a Roman? He said, Yea. 28 And the chief captain answered, with a great sum obtained I this freedom. And Paul said, But I was free born. 29 Then straightway they departed from him which should have examined him: and the chief captain also was afraid, after he knew that he was a Roman, and because he had bound him.

Jesus Is Crucified for the Breaking Jewish Law

Joh 19:1 Then Pilate therefore took Jesus and scourged *him.* 2 And the soldiers platted a crown of thorns, and put *it* on his head, and they put on him a purple robe, Joh 19:3 And said, Hail, King of the Jews! and they smote him with their hands. 4 Pilate therefore went forth again, and saith unto them, Behold, I bring him forth to you, that ye may know that I find no fault in him. 5 Then came Jesus forth, wearing the crown of thorns, and the purple robe. And *Pilate* saith unto them, Behold the man! 6 When the chief priests therefore and officers saw him, they cried out, saying, crucify *him,* crucify *him.* Pilate saith unto them, take ye him, and crucify *him:* for I find no fault in him. **Joh 19:7 The Jews answered him, WE HAVE A LAW, AND BY OUR LAW HE**

192

OUGHT TO DIE, because he made himself the Son of God. Joh 19:8 When Pilate therefore heard that saying, he was the more afraid; Joh 19:9 And went again into the judgment hall, and saith unto Jesus, Whence art thou? But Jesus gave him no answer.

Jesus challenged the hypocrisy and injustice of the Pharisees by his very presence and principle. For this they crucified him. He resisted the letter of the law for the spirit of the Law and brought to light on many occasions the injustice of the Jewish system of the letter of the law. Jesus challenged injustice both religiously, politically as well as spiritually with Love, non-violent resistance and justice for the oppressed. He would lay down his life for the release of Justice in the earth of all humanity both judicially, politically and spiritually.

Nation against Nation

At the heart of the Israeli, Arab dilemma, as well as at the heart of the middle - east peace dilemma is the ethnic issues that have plagued our nation and world for centuries. The signs of the times recorded in Matthew 24:7 nation against nation, is actually speaking of ethnic or racial wars that we still see rising up all over the world in places like Bosnia, Sudan, and throughout the continent of Africa, Asia, and India as well as the United States of America. At the heart of many of these racial wars are religious differences and beliefs that are fueling these conflicts. When we bring Christ to bare on these conflicts and allow the love and peace of God that surpasses all knowledge and understanding to invade these issues with God's wisdom we will position ourselves to answer the ultimate and final ethnic and religious conflict of all ages with peace in the middle east and Israel and the whole World.

Love for Peace Not Land for Peace

Soon after my second trip to Israel in 1994, where I was challenged to live in love with opposites to understand what it takes to live in peace in the middle-east, I was married in 1995. Over the next 15 years my wife and I had 5 children. We helped Pastor a five thousand member mega-church with a Caucasian Pastor, leadership and staff. We launched from that ministry 4 inner-city satellite churches that saw over 10,000 people saved and discipled on four sides of town, each from the government projects of our city of Columbus Ohio. We saw rival gangs unite and put down their weapons and gang paraphernalia and begin helping us evangelize the city. We travelled the world preaching the gospel of Jesus Christ to every nation, tribe and tongue. All of this was done because I had a mandate to learn how to live, and stay together with husband, wife, black, white, rich, poor, Baptist, Pentecostal and every other denomination through the Love of God.

Then after 17 years attempting to walk out this revelation in my life with my wife, family, church, neighborhood and city God called me back to Israel in 2011. I was invited on an all expenses paid trip to Israel through an organization called AIPAC – *The American Israel, Public Affairs Committee*. This is a lobbying organization seeking to educate African American Pastors and leaders in the Israeli–Palestinian land for Peace two-state process for peace in the middle-east. The organizations aim is to have these pastors lobby their congressmen and senators towards pro-Israeli legislation. On this trip there were about 30 Pastors from the Midwest, from every denomination coming to hear and learn about the issues in the middle-east. We met with members of the Israeli Government, members of the Palestinian government, members of the press and with ordinary citizens. We met with Caucasian Jews, Ethiopian Jews, Sephardic Jews, secular and Orthodox Jews. With all of them wanting to give us their view point on the Israeli, Palestinian situation. In one of the meetings with an Ethiopian Jewish member of the Israeli Government, we sat and listened to his attempt to give us what he thought Israel should do in giving up some of the land that was gained in the 1967 six-day war, for peace with the Palestinians. In the midst of his address I sensed the spirit of God speaking to me His wisdom concerning His peace policy. I heard the phrase, *MY POLICY IS NOT LAND FOR PEACE, BUT LOVE FOR PEACE*. I then felt to ask him a question, and depending on how he replied, I would share with him what I was hearing.

I felt to ask him if He was religious. If wasn't religious, I would just pray for him to become acquainted with his own religion that speaks of a coming Messiah to rule on the seat of the throne of David to bring peace to Jerusalem. If he was religious, I felt to ask him if he believes in the Messiah that will come to sit on the seat of the throne of David." If he did, I would tell him the wisdom I felt I was hearing; LOVE FOR PEACE! The fullness of what I was hearing to say if he was religious was this;

At the end of the age God is going to pour out His spirit on all flesh. This is coming in a short amount of time. During this time, the awesomeness and the terribleness of God will come upon all flesh in this region. (Joel 2:28-32; Acts 2:17-21) His spirit of Justice and Judgment will fall on Jews, Arabs, Palestinians, Christians, and Muslims. And the fruit of His spirit is; **LOVE,** *JOY* **PEACE***, LONGSUFFERING, TEMPERANCE, MEEKNESS, GENTLENESS, GOODNESS, FAITH. If the Love of His spirit is not received by all parties to bring peace, (reconciliation to Him and one another) His Jealous Love will bring Peace. Out of His Jealous Love many of His people will be violently and forcibly removed from the land and will not return until they say, blessed is he that cometh in the name of the Lord. At that time, He will return to them, when they return to Him, and He will bring Peace to this region and the whole world.*

When this governmental official finished speaking I asked him what I felt to ask him, Are you religious? He said No, I'm a Zionist. So I refrained from giving him a message from the Messiah that he doesn't believe in. But later on, after he left and as we debriefed with the Pastors present, I shared what I felt was the wisdom of God concerning peace in the middle-east that we might pray for all parties involved. Surprisingly enough many of those Pastors were unreceptive of this wisdom as being from God, saying that we must help them find a solution to this issue that is more practical and doable. This is a practical issue that needs practical answers, not spiritual apocalyptic answers, they said. However, what I found out between my first trip to Israel and this past trip to Israel 17 years later is that God wants to put within his people that seek his face and truly pray for the peace of Jerusalem, the answers to the peace, reconciliation and unity of the nations - LOVE FOR PEACE.

Love works. I saw it work in my marriage. I saw it work in my multi-ethnic church. I saw it work in the inner-city with rival gangs, as well as in the suburbs. I saw it work in inter-denominational faith gatherings. I saw in work in the Civil rights movement with Dr. Martin Luther King Jr. through the many videos and DVD's growing up. And if it can work in your marriage, and in your church, and in your neighborhood, and in African-American, Caucasian relationships, it can work in Israel with Arabs and Jews. The key to living out this revelation in the earth with Husband and wife, black and white, rich and poor, nation with nation is found in living out of an understanding of the fruit of the Spirit of Love and learning how to live with your flesh subjected to the spirit of God. Accentuating the Spirit over the flesh and receiving the Heart of God to Love the Lord our God with all our heart, mind, soul, strength and our neighbor as our selves is the key to coming together in unity and living in peace and harmony one with the other. This Love in action is best expressed in national and race relations in Jesus' account of how the Son of Man will Judge the sheep and goat nations in Matthew 25.

> *Mat 25:34 Then shall the King say unto them on his right hand, Come, ye blessed of my Father, inherit the kingdom prepared for you from the foundation of the world: 35 For I was an hungered, and ye gave me meat: I was thirsty, and ye gave me drink: I was a stranger, and ye took me in: 36 Naked, and ye clothed me: I was sick, and ye visited me: I was in prison, and ye came unto me.*

This account in Matthew 25 tells us what God requires in ministry to his brethren, the Jews. He's not requiring that we convert them, that's the Spirit's job. Our job is to release the operation of the Love of God to them to turn their hearts. And this, I believe is also what it's going to take to turn the hearts of all parties involved in the middle-east.

The Love of God is for Opposites

As I relayed in the introduction, the operation of the Love of God was revealed with a very common verse that I had heard all my life. John 3:16. With this simple verse God broke bitterness, hatred and unforgiveness that had been inbred in me in the African-American Church and community growing up. For *GOD so Loved the WORLD, that he GAVE his only begotten SON*. The three key words that set me free were GOD - (holy, separate, pure, righteous), WORLD - (unholy, unrighteous, sinful, wicked) brought together by LOVE. Two polar opposites brought together by THE LOVE OF GOD. God spoke to me and said "THE LOVE OF GOD IS FOR OPPOSITES" and the key to the coming together of the races, nations, and world, is the Love of God. He further said, people that say they have the love of God won't really know they have the Love of God until they're giving Love to someone that is not like them, that doesn't look like them, act like them, or think like them. It's not God's love until it continues to give to those that are unlike us, unlovely to us, hurt us, or do us wrong. It is this love that brings reconciliation and forgiveness in divided and distant relationships. Since the time when I received this revelation I've been free from reverse racism and have begun the process of being healed in productive relationships with the opposite sex *(My Wife)*, and opposite races *(Caucasian, Hispanic)*, and ethnically diverse friends, workers, ministers, where I continue to give the Love of God when there is not a basis or common ground for giving it.

Love is for Opposites is the foundational definition necessary for the Christian purpose, calling and responsibility of the Love of God in the ministry of reconciliation. John 3:16 says, For God so Love the World that he gave. A holy God, so loved a sinful World that he gave His only begotten son. The Love of God was expressed in the giving of his prized possession for a world that was unlike him, disconnected, alienated and at enmity with Him. The World and God are polar opposites, but God manifested His Love towards us in while we were yet still sinners he died for us. You don't know you have the Love of God until you're giving and spending time with someone that's not returning what you're giving. You don't know that you have the love of God until you're giving forgiveness and reconciliation to someone that has hurt you, abused you, talked about you or oppressed you. You don't know that you have the love of God until you are spending time giving of yourself to help someone that is a different color than you, a different socio-economic status than you, or from a different neighborhood than you, or a different race or ethnicity than you. The Love of God is for opposites.

Ascertaining this revelation and interjecting these principles into our everyday life, is the key to teaching blacks and whites to live together in America and abroad. It is the key to bringing peace to ethnic wars and tribal wars throughout Africa, and the nations of the world. It is the key to living together in harmony, making our world a brotherhood as well as a neighborhood. And this lifestyle, living by these principles, will be the light that shines on the Jews and Arabs teaching them how to live together in the same land. So this is what I've been doing for the last 16 years. I've been seeking to remain in right relationship with God in heaven and mankind (other races and sexes) in the earth, to the end that all mankind might be a light for salvation to Israel and truly come to the solution of the dilemma of how God expects us to live in the coming kingdom of God, and how to obtain eternal life; *Love the Lord thy God with all thy heart, thy mind, soul, and strength and love thy neighbor as thy self.*

CHAPTER 14

THE TIMES & SEASONS FOR REVELATION OF THE PURPOSE OF THE NATIONS

To everything there is a season, and a time to every purpose under the heaven: Ecclesiastes 3:1

As we come to a realization of who we are in Christ and begin to look to God for all that he has for us in the earth, knowing our purpose in the earth will become increasingly important. The purpose of the three sons of Noah and the knowledge and fulfillment of their purpose as related to the plan of God for the entire earth is the basis of the unity of the nations and the fulfillment of the will of God in the earth. In order for the nations to come into the unity of the Spirit to release the commanded blessing or fullness in the earth all parties involved must understand their part and know what their purpose is in the earth.

In every *season* of God there are *times* for the release of the measure of what he's promised us in the earth. But before God will release all that's been promised in a particular *season*, you must attain to the *purpose* in the earth that he has called you to under the *heaven.* In the end-time season as God prepares to release more of his promised presence and power in the earth he first has to release more of the revelation of his person and purpose for mankind in the earth. If we don't receive more revelation of Him to receive more of his purpose, when He releases His promised power or provision to a people, to the church and/or to the nations in the world we will be unable to handle the release of His glory in our lives. If we don't know why we are here, and what were supposed to be doing here, when His glory comes we will not be able to make sense of all that God is doing, therefore squandering what he's given us. God wants to release promises in season for individuals, for His Church and for the nations of the world. However, the promise must be tied to Him and his purpose for our lives, in the right season. Everything God wants to do in the nations and through the nations is related to Him and His purpose for the earth.

199

And everything God has called the nations to be and do in the earth is the purpose of the nations. The promised *thing* comes in seasons, but the promise coming is dependent upon mankind coming to his purpose. You've got to connect with him before you can connect with your purpose if you want to get the promised thing, because He, the promised thing and the purpose are one.

> *To everything there is a season, and a time to every purpose under the heaven Ecc 3:1*

When it's <u>time</u> for a breakthrough in your life you're going to have to come into more revelation of the <u>thing</u> in season to come into more of your <u>purpose</u> in the earth, to bring forth the <u>thing</u> you need to accomplish your purpose. All the resources for the nations of the world are connected to the nations understanding 1) The thing or things God has for them, 2) The seasons and times and 3) knowing their purpose. All the energy, power, minerals, natural resources, and wealth in the earth are all tied to the **thing**, **the seasons and times** and **purpose**. **Your purpose** is not just something you do, it's who you are. It's who you're called to become. Your purpose is not an inordinate object or just something you do, your purpose is a person. YOU are the purpose. **The thing promised** is what we are given by God to accomplish or become purpose. So if you can tap into the thing promised you can tap into your purpose and you will receive everything that belongs to you in your life, your family, your city, your nation, etc. Your purpose leads you to seek after the thing that will bring forth who you are and what you need to do what you are called to do. But what or who is the thing that comes in season to bring forth purpose?

What or Who is the Thing

> *And the angel answered and said unto her, The Holy Ghost shall come upon thee, and the power of the Highest shall overshadow thee: therefore also <u>That Holy Thing</u> which shall be born of thee shall be called the Son of God. Luke 1:35*

The main thing that God wants to release to people, families, and nations to bring them into purpose is not an object but it's a person. That person is Jesus. Haggai says that the purpose for the shaking of nations is to cause Jesus, the desire of the nations to come and fill the earth with glory. *And I will shake all nations, and the desire of all nations shall come: and I will fill this house with glory, saith the LORD of hosts. Hag 2:7* Many people pray more for the Glory than they do for the desire of the nations. Jesus, the desire of the nations will come before the glory fills our houses, or the earth. This is why we must desire him more than we do the glory, or the promise, etc. The best definition in scripture I can find to define what glory is, is in John 1:14. John 1:14 says, *and the Word was made flesh, and we beheld HIS GLORY as the glory of the only begotten of the father full of grace and truth.* The glory is the word made flesh. The purpose of the nations is the magnifying and worship of Jesus to release glory, grace and truth – the word made flesh into the earth. He is everything, and when we make everything about him and his hope for our lives we receive revelation of who he is and we are able to receive revelation of what we are called to be and do in him. One of the main prayers we pray at the International House of Prayer in Kansas City is Paul's Apostolic prayer over the Ephesians Church in Ephesians 1:17

> *That the God of our Lord Jesus Christ, the Father of glory, may give unto you the spirit of wisdom and revelation in the knowledge of him: 18 The eyes of your understanding being enlightened; that ye may know what is the hope of his calling, and what the riches of the glory of his inheritance in the saints,*

When God releases His spirit of wisdom and revelation in the knowledge of who he is, our eyes are opened to the hope of His calling. When our eyes are opened to the hope of His calling riches in glory are released, which are the inheritance of the saints. The word riches is the Greek word ploo-tos which means, *fullness, wealth, money, possessions, abundance, richness.* The riches of the glory of His inheritance are released when we get his knowledge on Him and what we are called to be and do in him. So it is with the nations. When the nations receive the spirit of wisdom and revelation in the Knowledge of Jesus they will know their calling or purpose in him and all the resources of heaven and earth will be released to them. Things about God and from God are released in specific seasons and times for the accomplishment of every purpose under the heaven when we get a revelation of the Son of God. The more we see Jesus, the more we will see of our purpose in the earth. This is what the church was built for. The Church was built upon an encounter with Jesus that would release authority to the nations to accomplish the purpose of binding the kingdom of darkness in the earth and releasing the kingdom of Heaven to the earth.

> *Mat 16:15 He saith unto them, But whom say ye that I am? 16 And Simon Peter answered and said, Thou art the Christ, the Son of the living God. 17 And Jesus answered and said unto him, Blessed art thou, Simon Barjona: for flesh and blood hath not revealed it unto thee, but my Father which is in heaven.*

> *18 And I say also unto thee, That thou art Peter, and upon this rock I will build my church; and the gates of hell shall not prevail against it. 19 And I will give unto thee the keys of the kingdom of heaven: and whatsoever thou shalt bind on earth shall be bound in heaven: and whatsoever thou shalt loose on earth shall be loosed in heaven.*

When Peter received a revelation of Jesus, Jesus gave Peter a revelation of who he was. Peter said, "Thou are the Christ, the Son of the living God," and Jesus said, "Thou art Peter," and upon this Rock – *Who I am, and who you are in me* – I will build my Church; and I will give unto you the keys to the kingdom of Heaven, and whatever you bind on earth will be bound in heaven, and whatever you loose on earth will be loosed in heaven. God wants to pour out his spirit of revelation on the nations, to reveal Jesus to them, as he did to Peter, so he can reveal their purpose and release His blessing on them. This will happen as forerunners Pray Ephesians 1:17 over their nations. When we do, Luke 1:35 says; *The Holy Ghost shall come upon (the nations), and the power of the Highest shall overshadow them, and that Holy thing which shall be born of them shall be called the Son of God.* The desire of all nations wants to come into covenant with all nations for the accomplishing of the purpose of the nations in the earth – *worship and exaltation of Jesus for the releasing of heaven on earth.* Encountering and coming into covenant with Jesus, *the Holy Thing* releases the Holy Ghost to come upon us, that we may be overshadowed by the power of the Highest. This process of *Encounter, Revelation* and the release of *Purpose, Power,* and *Provision* comes to us in seasons like the rain as we return unto the Lord out of the shaking of the nations and pursue a revelation of the Christ. He shakes the nations to get them to look to Him that He may come unto us like the rain. Hosea 6:1 says;

> *Come, and let us return unto the LORD: for he hath torn, and he will heal us; he hath smitten, and he will bind us up. 2 After two days will he revive us: in the third day he will raise us up, and we shall live in his sight. 3 Then shall we know, if we follow on to know the LORD: his going forth is prepared as the morning; and he shall come unto us as the rain, as the latter and former rain unto the earth.*

The seasons in which he comes to us are called the latter and the former rain. The former rains are the spring rains, and the latter rains are the fall rains. These are the seasons set in the earth by God for the release of revelation of who he is for fruitfulness of nations and geographical regions as the nations in those regions return unto the Lord. The seasons are set in the earth naturally, as well as spiritually in order that we may experience new life in Christ. The natural cycles of the seasons in the earth are symbolic of the death, burial, and resurrection of Jesus Christ. Winter, Spring, Summer and Fall, are all seasonal signs to reveal the life of Christ to humanity. As all four of these seasons play a part in the process of the growth in the vegetation, the geology, the topography and the human and animal life of the earth, so that humanity can exist and be fruitful and multiply in the earth, it is symbolic of what the release of the revelation of God will do in seasons for the inner life of mankind. The spiritual seasons of God are set in order that we may actually receive this revelation that we may experience the new life of God through Jesus Christ. What are the spiritual seasons of God? If we know what these seasons are, it's these seasons that releases the revelation of Jesus that will release our purpose in the earth.

The Feast Seasons – Due Season

The spiritual seasons are recorded in Leviticus 23, and Deuteronomy 16 and they are known as the Feasts of the Lord. They are **Passover** – the Spring harvest, or *the rainy season*, **Pentecost**– the Summer Harvest, or *the former rains* and **Tabernacles** – the Fall Harvest or *the latter rains*. Joel describes the release of all three of these seasons all in one month in Joel 2:23 saying;

> Be glad then, ye children of Zion, and rejoice in the LORD your God: for he hath given you the former rain moderately, and he will cause to come down for you 1) the rain, 2) the former rain, and 3) the latter rain in the first month.

These three Feast enumerated in the Old Testament are fulfilled in the revelation of Jesus in the New Testament. These were the three main feasts that were to be kept in the Hebrew economy for the purpose of the release of the revelation of the Messiah Jesus Christ, the King of all the earth. Feast of Passover, Pentecost, and Tabernacles were all significant signs of the coming of Jesus and were to be recognized and passed on to the succeeding generations. Feast of Passover was instituted to memorialize when God brought them out of Egypt with a mighty right arm Exodus 12. They were to place the blood on the door posts and lintel of their houses, and when the death angel saw the blood he would Passover their homes while slaying the firstborn of the Egyptians homes. The Feast of Pentecost or Feast of Weeks was 50 days after Passover, and signified the giving of the Law to Moses at Mount Sinai, in the wilderness. Exodus 24:16. This Feast was also correlated with the wheat harvest. The Feast of Tabernacles signified God coming down and living with them in the wilderness within the Ark of the Covenant, and being a cloud by day and a fire by night to lead them to the Promised Land, Exodus 40:38.

These three main feasts were to be observed as a means of continuing to pass on to the next generation the testimony of God's favor to His people, and to show the power of the God they served. These feasts also were given to reveal and to release to them a revelation of the coming Messiah – Jesus the Christ. Every season they were to be positioning themselves to see and recognize their Messiah in the Land. They were to only be observed once they came out of Egypt and were specifically for the promise Land. They were given that once they got into the land they would begin preparing the land for their coming Messiah to the Land, giving the land new life.

In the New Testament to the believer in Christ they are given to us to release to us the Revelation of Jesus Christ and His ultimate coming kingdom in the earth. Jesus was Crucified as our Passover Lamb in the Feast of Passover, He released the Holy Ghost for the empowering of the Church to bind the kingdom of darkness and release the kingdom of God in the Feast of Pentecost, and He's coming back to dwell with man in the earth in the Feast of Tabernacles. These three seasons are what Galatians 6:7 refer to as *due season*.

> *Gal 6:7 Be not deceived; God is not mocked: for whatsoever a man soweth, that shall he also reap. 8 for he that soweth to his flesh shall of the flesh reap corruption; but he that soweth to the Spirit shall of the Spirit reap life everlasting. 9 And let us not be weary in well doing: **for in due season** we shall reap, if we faint not.*

In these three seasons we are able to receive more of Jesus – *The Holy Thing* – that we may come into the fullness of our purpose in Jesus for the earth. This Holy *thing* does not just speak of Jesus alone, but more accurately it speaks of the covenant relationship with Jesus that is strengthened in every season by more of the revelation of Jesus Christ. When we come into Covenant relationship with Jesus, it releases Revelation of Jesus, which releases our purpose under the heaven. *He that finds a wife finds a good thing Prov. 18:21.* The good thing is not the wife but the covenant that comes when we find a wife. This good thing is released in the season when the man is pursuing his purpose. This good thing will come in season as a man is pursuing the revelation of Jesus Christ that brings him into his purpose in the body of Christ. Someone's asking, so how do I know the season for this good thing that I believe to come into my life? The thing is tied to a purpose. God gave me a word as a single man in ministry at 26 years old, when I was asking this same question. He said, "*You come into covenant with me, and prepare my bride for my coming and I will prepare your bride for your coming.*"

His High calling for us - Jesus

When we get to God's purpose for our life, which is Jesus, everything else will fall in line and begin to work for us. The purpose of God's call is not doing for him, but being with Him. And being with him will make us like him. Being like Jesus in the earth is his high calling on our lives. It's what he was hoping for when he called us. What he was hoping for when he saved us was Christ in us the hope of glory. So when Christ saved us he saw us being just like Jesus. He saw us thinking like him, talking like him, walking like him, and living like him. He saved us and prayed over us that God would give unto us the spirit of wisdom and revelation in the knowledge of him: the eyes of our understanding being enlightened; that we might know the hope of his calling. Before we get the good thing that we've been praying for we've got to become the person that he's been praying for - Jesus.

CHAPTER 15

THE PURPOSE OF AFRICA & THE NATIONS IN HIS HOUSE OF PRAYER

*1Jn 4:17 Herein is our love made perfect, so that we may have boldness in the day of judgment: **because as he is, so are we in this world.***

How do you become the person he's been praying for you to become? You must return to the source both in Heaven – Christ, and in the Earth – Your earthly Heritage. We must know what God has called us to do as related to our heavenly, eternal purpose. This deals with our calling to be a priest after the order of Melchizedek, calling heaven to earth. We must also know what God has called us to be after our earthly purpose. This deals with where we've come from in the earth as related to our geographical origin, which releases our earthly heritage.

We must study the Son of God, Jesus Christ, to know and enter into our eternal purpose for bringing heaven to earth. And we must study and know where we've come from in the earth as related to the three sons of Noah – Shem, Ham and Japheth, to know where in the body of Christ in the earth we will operate in that purpose.

How to Know National Purpose

How do the nations come to know their purpose so that God can release more of the things he's promised for the earth through our intercession? Our purpose is tied to where we've come from, both spiritually and naturally. Spiritually we've all come from God. Naturally we've all come from a particular geographical region in the earth, based on the migration of the three sons of Noah, Shem, Ham and Japheth, from which all nations originate from. (Acts 17:26) With each of the sons in the triune nature of humanity in the earth being correlated to the triune nature of the persons in the Godhead, we can come to know the purpose of each son from the three sons of Noah.

By correlating them to the revelation of the responsibilities of each of the three persons of the Godhead – Father, Son and Holy Ghost we can know national purpose in the earth.

In Earth As It Is In Heaven

1 John 4:17 Herein is our love made perfect, that we may have boldness in the day of judgment: because as he is, (in heaven) so are we in this world.

1 John 5:7, 8 say it like this, 7. For there are three that bear record in heaven, the Father, the Word, and the Holy Ghost: and these three are one.

8. And there are three that bear witness in earth, the Spirit, and the water, and the blood: and these three agree in one.

These three verses show the correlation of heaven and earth and how what's in heaven is connected to and mirrors what's in the earth. When Jesus taught us to pray, he begins by teaching us the connection, mirror principle when he says, Pray, Our father, which art in heaven, Hallowed be thy name, thy kingdom come, *thy will be done, in earth, as it is in heaven.* Heaven and earth were created to mirror one another, and are to be connected to one another. *In the beginning God created the heavens and the earth.* This principle is at the root of the fall and restoration of man and the earth. When man fell he was disconnected from God, his image, and the earth from heaven its' image.

The Mirror Principle of Heaven & Earth

Our prayers are to be focused on bringing these two, man back to God, and heaven back to earth to be united together once again. These two verses in 1 John 5:7, 8 are connected by the conjunction *"and"* to show the mirror principle of how God in heaven functions, and how man in earth is to come to function. Verse 7 says, *there are three that bear record in heaven, the Father, the word, and the Holy Ghost and these three ARE one.* Verse 8 says, *AND there are three that bear witness in the earth, the Spirit, and the water, and the blood: and these three AGREE in one.*

These three ARE ONE in Heaven

One verse, verse 7, speaking of the Mystery of the Godhead says, *"These three ARE ONE"*, the next verse speaking of man in the earth says, *"AND....these three AGREE IN ONE."* The word "ARE ONE" in verse 7 is the Greek word *"EISI"(pronounced I see)* which means *to "exist," "they are",* or *"to always have been."* So verse 7 is actually saying, *THESE THREE IN HEAVEN, THE FATHER, THE WORD AND THE HOLY SPIRIT ARE ONE, AND HAVE ALWAYS EXISTED AS ONE.*

These three ARE BECOMING ONE in Earth

In verse 8 the word AGREE IN ONE is stated together unlike verse 7, which simply says, they ARE ONE. But when you put the word "AGREE" with the word "IN," it's the Greek word *"eis"* (pronounced ice) which means *"to" or "into."* This is indicating a point reached or entered, of time, place or purpose. This makes verse 8 actually say, *"THERE ARE THREE THAT BARE RECORD IN EARTH....AND THESE THREE ARE BECOMING ONE, OR THEY ARE LEARNING TO EXIST AS ONE AS THEY ENTER INTO COVENANT AND STAY CONNECTED WITH THE THREE THAT ARE ONE IN HEAVEN."*

Something Happening on Earth that has always been in Heaven

Verse 7 being connected with verse 8 by the conjunction "AND" makes the responsibility of the three in earth to stay connected to the three in heaven in order to learn how to achieve oneness in the earth. It is the purpose of the three in the earth to gaze on, study, investigate, and gain revelation on how the Father, the Word, and the Holy Ghost operate as one so as to operate as one in the earth. This is achieved by corporate worship. Until the three in earth come together within the body of Christ in worship to agree in one place on who God is and that

209

will never truly understand our purpose. We come to understand our purpose as we worship the one who is worthy, because there's no one in earth that is perfectly ONE as he is in the Godhead. We need the one God in order to come together with one another, to accomplish our purpose in the earth. Our purpose is insignificant and impossible without each other.

This mystery has been revealed and will continually be revealed to a people that behold him for the purpose of becoming like him the earth. The purpose of understanding the triune nature of God is to understand how man in the earth is to be in agreement with God and one another to accomplish God's purposes in the earth, and to call Jesus back to man, and heaven back to the earth. As we worship together, all races, nations, ethnicities in one place, in one body we will become one, as God is in heaven, Father, Son, and Holy Ghost, one God – and we will come to understand who we are and our purpose in him.

How Do We Receive a Revelation of Our Earthly Responsibilities

How do we receive a revelation of our earthly responsibilities in the triune nature of mankind correlated to the triune nature of God? I john 5:8 says, There are three that bear witness in earth, The Spirit, and the Blood, and the Water, and these three agree in one. The Spirit of man in earth comes from the Father, so it correlates to the Father in heaven; the Blood comes from the body of Christ, which was applied to the mercy seat in heaven, so the blood correlates to the Son in heaven. And the Water in the earth comes from the Holy Ghost. John 7:38, 39 says, *He that believeth on me, as the scripture hath said, out of his belly shall flow rivers of living water. 39 (But this spake he of the Spirit, which they that believe on him should receive: for the Holy Ghost was not yet given; because that Jesus was not yet glorified.)* so the Water in the earth correlates   with   the   Holy   Ghost   in   heaven. Each of these witnesses in the earth, the Spirit – *Father*, the Blood – *the Son*, and the Water – *The Holy Ghost* correlate to one of the three sons of Noah, from which all nations have come from. So if we find out which witness in the earth correlates with which son – Ham, Shem or

Japheth, we can find the purpose of the nations by attributing to each son of Noah the purpose in earth of one of the 3 persons in the Godhead in heaven.

Which person of the Godhead relates to the person and purpose of the three sons of Noah? It is my humble opinion that we can find which son of the three sons of Noah correlate to one of the persons of the Godhead by recognizing the sons of Noah that went forth first, second, or third from the land of God-Jerusalem, to rule and attempt to exercise dominion in the earth in the six thousand years of humanity in the earth. Who dwelled and ruled in the land of God the first two thousand years, and which one dwelled and ruled in the land the second two thousand years, and which son went forth in the third two thousand years? We can distinguish the order and purpose of the nations with a Fatherhood anointing, a Son-ship anointing, and a Holy Ghost anointing by determining the order by which they inhabited the land of God. By recognizing the order of the two-thousand-year reign of each son of Noah and correlating them to the personalities of each person in the Godhead we can know the general purpose of the nations in the earth.

The Order of the Sons Possessing the Land of God

The nations from Ham were the first inhabitants of what is known now as Jerusalem, the city of God. The land of Israel was originally known as the land of Canaan. Canaan was the fourth son of Ham.

> Genesis 10:15 says, *And Canaan beget Sidon his first born, and Heth* (Hittite tribe from whence cometh Uriah, the husband of Bathsheba) *and the Jebusite, and the Amorite, and the Girgasite, and the Hivite, and the Arkite, and the Sivate. And the Arvadite, and the Zemarite, and the Hanathite and afterward were the families of the Canaanites spread abroad. And the border of the Canaanites was from Sidon, as thou comest to Gerar, unto Gaza; as thou goest, unto Sodom, and Gomorrah, and Admah, and Zeboim, even unto Lasha.* Verse 20, *These are the sons of Ham, after their*

families, after their tongues, in their countries, and in their nations.

This land given in Genesis 10:19 is the land now known to us as Jerusalem. It was called during the time of the possessing of the land by the children of Israel the Promise land. It was a land flowing with milk and honey. It was a land of prosperity and blessing, I believe, because of Abraham's encounter in that land with Melchizedek, the priest of the most-High God. The land was originally the land of the Canaanites from Ham. After Canaan inhabited the land for approximately two thousand years, it was given by God to Abraham's descendents from Shem. The Children of Israel lived in the land for the next two thousand years, as David established Zion in Jerusalem, until 70A.D. When Jerusalem was destroyed and overrun by the Romans the Japhetic reign began. From this time this land was in the hands of the Europeans from Japheth until God returned the Jews back to their promised homeland Israel, in 1948 and back to Jerusalem as it capital in 1967, after the six-day war.

The nations from the three sons of Noah, Ham, Shem and Japheth, are able to see their purpose in the earth as they study the three personalities of the God-head and recognize that not only was man created in His image and likeness, but mankind – *the nations* - were created in His image and likeness. The Father that sent his Son, initiates, imparts and releases *the sowing of the seed* of the word of God, and covers and protects that seed. The Son as God is the seed sown into the earth. He humbles himself and gives his life for *the reconciling of the World* back to the father. The Holy Ghost as God releases his power to his church, his bride, to be the womb to reproduce the seed sown by the father. He gives this Holy Ghost empowered Church the keys of authority back from Satan, *to subdue the earth*. Each of the nations from the three sons of Noah can find their purpose in the earth as the *Father* that sows the seed, the *Son* that gives his life for the reconciling of the world, or the *Holy Ghost* that unlocks authority to the church to reproduce the seed, to subdue the earth.

The Hametic Purpose – The Fatherhood Covering Anointing – A People of Refuge

In relation to mankind – *the nations* in the earth, being created in the image of God – *Father, Son & Holy Ghost*, and the three sons of Noah, the nations from Ham, having been the first inhabitants of the promise land are in the image of Father. They are initiators in the spirit, Apostolic Fathers, a people of refuge, to cover and preserve, with a fatherhood anointing. As fathers in the nations they have a covering anointing. The fatherhood nations from Ham when restored in the body of Christ with the other two sons, can find their purpose and fulfill their part in the earth coming to its purpose. Matthew 18:20 says where two or three are gathered together in my name there am I in the midst of them. As the sons of Ham are gathered together in the body of Christ with the other two sons from Noah their purpose as Apostolic Fathers in the earth will begin to be seen and manifest in the nations.

The Unique Calling on Africa – Cities of Refuge for Persecuted Jews

Africans around the world have a unique calling at the end of the age. One IHOP-KC leader, Samuel Clough, shared with me how Africans and those from the land of Ham will operate in this fatherhood, covering anointing at the end of the age, ministering to and sheltering the Jews in the hour of trial. The Prophet Isaiah in Isaiah 18 clearly gives this message to Africa. It is referring to an area of Africa south of Egypt that is in the general area of Nubia, Sudan, or Ethiopia, and Isaiah 18:7 specifically tells us that these Africans will bring a unique present to the Lord. Zephaniah 3:10 tells us that dispersed Jews will come up from "beyond the rivers of Ethiopia" at the end of the tribulation and this gives us insight into the gift of Isaiah 18:7. The gift that the African people bring the Lord is very likely the gift of Jews sheltered during the final tribulation at the end of the age. Egypt has always been the place of refuge for the Jewish people. It was the place where the nation was built in the centuries before the Exodus. It was also the land that sheltered Jesus when Herod sought to slaughter Him.

*"When Israel was a child, I loved him, and out of Egypt
I called My son". (Hosea 11:1 NKJV)*

The nation of Israel grew as a child in Egypt and was then called out during the Exodus under Moses. In the same manner, Jesus was sheltered in Egypt as a small child until He was called out of Egypt. While these are both fulfillments of Hosea 11:1, there will be a greater fulfillment of Hosea 11:1 at the end of the age. Israel at the end of the age will be a "child" compared to the maturity she will grow to in the Millennium and Jesus will lead the greater Exodus out of Egypt (Africa). The Biblical language around the second coming of Jesus is the language of the Exodus and it will be a second, and greater, exodus led by the greater Moses. Once again Israel, whom God desperately loves, will emerge through Egypt and God will call His Son out of Egypt as Jesus marches out of Egypt as a greater Moses liberating oppressed Jews in prison camps and approaching Jerusalem for the final battle with Jerusalem (Psalm 14:7; 102:13,19, 20; Isaiah 11:11-16; 27:12-13; 42:6-24; 49:5-25; 61:1-2; Jeremiah 30:3-24; 31:1-23; Ezekiel 20:33-44; 39:25-29; Hosea 11:10-11; Micah 4:6; 5:6; 7:12; Amos 9:8-15; Joel 2:32-3:1-2; Zephaniah 3:19-20; Zechariah 9:10-14; 10:10-11;). This will be the ultimate fulfillment of the passage.

The Exodus is the largest single event in the Scripture but 150 chapters, more than describe the Exodus, are given to describing the ultimate Exodus that will happen at Jesus return. When Hosea 11:1 is viewed in light of Isaiah 18:7 and Zephaniah 3:10 it is easy to see that while the Jews will be specifically "called out of Egypt," Egypt will be the gateway to Africa for Jews in flight at the end of the age and many Jews will travel further south in Africa seeking refuge from the terrors of the great tribulation. The LORD obviously intends both the African people in general and the continent of Africa in particular to take a primary role in ministering to and covering (sheltering) the Jews at the end of the age.

The Fatherhood Anointing Restored to the People of African Descent and their Communities

As African, African-American/Diaspora men & women begin to operate in their true fatherhood anointing, the curse that has been on

this people group, as well as in the earth, is going to be broken. God is raising up young African, African-American/Diaspora men to once again walk in the anointing to father - *Protect, And Provide*, both in the natural and the spirit, raising their families, churches, businesses, and nations in the fear and admonition of the Lord. He's turning their hearts back to their children to begin living for the raising up and releasing of sons in the earth. They will begin to walk in their purpose as Apostolic Fathers and Priests praying the priestly prayer of Jesus for unity in John 17.

The Urgency of the Crisis

The Scripture is clear that the Jews will face a trial at the end of the age unlike any other in history. Zechariah's description of Israel's trial is terrifying (Zechariah 12-14). Daniel warns that the events will continue until the Jews are scattered (Daniel 12:7). Jesus warns of a time unlike any in human history that would be impossible to survive unless it was shortened. He calls the Jews to run from the city when they begin to see the events unfold (Matthew 24:15-22). Just as Jesus warned, the Jews will have to flee Israel as the antichrist begins to bear down on the land. The critical question is where will the Jews go? The Jews cannot go north. Turkey has traditionally been the seat of the Islamic empire and will not be friendly to Jews in flight. The Jews cannot go east. East is ancient Babylon and modern Islamic nations that will not be friendly to the Jews. Southeast is the land of Arabia, a peninsula consumed with anti-Semitism.

The Jews cannot go west because of the Mediterranean. The Jews will be forced to go south through Egypt into Africa. It was 7 lean years of famine that caused Jacob and His sons to go to Egypt before the first Exodus and the last 7 years will create pressure on the earth that will again cause Jacobs sons to flee south to Egypt. Just as He did by sending Joseph, God will prepare intercessors in Egypt to open the door for the Jews to flee to Africa. This time it will be a praying church that opens the heavens over Egypt to provide a moment of safe passage into Africa for the Jews.

However, just as before, Egypt will both shelter and finally oppress the Jews as well, as the antichrist tightens his grip on the Middle East. Because Africa is the only way of escape Jews in the land will have, the religious climate of Africa is an eschatological issue. We must begin to sound an alarm to the church with regard to the crisis that is brewing both in the continent of Africa and among Africans in Diaspora. As friends of the Bridegroom, we must actively participate in His plan to make provision for His brothers in their chief hour of trial.

In the spirit of a forerunner, we must sound an alarm. The implications of Islam's assault on Africans are beyond what we can presently understand. The lack of eschatological understanding has caused us to not perceive what the enemy is doing in our generation. While we want to always carry the Lord's zeal for revival and for the salvation of all people, we must ask some serious questions about the growth of the gospel in Africa as it is related to the Land and people of the promised land.

The Release of the Land to Shem

In relation to mankind – *the nations* in the earth, being created in the image of God – *Father, Son & Holy Ghost*, and the three sons of Noah, after Ham's descendants occupied and lived in the land of God, this land was taken from the Canaanites and promised and given to the seed of Abraham, because of idol worship by the Canaanites in that land. They were to be completely destroyed. Leviticus 18 tells of the sins of the Canaanites.

> Lev.18:1-3, 24, 25 *And the Lord spake unto Moses, saying, Speak unto the children of Israel, and say unto them, I am the Lord your God. After the doings of the land of Egypt, wherein ye dwelt, shall ye not do: and after the doings of the land of Canaan, whither ye go in to possess shall ye not do: for in all these the nations are defiled which I cast out before you: And the lands is defiled: therefore I do visit the iniquity thereof upon it, and the lands itself vomits out her inhabitants.*

The next son of Noah, Shem, begins to arise in the earth through Abraham. Abram was the son of Terah, the son of Nabor, the son of Serug, the son of Reu, the son of Peleg, the son of Eber, the son of Salah, the son of Arphaxad, the son of Shem. Abraham is called and set apart by God to enter into covenant with him in Genesis 12 as Abram.

> *God said unto Abram, Get thee out of thy country, and from thy kindred, and from thy father's house, unto a land that I will shew thee: And I will make of thee a great nation, and I will bless thee and make thy name great; and thou shalt be a blessing: And I will bless them that bless thee, and curse him that curseth thee: and in thee shall all families of the earth be blessed.*
> Genesis 12:1

The Semitic Purpose – The Son-ship Reconciling Redeeming Anointing

This begins the rise of the second son of Noah, Shem, to begin to be the mighty one in the earth. It was through Abraham's seed that all the nations of the earth would be blessed and reconciled to God. And from his line the Messiah, the Savior of the world would come. It was during this period that the Kingdom of David was established in the earth. This kingdom ruled during his lifetime and his son Solomon's lifetime as the greatest kingdom in the earth. This was the second two-thousand years of the Semitic reign. The Semitic reign represents the second person of the God head, the Son of God, Jesus Christ, whose blood would be shed to take away the sins of the world. So it would be for the descendants of

Shem with the Jews and many others of the descendants of Shem. Their casting away (persecution, affliction and tribulation) over the years as a result of Judgment for sin was symbolic and correlates to God's judgment on His Son for the sins of the world, to reconcile the world back to God.

> *Rom 11:12 Now if the fall of them be the riches of the world, and the diminishing of them the riches of the Gentiles; how much more their fullness? 13 For I speak to you Gentiles, inasmuch as I am the apostle of the Gentiles, I magnify mine office: 14 If by any means I may*
>
> *provoke to emulation them which are my flesh, and might save some of them. 15* **For if the casting away of them be the reconciling** *of the world, what shall the receiving of them be, but life from the dead?*

These nations would be nations whose fall would be for the reconciling of the nations. However, their receiving would be life from the dead of the whole earth. In the end they would indeed fulfill the prophecy spoken unto them by God to Abraham, that, *I will bless thee, and make thy name great; and thou shalt be a blessing; and in thee shall all families of the earth be blessed.* The ultimate purpose of the sons from Shem as redeemer, reconciler people will eventually bring together and bless the nations of the world. However, before the blessing there would be the breaking. Before the resurrection there always comes the crucifixion. This first began in Genesis 22:1-8 when Abraham offered up Isaac, the promised seed, unto God on Mount Moriah; because Abraham would be willing to offer up his only son, God cut covenant to release His only Son into the earth. The nations from Shem represent the Son of man through Abraham's seed. They would be seen throughout the lines of time as redeemer nations, that as a result of their casting away they would be for the reconciling of man to God and eventually to one another.

From the purpose of the Son of God, the nations from the sons of Abraham, would find their purpose in the earth. The Son of God said in John 14:6 *I AM the way*, the truth and the life. So it's been for the sons of Abraham, as they have given all religions their great moral code, through the Ten Commandments. The Son came to give His life for the sins of the world. The Son said I *AM the door*. The Son said *I AM the bread of life*. The purpose of the Son is the salvation of the world. From these characteristics of the Son of God and many more, the nations from the sons of Shem can understand their purpose in the earth; and fulfill that purpose, coming into unity with the other brothers, Ham and Japheth in the house of prayer to help bring the earth to its destiny and purpose.

The Japhetic Purpose – The Holy Ghost, Helper anointing for the preaching of the Gospel in the whole world

Japheth was the last son of Noah to reign of the three. The scripture declares, the first shall be last, and the last shall be first. Japheth was the eldest, first born son to Noah, but was the last to rule in the earth and occupy the land of God. The baton was passed onto Japheth, in the book of Acts, as Peter was summoned by the Roman Centurion Cornelius, to speak unto him the words of life in Acts 10, and as Paul, the Apostle of Jesus Christ declared His intention and call to be a light to the Gentiles. It was here that the European nations of the Japhetic line would begin the preaching and spreading of the gospel in the 3rd two-thousand-year period.

Peter Unlocks the Door to the Gentiles to Receive the Message and Mantle for the Spreading of the Gospel in Acts 10:1

Acts 10:1 There was a certain man in Caesarea called Cornelius, a centurion of the band called the Italian band, 2 A devout man, and one that feared God with all his house, which gave much alms to the people, and prayed to God always. 3 He saw in a vision evidently about the ninth hour of the day an angel of God coming in to him, and saying unto him, Cornelius. 4 And when he looked on him, he was afraid, and said, what is it, Lord? And he said unto him, Thy prayers and thine alms are come up for a memorial before God. 5 And now send

men to Joppa, and call for one Simon, whose surname is
Peter: 6 He lodges with one Simon a tanner, whose
house is by the sea side: he shall tell thee what thou
oughtest to do.

Paul's Call to the Gentiles in Acts 13:46-48

*Then Paul and Barnabas waxed bold, and said, It was
necessary that the word of God should first have been
spoken to you: but seeing ye put it from you, and judge
yourselves unworthy of everlasting life, lo, we turn to
the Gentiles. 47 For so hath the Lord commanded us,
saying, I have set thee to be a light of the Gentiles, that
thou shouldest be for salvation unto the ends of the
earth. 48 And when the Gentiles heard this, they were
glad, and glorified the word of the Lord: and as many as
were ordained to eternal life believed.*

The Japhetic - *European nations* - began ruling, reigning and
attempting to take dominion in the earth, with the rise of Alexander the
Great in 300 B.C. but was consummated with these two incidents, I call
a baton hand-off with Peter and Paul. And even though the Roman
Empire and many other European dynasties went forth to conquer and
overrun the nations from Ham and Shem in the 3rd two-thousand years,
they also carried the mantle and message of the gospel in this 3rd two-
thousand-year period, keeping the light of the message of salvation
through Jesus Christ shining to be given to the ends of the earth. Each
son from Noah has taking turns attempting to overthrow, overtake and
oppress the other two sons, to have dominion in the earth. However,
each son has also taking turns in helping take the message of a coming
savior to the world.

It was the European nations from Japheth that would take the gospel
throughout the world in the last 2000 years and be responsible for
spreading it to the four corners of the earth. It would be the European
Nations from Japheth that would reign in the earth over this last 2000
year period. It would be these nations that would take the gospel back
to the dark regions of Africa and renew and restore the Christian faith

that was lost during the 7th century onward when Muslims begin to violently spread Muhammad's religion of Islam throughout Africa. As the result of the loss of an expression of the Christian faith in the regions of Africa, the regions on this continent would be darkened for centuries with witch-craft and necromancer and indigenous religions.

These European Nations from Japheth would represent the power and anointing of the third person of the Godhead, the Holy Ghost to be released as rivers of living water throughout the world. They would be most responsible for the spread of the gospel to the four corners of the earth. The European nations from Japheth would be missionary nations that would send missionaries all over the globe with the message of Jesus Christ's death burial and resurrection. They would be the distributors of the Gifts to the Nations in the last 2000 years. They would be the Helper nations that would be the possessors of the wealth for the taking of the gospel to the ends of the earth in the last 2000 years. They would be the nations that would make intercession by the spirit for the other two sons to come to the knowledge of Jesus Christ through missionaries being sent throughout the world.

> *Rom 8:26 Likewise the Spirit also helpeth our infirmities: for we know not what we should pray for as we ought: but the Spirit itself maketh intercession for us with groanings which cannot be uttered.*

The nations from Japheth would have the mantle in the last 2000 years to unlock the door of the Gospel to the earth. Just as the nations from the Hametic, peoples were the predominant son in the earth in the first two thousand years, and just as the nations from the Semites were the predominant son in the second 2000 years, the Europeans from Japheth would be the predominant son instrumental in the preaching of the gospel in the entire world in the third 2000 years. Even though the gospel, in many cases was spread through the oppression of slavery and colonialism, it was none the less spread. God had a plan in the slavery of the African nations by the Europeans, just as God had a plan in the slavery of the Jews in Egypt, an African nation – *The Worship of Jehovah God.* God did not enslave any people, but he did allow it to accomplish his purposes. He allowed it to cause the children of Israel in

Egypt to cry out to him for deliverance. And he allowed it to get those from the nations from Ham to cry out to Him, and to get those of the nations from Ham all over the world, into all the nations of the world. He allowed it so that Africans, who were in Islam or dark, indigenous, ancestral worship of devils, or nature, or animals, would hear the gospel preached to them by their Japhetic, European brothers and cry out to Jesus, the true and the living God, for their deliverance. This preaching of the gospel in Africa and in the European nations of the world would be strategic at the end of the age for that continent to be able to fulfill their Apostolic covering anointing as cities and places of Refuge for Jews in flight at the persecution of the Anti-Christ during the last 3 ½ years of human history.

The Resurgence and Growth of the Gospel in Africa

Is it possible that the mega meetings that Reinhard Bonnke and Daniel Kolenda have seen in Africa in the 20th and 21st centuries, with hundreds of thousands and even over a million in single meetings are not only for the salvation of the African people, but the fulfillment of the release of the Holy Ghost, helper nations being released to the sons of Ham from the sons of Japheth, fulfilling their end-time calling for rivers of living water to be released in all the earth? Could it be possible that Bonnke's vision of a blood washed Africa was given by God specifically as an answer to the plan of an Islamized Africa?

Could it be that in gospel crusades with over a million in attendance and in the large revival movements in Africa we are seeing something far deeper than evangelical crusades?

Could we actually be seeing the manifestation of a spiritual conflict that is far larger and far more serious than we have anticipated? Could it be that a million people in a meeting or a revival movement in Mozambique is the visible manifestation of a deep battle where darkness is actively preparing the earth for the antichrist while Jesus is seeking to prepare a sanctuary for His people in their hour of trial? Could the blood line dividing the gospel and Islam in Africa actually be the front line of Satans rage against Israel? Could it actually be the beginning of the battle to exterminate the Jews at the end of the age?

This is the crisis in the church that no one is talking about. Due to the gravity of the issues, we must begin to ask these questions and ask the Holy Spirit to give clarity. We must see the emergence of a forerunner ministry in our generation that will speak with clarity to the call of the African Descent Community while also confronting antichrist religious movements that have eschatological implications. If God is truly preparing Africa as a refuge for the Jews, are we cooperating with that plan in our generation?

It is time for eschatological understanding to go beyond understanding and be translated into action. Because of the hour we live in, eschatological understanding must begin to influence our missiology and the way we view the movement of the gospel among regions and unique people groups across the earth. The Lord is calling us to both <u>understand</u> and also begin to <u>engage</u> in the end-time conflict in that region of the descendants from Ham. *It is already underway.*

The Purpose of Worship in the Uniting of the Nations from the 3 sons of Noah

In the 21st century, the 6000th year of man in the earth, and the beginning of the 7000 thousandth year of God's rest, after we engage in the battle for the African Continent and the destiny and purpose of Africa, and after the coming down of the barriers to reconciliation, all three brothers from Noah, the holy, earthly trinity from which all nations come from, will be able to come together once again in His house of prayer for all nations. They will begin to worship God in heaven for the purpose of man being able rule and reign together in unity with the Heart of God through intercessory prayer as a kingdom of Priests in the earth. As God is Father, Son and Holy Ghost in Heaven, mankind from the nations of Noah's sons that come together in one body, the body of Christ to worship will now begin moving into that dimension of unity and oneness in the earth, in race relations, and national relations that will bring forth the will of God in the earth. It is during this time that we will make our world one, reconciling the world to God and to one another in the earth. It is during this time that forerunners will begin to go forth preparing the earth for the presence of the Lord. The Ultimate purpose of the nations of the earth is the worship of the God of heaven and earth as one new man. Once we understand who we are and what we're called to do and come together, recognizing that we can't be or do without one another, we will enter into a worship session on the earth that releases rain that causes every nation to know the Lord. Zechariah gives us this picture of the nations that are brought to their purpose in worship during the feast of tabernacles yearly saying;

> *Zec 14:9 And the LORD shall be king over all the earth: in that day shall there be one LORD, and his name one. 10 All the land shall be turned as a plain from Geba to Rimmon south of Jerusalem: and it shall be lifted up, and inhabited in her place, from Benjamin's gate unto the place of the first gate, unto the corner gate, and from the tower of Hananeel unto the king's winepresses. 11 And men shall dwell in it, and there shall be no more utter destruction; but Jerusalem shall be safely inhabited.*

> *12 And this shall be the plague wherewith the LORD will smite all the people that have fought against Jerusalem; Their flesh shall consume away while they stand upon their feet, and their eyes shall consume away in their holes, and their tongue shall consume away in their mouth. 13 And it shall come to pass in that day, that a great tumult from the LORD shall be among them; and they shall lay hold everyone on the hand of his neighbor, and his hand shall rise up against the hand of his neighbor.*

> *14 And Judah also shall fight at Jerusalem; and the wealth of all the heathen round about shall be gathered together, gold, and silver, and apparel, in great abundance. 15. and so shall be the plague of the horse, of the mule, of the camel, and of the ass, and of all the beasts that shall be in these tents, as this plague. 16*

> *And it shall come to pass, that every one that is left of all the nations which came against Jerusalem shall even go up from year to year to worship the King, the LORD of hosts, and to keep the feast of tabernacles.*
>
> *17 And it shall be, that whoso will not come up of all the families of the earth unto Jerusalem to worship the King, the LORD of hosts, even upon them shall be no rain. 18 And if the family of Egypt go not up, and come not, that have no rain; there shall be the plague, wherewith the LORD will smite the heathen that come not up to keep the feast of tabernacles.*
>
> *19 This shall be the punishment of Egypt, and the punishment of all nations that come not up to keep the feast of tabernacles. 20 In that day shall there be upon the bells of the horses, HOLINESS UNTO THE LORD; and the pots in the LORD'S house shall be like the bowls before the altar. 21 Yea, every pot in Jerusalem and in Judah shall be holiness unto the LORD of hosts: and all they that sacrifice shall come and take of them, and seethe therein: and in that day there shall be no more the Canaanite in the house of the LORD of hosts.*

Worship of the nations every year at the Feast of Tabernacles will be how the nations are able to remain as one, operating in a holy earthly trinity. This will truly be the international house of prayer and worship. As we operate in the mirror principle and worship the Lord as the nations come together in His name we will become like who we worship and become one. Heaven will come to earth, and as he is, so will we be in the earth. *1 Jn 4:17 Herein is our love made perfect, that we may have boldness in the day of judgment: because as he is, so are we in this world.* International corporate worship will also be how those nations receive the blessing of rain. The Bible speaks of rain on many occasions. In the majority of these instances, it is referring to the blessings of rain. This release of international worship of the nations of the King of kings will be the worship of the Name of the Lord – Jesus Christ. Zechariah says, in that day there shall be one Lord and His name will be one. The

225

name of Jesus will be on the lips of every human being. As we worship the Lord of Hosts, and as the purpose of the nations are made clear and plain all nations will receive rain. There are eight references to what rain is associated with in the Bible

Here Comes the Rain

1. **BREAD (substance, money) – Exodus 16:4** Then said the Lord unto Moses, Behold, I will rain bread from heaven for you; and the people shall go out and gather a certain rate every day, that I may prove them whether they will walk in my law, or no.
2. **BLESSING – Malachi 3:10** Bring ye all of the tithes into the storehouse, that there may be meat in mine house, and prove me now herewith, says the Lord of hosts, if I will not open you the windows of heaven, and pour you out a blessing, that there shall not be room enough to receive it.
3. **DOCTRINE – Deuteronomy 32:2** My doctrine shall drop as the rain, my speech shall distil as the dew, as the small rain upon the tender herb, and as the showers upon the grass.
4. **RIGHTEOUSNESS – Hosea 10:12** Sow to yourselves in righteousness, reap in mercy; break up your fallow ground: for it is time to seek the LORD, till he come and rain righteousness upon you.
5. **JUDGEMENT – Psalm 11:6** Upon the wicked he shall rain snares, fire and brimstone, and a horrible tempest: this shall be portion of their cup.
6. **THE WORD OF GOD – Isaiah 55:10** For as the rain cometh down, and the snow from heaven, and returns not thither, but waters the earth, and makes it bring forth and bud, that it may give seed to the sower, and bread to eater: So shall my word be that goes forth out of my mouth.
7. **GOD – Hosea 6:3** Then shall we know, if we follow on to know the LORD: his going forth is prepared as the morning; and he shall come unto us as the rain, as the latter and the former rain unto the earth.
8. **FAVOR – Proverbs 16:15** In the light of the king's countenance is life; and his favor is as a cloud of the latter rain.

Who Will Take the Initiative to be
Forerunners to Every Nation of the Earth

For all of this to happen; For the purpose of all nations coming together preparing the earth for the Lord to inhabit it, where all nations will come up to Jerusalem to worship the King of kings, Africans and the African Diaspora world-wide must be forerunners and be the first to submit, to serve the purposes of God in the coming together of all nations. This people group was first in the building of the great humanistic civilizations of antiquity in Egypt, Babylonia, and Ethiopia, and we must take the lead at the end of the age in the building of the civilization that ushers back into the earth the King of kings and the Lord of Lords. God is looking for Modern day Forerunners out of Africa, who will stand on the side of God when it comes to the things of His heart in the civic and social arena in this end-time generation. God is looking for Forerunners that will stand up for the Life of the unborn, for Marriage, and Social justice. He's looking not only for forerunner messengers, but for forerunner intercessors, Kings and Priests after the order of Melchizedek to pray to reconcile God to man, mankind back to one another, and heaven to earth. When those of African descent take up this ministry and submit ourselves to God and man to serve man and God's purposes in the coming together of all nations, it will start a domino effect in the nations of the world with the release of Forerunners out of every nation, tribe and tongue.

The 7 commitments of a Forerunner - the Sacred Charge

The Sacred Charge is vital to this Forerunner mandate. It is a prophetic call to refuse to settle for anything less than radical pursuit of God and His purposes for this end-time generation. It is a challenge to live in wholehearted pursuit of Jesus as forerunners who operate in the power of the Holy Spirit today, as we prepare ourselves to prepare others for the Lord's return. At the International House of Prayer we have identified seven foundational commitments to walk out this sacred charge in everyday life, with insights and practical steps on how to do this.

The Sacred Charge

1. **Pray Daily**: Connecting with God while Changing the World

2. **Fast Weekly**: Positioning Ourselves to Receive More from God

3. **Do Justly**: Being Zealous for Good Works that Exalt Jesus

4. **Give Extravagantly**: The Joy of Financial Power Encounters

5. **Live Holy**: Living Fascinated in the Pleasures of Loving God

6. **Lead Diligently**: Taking Initiative to Minister to Others

7. **Speak Boldly**: Being a Faithful Witness of the Truth

APPENDIX

KEY PROPHETIC PROMISES TO PRAY FOR ISRAEL AND THE CHURCH TO PRE-PRAYER US FOR HIS PRESENCE

A Promise that though the Lord scatters you (Israel & the Church) among the nations, If from there we will seek the Lord with all our hearts, and souls when we are in tribulation, even in the latter days (The End-Times) if we will turn to the Lord and obey his voice, he will be merciful unto us .

> *Deu 4:27-31 And the LORD shall scatter you among the nations, and ye shall be left few In number among the heathen, whither the LORD shall lead you. 28 And there ye shall serve gods, the work of men's hands, wood and stone, which neither see, nor hear, nor eat, nor smell.*

A Promise for our captivity to be turned (deliverance) when we obey His voice.

> *Deu 30:1-10 And it shall come to pass, when all these things are come upon thee, the blessing and the curse, which I have set before thee, and thou shalt call them to mind among all the nations, whither the LORD thy God hath driven thee, 2 And shalt return unto the LORD thy God, and shalt obey his voice according to all that I command thee this day, thou and thy children, with all thine heart, and with all thy soul;*

A Promise that if we turn aside from the Great Commandment to do evil in the sight of the LORD, evil will befall us in the latter days (end-times).

> *Deu 31:29 For I know that after my death ye will utterly corrupt yourselves and turn aside from the way which I have commanded you; and evil will befall you in the latter days; because ye will do evil in the sight of the LORD, to provoke him to anger through the work of your hands.*

A Promise of Protection, Safety and Happiness before our Enemies from the God of Jeshurun (Israel)

Deu 33:26-29 There is none like unto the God of Jeshurun, (to be straight or even; figuratively to be, to make right, pleasant, prosperous: - direct, fit, seem good) who rideth upon the heaven in thy help, and in his excellency on the sky. 27 The eternal God is thy refuge, and underneath are the everlasting arms: and he shall thrust out the enemy from before thee; and shall say, Destroy them.

A promise to Recover and Assemble the remnant of His people, (Israel, & The Church) which shall be from the Nations; Assyria, Egypt, Cush (Africa), and to set them up an Ensign for the Nations

Isa 11:10-16 And in that day there shall be a root of Jesse, which shall stand for an ensign of the people; to it shall the Gentiles seek: and his rest shall be glorious. 11 And it shall come to pass in that day, that the Lord shall set his hand again the second time to recover the remnant of his people, which shall be left, from Assyria, and from Egypt, (Africa) and from Pathros,(Upper Eygpt) and from Cush, (Africa) and from Elam, and from Shinar,(Iraq and/or Iran) and from Hamath, (Lebanon/Syria)and from the islands of the sea.

A Promise that God will do a marvelous work among his people by causing the wisdom of the wise to perish and understanding of their prudent to be hid.

Isa 29:14 Therefore, behold, I will proceed to do a marvelous work among this people, even a marvelous work and a wonder: for the wisdom of their wise men shall perish, and the understanding of their prudent men shall be hiding.

Promise of Fruitfulness for Lebanon, and for the ears of the deaf to be opened and the eyes of the blind (both natural, literal ears and eyes, and spiritual, Israel and the nations)

Isa 29:17-21 Is it not yet a very little while, and Lebanon shall be turned into a fruitful field, and the fruitful field shall be esteemed as a forest? 18 And in that day shall the deaf hear the words of the book, and the eyes of the blind shall see out of obscurity, and out of darkness. 19 The meek also shall increase their joy in the LORD, and the poor among men shall rejoice in the Holy One of Israel.

A Promise that Israel shall not be ashamed and that they shall sanctify the Name of the Lord and Fear the Lord

Isa 29:22-24 Therefore thus saith the LORD, who redeemed Abraham, concerning the house of Jacob, Jacob shall not now be ashamed, neither shall his face now wax pale. 23 But when he seeth his children, the work of mine hands, in the midst of him, they shall sanctify my name, and sanctify the Holy One of Jacob, and shall fear the God of Israel.

A Promise of the Lord to wait that He may be gracious to Israel and the Church, that he will have mercy during the time of Judgment for those that wait for Him.

Isa 30:18-19 And therefore will the LORD wait, that he may be gracious unto you, and therefore will he be exalted, that he may have mercy upon you: for the LORD is a God of judgment: blessed are all they that wait for him. 19 For the people shall dwell in Zion at Jerusalem: thou shalt weep no more:

A promise of divine direction through the coming forth of anointed Teachers, and answered prayers in the midst of the end-time tribulation.

Isa 30:20-22 And though the Lord give you the bread of adversity, and the water of affliction, yet shall not thy teachers be removed into a corner any more, but thine eyes shall see thy teachers: 21 And thine ears shall hear a word behind thee, saying, this is the way, walk ye in it, when ye turn to the right hand, and when ye turn to the left.

The Promise of the release of rain for the harvest of the seed, of divine provision and prosperity in the midst of famine

Isa 30:23, 24 Then shall he give the rain of thy seed, that thou shalt sow the ground withal; and bread of the increase of the earth, and it shall be fat and plenteous: in that day shall thy cattle feed in large pastures. 24 The oxen likewise and the young asses that ear the ground shall eat clean provender, which hath been winnowed with the shovel and with the fan.

The promise of provision and prosperity upon Houses of Prayer during the day and time of the collapse of the systems of this world

Isa 30:25, 26 And there shall be upon every high mountain, and upon every high hill, rivers and streams of waters in the day of the great slaughter, when the towers fall. 26 Moreover the light of the moon shall be as the light of the sun, and the light of the sun shall be sevenfold, as the light of seven days, in the day that the LORD bindeth up the breach of his people, and healeth the stroke of their wound.

A Promise of the Lord to sift the nations through the words of his mouth (His Prophets) and his fiery Judgments

Isa 30:27, 28 Behold, the name of the LORD cometh from far, burning with his anger, and the burden thereof is heavy: his lips are full of indignation, and his tongue as a devouring fire:

A Promise of a song from his worshippers and singers that will cause his voice to be heard and to release his judgments against the nations in the earth.

Isa 30:29-33 Ye shall have a song, as in the night when a holy solemnity is kept; and gladness of heart, as when one goeth with a pipe to come into the mountain of the LORD, to the mighty One of Israel. 30 And the LORD shall cause his glorious voice to be heard, and shall shew the lighting down of his arm, with the indignation of his anger, and with the flame of a devouring fire, with scattering, and tempest, and hailstones.

A Promise that the Spirit will release fruitfulness and Judgment in the wilderness, but that righteousness will continue in the fruitfulness during the time of Tribulation.

Isa 32:15, 16 Until the spirit be poured upon us from on high, and the wilderness be a fruitful field, and the fruitful field be counted for a forest. 16 Then judgment shall dwell in the wilderness, and righteousness remain in the fruitful field.

A promise that the work and effect of righteousness shall be peace, quietness and assurance and that the people of God shall dwell in a peaceable habitation, in sure dwellings, and in quiet resting places during times of judgment and tribulation.

Isa 32:17-20 And the work of righteousness shall be peace; and the effect of righteousness quietness and assurance forever. 18 And my people shall dwell in a peaceable habitation, and in sure dwellings, and in quiet resting places; 19 When it shall hail, coming down on the forest; and the city shall be low in a low place.

A Promise and Prayer for the Lord to be gracious for those who wait upon Him in the time of Trouble, judgment, and tribulation.

Isa 33:2-6 O LORD, be gracious unto us; we have waited for thee: be thou their arm every morning, our salvation also in the time of trouble. 3 At the noise of the tumult the people fled; at the lifting up of thyself the nations were scattered. 4 And your spoil shall be gathered like the gathering of the caterpiller: as the running to and fro of locusts shall he run upon them.

The Promise that our eyes shall see the king in his beauty, and behold the land afar off

> *Isa 33:17* Thine eyes shall see the king in his beauty: they shall behold the land that is very far off.

A promise of Joy singing and gladness in the wilderness. A promise to see the glory of the Lord in the wilderness

> *Isa 35:1, 2* The wilderness and the solitary place shall be glad for them; and the desert shall rejoice, and blossom as the rose. 2 It shall blossom abundantly, and rejoice even with joy and singing: the glory of Lebanon shall be given unto it, the excellency of Carmel and Sharon, they shall see the glory of the LORD, and the excellency of our God.

A promise of strength for weak hands, and feeble knees. Strength for the fearful, and the coming of God with vengeance to his people. A promise of miracles of the opening of blind eyes, deaf ears, and the lame walking

> *Isa 35:3-6* Strengthen ye the weak hands, and confirm the feeble knees. 4 Say to them that are of a fearful heart, Be strong, fear not: behold, your God will come with vengeance, even God with a recompence; he will come and save you. 5 Then the eyes of the blind shall be opened, and the ears of the deaf shall be unstopped.

A promise of water in the wilderness and a highway of holiness for the redeemed to walk in

> *Isa 35:7-10* And the parched ground shall become a pool, and the thirsty land springs of water: in the habitation of dragons, where each lay, shall be grass with reeds and rushes. 8 And an highway shall be there, and a way, and it shall be called The way of holiness; the unclean shall not

234

pass over it; but it shall be for those: the wayfaring men, though fools, shall not err therein.

A promise of the singing of a new song and praise in the wilderness to give glory to the Lord that releases the LORD to go forth as a mighty man of war to stir up jealousy and prevail against his enemies

Isa 42:10-17 Sing unto the LORD a new song, and his praise from the end of the earth, ye that go down to the sea, and all that is therein; the isles, and the inhabitants thereof. 11 Let the wilderness and the cities thereof lift up their voice, the villages that Kedar doth inhabit: let the inhabitants of the rock sing, let them shout from the top of the mountains.

A promise that when we pass through the waters, rivers, and fire he will be with us, and that the waters will not overflow us and the fire will not burn or kindle upon us.

Isa 43:1, 2 But now thus saith the LORD that created thee, O Jacob, and he that formed thee, O Israel, Fear not: for I have redeemed thee, I have called thee by thy name; thou art mine. 2 When thou passest through the waters, I will be with thee; and through the rivers, they shall not overflow thee: when thou walkest through the fire, thou shalt not be burned; neither shall the flame kindle upon thee.

A promise that Africa would be a covering for Israel and the church. A promise of God's love so for his chosen people that he will use gentile nations to cover them and protect them from persecution,

Isa 43:3, 4 For I am the LORD thy God, the Holy One of Israel, thy Saviour: I gave Egypt for thy ransom, Ethiopia and Seba for thee. 4 Since thou wast precious in my sight, thou hast been honourable, and I have loved thee: therefore will I give men for thee, and people for thy life.

<u>A promise that God will be with His people (Israel & the Church) during their trouble and tribulation, and that He will bring them together from the nations of the earth to keep them and cover them from their persecutors.</u>

> *Isa 43:5-7* Fear not: for I am with thee: I will bring thy seed from the east, and gather thee from the west; 6 I will say to the north, Give up; and to the south, Keep not back: bring my sons from far, and my daughters from the ends of the earth;

<u>A promise of Help and supernatural provision and sustenance for his chosen people, of water upon the thirsty and floods upon dry grounds. A promise of the pouring out of his spirit and blessing upon the children of his chosen (Israel & the Church) for salvation and the calling on the name of the Lord</u>

> *Isa 44:1-5* Yet now hear, O Jacob my servant; and Israel, whom I have chosen: 2 Thus saith the LORD that made thee, and formed thee from the womb, which will help thee; Fear not, O Jacob, my servant; and thou, Jesurun, whom I have chosen. 3 For I will pour water upon him that is thirsty, and floods upon the dry ground: I will pour my spirit upon thy seed, and my blessing upon thine offspring:

<u>A promise of Israel's salvation in the Lord with an everlasting salvation, that his people would not be ashamed, nor confounded.</u>

> *Isa 45:17* But Israel shall be saved in the LORD with an everlasting salvation: ye shall not be ashamed (disappointed or confused by the the delay) nor confounded (wounded, insulted, hurt) world without end.

<u>A promise that all the ends of the earth that look unto him would be saved, A promise that every knee would bow and every tongue shall confess Jesus to be LORD, and that all the chosen of God (Israel & the Church) would be justified and shall glory.</u>

> *Isa 45:22-25* Look unto me, and be ye saved, all the ends of the earth: for I am God, and there is none else. 23 I have

sworn by myself, the word is gone out of my mouth in righteousness, and shall not return, That unto me every knee shall bow, every tongue shall swear.

A Promise of the Lord to comfort his people (Israel & The Church) in all of her desolation, drought and destruction. A promise that he will make her wilderness fruitful and restore the earth back to the garden of Eden, and that joy and gladness would be found in them again

Isa 51:3, 4 For the LORD shall comfort Zion: he will comfort all her waste places; and he will make her wilderness like Eden, and her desert like the garden of the LORD; joy and gladness shall be found therein, thanksgiving, and the voice of melody.4 Hearken unto me, my people; and give ear unto me, O my nation: for a law shall proceed from me, and I will make my judgment to rest for a light of the people.

A promise that his righteousness would be near and his salvation would go forth and his arms would judge the people. A promise that the islands, coast and dry lands would wait upon Him and on his arm they would trust.

Isa 51:5-8 My righteousness is near; my salvation is gone forth, and mine arms shall judge the people; the isles shall wait upon me, and on mine arm shall they trust. 6 Lift up your eyes to the heavens, and look upon the earth beneath: for the heavens shall vanish away like smoke, and the earth shall wax old like a garment, and they that dwell therein shall die in like manner: but my salvation shall be for ever, and my righteousness shall not be abolished

A promise that the redeemed of the LORD will return and come with singing and with everlasting joy on their head, for all that Awake, and put on their strength.

Isa 51:9, 11 Awake, awake, put on strength, O arm of the LORD; awake, as in the ancient days, in the generations of old. Art thou not it that hath cut Rahab, and wounded the dragon? 10 Art thou not it which hath dried the sea, the waters of the great deep; that hath made the depths of the sea a way for the ransomed to pass over?.

A promise of fruitfulness to the barren that sing. A promise to break forth on the right hand and left and for their children to inherit the nations of the heathen, to all those that enlarge their tents, and make room for increase the salvation of the nations.

Isa 54:1-4 Sing, O barren, thou that didst not bear; break forth into singing, and cry aloud, thou that didst not travail with child: for more are the children of the desolate than the children of the married wife, saith the LORD. 2 Enlarge the place of thy tent, and let them stretch forth the curtains of thine habitations: spare not, lengthen thy cords, and strengthen thy stakes;

A promise that the Lord would be the husband of his people and their Kinsmen redeemer. A promise that with great mercies will he gather his people.

Isa 54:5-8 For thy Maker is thine husband; the LORD of hosts is his name; and thy Redeemer the Holy One of Israel; The God of the whole earth shall he be called. 6 For the LORD hath called thee as a woman forsaken and grieved in spirit, and a wife of youth, when thou wast refused, saith thy God. 7 For a small moment have I forsaken thee; but with great mercies will I gather thee.

A Promise that he would no longer be wroth with his people, nor rebuke them any longer and that his covenant of peace would not be removed.

Isa 54:9, 10 For this is as the waters of Noah unto me: for as I have sworn that the waters of Noah should no more go over the earth; so have I sworn that I would not be wroth with thee, nor rebuke thee. 10 For the mountains shall depart, and the hills be removed; but my kindness shall not depart from thee, neither shall the covenant of my peace be removed, saith the LORD that hath mercy on thee.

A Promise to the afflicted and tossed that he would place upon them the stones of favor and prosperity and that their children would be taught of the Lord and that their peace would be great.

> *Isa 54:11-13 O thou afflicted, tossed with tempest, and not comforted, behold, I will lay thy stones with fair colours, and lay thy foundations with sapphires. 12 And I will make thy windows of agates, and thy gates of carbuncles, and all thy borders of pleasant stones. 13 And all thy children shall be taught of the LORD; and great shall be the peace of thy children.*

A Promise for his people to be established in righteousness and be far from oppression and fear. And that all that gather together against them and form weapons against them will not prosper.

> *Isa 54:14-17 In righteousness shalt thou be established: thou shalt be far from oppression; for thou shalt not fear: and from terror; for it shall not come near thee. 15 Behold, they shall surely gather together, but not by me: whosoever shall gather together against thee shall fall for thy sake. 16 Behold, I have created the smith that bloweth the coals in the fire, and that bringeth forth an instrument for his work; and I have created the waster to destroy. 17 No weapon that is formed against thee shall prosper; and every tongue that shall rise against thee in judgment thou shalt condemn. This is the heritage of the servants of the LORD, and their righteousness is of me, saith the LORD.*

A promise that all the nations that join themselves to the Lord to serve him and to Love the name of the LORD to be his servants and take hold of his covenant, he will bring them to His House of Prayer and that his house would be called a house of prayer for all people (nations)

> *Isa 56:6-8 Also the sons of the stranger, that join themselves to the LORD, to serve him, and to love the name of the LORD, to be his servants, every one that keepeth the sabbath from polluting it, and taketh hold of my covenant; 7*

Even them will I bring to my holy mountain, and make them joyful in my house of prayer: their burnt offerings and their sacrifices shall be accepted upon mine altar; for mine house shall be called an house of prayer for all people (nations). 8 The Lord GOD which gathereth the outcasts of Israel saith, Yet will I gather others to him, beside those that are gathered unto him.

A Promise to those that fear the name of the Lord that when the enemy shall come in like a flood, the Spirit of the LORD shall lift up a standard against him.

Isa 59:19 So shall they fear the name of the LORD from the west, and his glory from the rising of the sun. When the enemy shall come in like a flood, the Spirit of the LORD shall lift up a standard against him.

A Promise to those that turn from their transgressions that the Redeemer shall come to his people (Israel & the Church), and that His Spirit would be upon them, with his words in their mouths and not depart.

Isa 59:20, 21 And the Redeemer shall come to Zion, and unto them that turn from transgression in Jacob, saith the LORD. 21 As for me, this is my covenant with them, saith the LORD;

The Coming Forerunner Ministry Out of Africa

Contact info:
Brondon Mathis
614 745-9683, office
614-425-7427, cell
yeshuamovement@gmail.com
facebook/brondonmathis.com

For other Book Releases by Brondon Mathis:
Go to www.Amazon.com to order

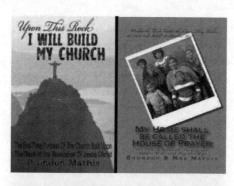

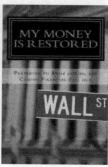

1. *Upon This Rock I will Build My Church*. The end-time purpose of the church built upon the book of the Revelation

2. *My Home shall be called a House of Prayer.* Our Family vision for training our children in the way they should go.

3. *My House shall be called the House of Prayer*. 7 Principles to becoming a Praying Church.

4. *My Money is Restored* – Preparing to Arise during the Coming Economic Fallout. This book presents the story of Joseph and the principles for the transference of wealth from the hands of the wicked to the hands of the righteous for the preservation of the Church and Israel

Made in the USA
Columbia, SC
04 December 2024